ST. JOHNS STREETCARS

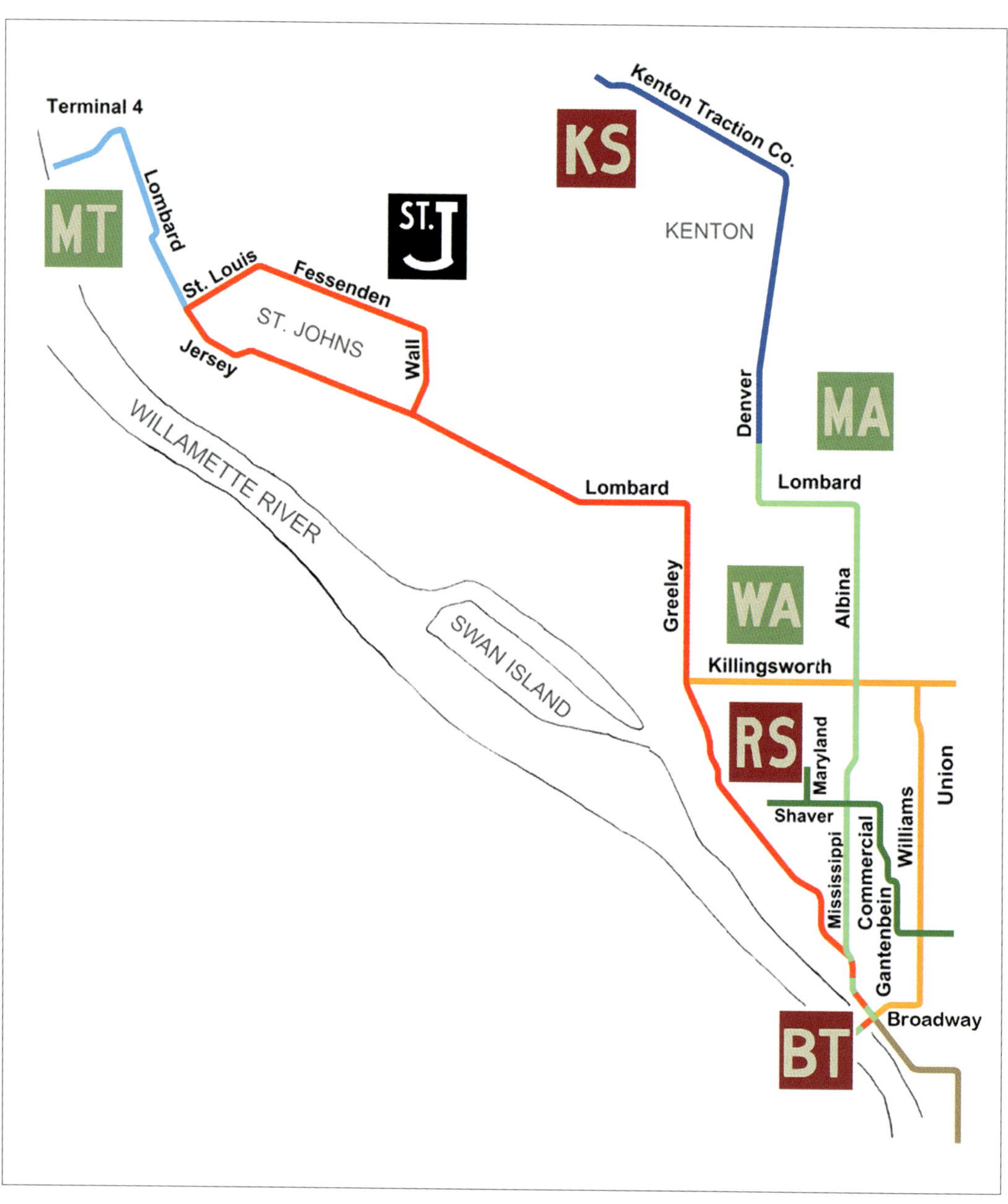
Terminal 4
MT
Lombard
ST. J
KS
Kenton Traction Co.
KENTON
St. Louis
Fessenden
ST. JOHNS
Jersey
Wall
WILLAMETTE RIVER
Denver
MA
Lombard
Lombard
Greeley
WA
Albina
SWAN ISLAND
Killingsworth
RS
Maryland
Union
Shaver
Mississippi
Commercial
Williams
Gantenbein
Broadway
BT

ST. JOHNS STREETCARS

THE STREETCARS OF NORTH PORTLAND

RICHARD THOMPSON

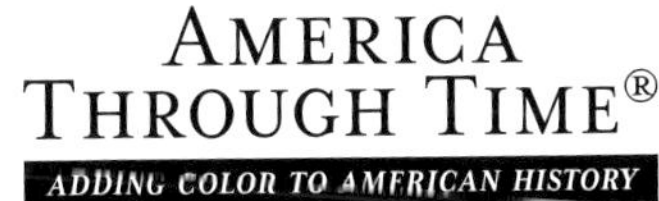

This book is dedicated to William H. "Bill" Binns, whose tireless devotion to the cause of railway history and the operation of restored streetcars has inspired a generation of volunteers at the Oregon Electric Railway Museum.

Frontispiece: Nine streetcar lines served North Portland over the years including (in alphabetical order): Albina, 1903; Kenton (K), 1909–1912; Kenton Stockyards (KS), 1909–1928; Lower Albina (L), see Mississippi Avenue; Mississippi Avenue (MA), 1892–1940; Municipal Terminal (MT), 1920–1929; Portland & Albina, 1889–1891; Russell-Shaver (RS), 1903–1936; St. Johns (SJ), 1889-1937; Upper Albina (U), see Williams Avenue; and Williams Avenue (WA), 1892–1937. In addition, the Bridge Transfer Line (BT), 1915–1937, connected with North Portland lines at the east end of the Broadway Bridge, although it did not run out the Portland Peninsula. Until 1903 St. Johns Line passengers had to transfer between electric streetcars and steam trains of the St. Johns Motor Line. In 1904, the Lower Albina and Upper Albina lines became the Mississippi Avenue and Williams Avenue lines, respectively. This map illustrates the North Portland lines during their peak years in the 1920s.

America Through Time is an imprint of Fonthill Media LLC
www.through-time.com
office@through-time.com

Published by Arcadia Publishing by arrangement with Fonthill Media LLC
For all general information, please contact Arcadia Publishing:
Telephone: 843-853-2070
Fax: 843-853-0044
E-mail: sales@arcadiapublishing.com
For customer service and orders:
Toll-Free 1-888-313-2665

www.arcadiapublishing.com

First published 2022

ISBN 978-1-63499-375-3

Typeset in Sabon LT Std
Printed and bound in England

Acknowledgments

With the completion of my eighth book on the subject of Oregon street and interurban railways, I can attest to the difficulty of gathering needed photographs, plans, memorabilia, and maps. As always, the reward for this labor of love has been self-satisfaction, but I could not have done it without help from fellow enthusiasts.

I wish to thank Norm Gholston, Mark Gilmore, Dan Haneckow, Martin Hansen, Mark Moore, Don Nelson, Steve Morgan, Bill Volkmer, and David Wilson for sharing their knowledge and images. As with previous volumes, I also want to acknowledge my late friends William K. "Bill" Hayes and G. Charles "Chuck" Bukowsky for their unflagging support for my books.

I am also grateful to Tracy Brown and Steve Morgan for proofreading the manuscript, and to my editor at Fonthill Media, Jamie Hardwick, for help with planning.

Unless otherwise noted, all pictures in this book are from the author's personal collection. Original photographers are cited wherever possible. Further information can be found on the author's website: vintagetrolleys.com.

Contents

Introduction

Most of what is now North Portland is encompassed by the Portland Peninsula. This fine stretch of level land, bounded by the deep waters of the Columbia River to the north and the Willamette River to the south, has been a favored place to settle since time immemorial. It is first mentioned in the journals of the 1805 Lewis and Clark Expedition, in which a Chinookan camp near today's Cathedral Park is recorded.

Immigrant settlers established a number of important towns along the banks of the Willamette River during the 1840s. One of these was a small townsite founded by James Johns, who had come to Fort Vancouver from California in 1841. The former Missourian filed a land claim on the Peninsula in 1847 and was soon running a general store. By 1865, Johns was selling lots. Some called him "Saint" Johns for his willingness to donate small parcels of his land to poor settlers. On November 28, 1868, an eight-block townsite was dedicated in his honor. Today, St. Johns is a district rather than a municipality, having been annexed into Portland in 1915.

As it grew, St. Johns and the surrounding Portland Peninsula developed into a manufacturing center. According to *The Oregonian*, the first electric sawmill in the United States was constructed here in 1903. By 1910, the area was home to nearly thirty factories and warehouses, including a woolen mill, planing mill, collapsible box factory, machine works, stove works, furniture factory, cooperage, and several lumber companies.

In 1904, the Bureau of Information described St. Johns as "essentially a working man's town." However, it also became known for its fine parks and university. Part of that can be credited to James Johns, whose will stipulated that his assets be used for building a new public school where children of all religious denominations could receive an education. The Peninsula's highest institute of learning, Portland University (at what is now the site of the University of Portland), was founded here in 1891, and many fine homes were soon built in the adjacent University Park neighborhood.

Transportation to the Portland Peninsula began on the river. In the years before the magnificent Gothic-style St. Johns Bridge opened on June 13, 1931, ferries provided an important link across the Willamette River. In fact, James Johns introduced its first ferry service in 1852. Shipyards along the St. Johns waterfront, and on Swan Island, built many river- and ocean-going craft and contributed vital cargo ships to both world wars. The City Dry Dock was located in St. Johns, and construction began on a new Municipal Terminal in 1917. From 1927 to 1940, Swan Island was the site of Portland's airport.

Next came the railroads. In 1902, the Oregon Railroad and Navigation Company (OR&N) built a branch along the St. Johns waterfront. The harbor bustled with activity after the 5.5-mile route opened and additional tracks soon encircled the city. Between 1909 and 1911, the successor Oregon and Washington Railroad and Navigation Company (OWR&N) built a mile-long railroad tunnel between N Columbia Boulevard and Mock's Bottom, expediting the movement of trains between Portland and Vancouver, Washington.

Ironically, electric streetcars were both early and late arrivals in North Portland. The first trolley line in Oregon began running from the west end of the Steel Bridge in Portland to the city of Albina on November 1, 1889. The last steam streetcar branch ceased operation in 1903, when the St. Johns Line was electrified.

Neighborhoods developed as the streetcar tracks spread. The Piedmont subdivision was among the first of these, having been platted in 1889. A few more housing additions sprang up once the loop through Albina was completed in 1891, and a new branch extended into the Overlook Neighborhood in 1903. Settlement along the bottom of the Portland Peninsula was steady by the twentieth century in spite of grades and gullies.

The Willamette Bridge Railway Company, a subsidiary of the Pacific Bridge Company, obtained an exclusive franchise to operate streetcars across the first Steel Bridge. By 1891, they had built the largest street railway system on the West Coast and were planning a unified system powered by electricity. Those tracks would become part of a consolidation of independent street railway companies that accelerated with establishment of the City & Suburban Railway Company in 1891 and the Portland Railway Company in 1900. Those two competing city streetcar systems merged into the Portland Consolidated Railway Company in 1904. Two years later, the massive Portland Railway, Light and Power Company (PRL&P) completed the process by absorbing all remaining lines, both interurban and city.

PRL&P inherited twenty-three city streetcar lines from predecessor companies, four of which served North Portland. The City & Suburban Railway had added three lines and the Portland Railway added one. By 1920, there were nine lines on the Peninsula. In this land of contrasts, North Portland had the fewest lines of any city district but was also home to the largest carbarn and the city's final new trolley line.

This is the story of the classic streetcar lines that traversed North Portland between 1887 and 1948. A final chapter celebrates the return of streetcars here, beginning in 2004. It is the history of a diverse system that evolved from horse-drawn streetcars to Oregon's first electric trolleys, and from trolleybuses to light rail vehicles. Nearly every North Portland neighborhood was connected by trolley, including Arbor Lodge, East St. Johns, Kenton, Overlook, Piedmont, Portsmouth, and University Park. To avoid confusion, modern street names have been used where possible to describe locations. Additional information, historic car rosters, and line maps, can be found on the author's website: vintagetrolleys.com

1

The First Albina Lines

At the dawn of the trolley era, two Albina lines served North Portland. The initial line was the first electric street railway in the state of Oregon. It was built by the Willamette Bridge Railway Company, whose horse-drawn streetcars had been crossing the Morrison Street Bridge since March 29, 1888, eleven months after the first span across the Willamette River opened. The pioneering Bridge Company also obtained an exclusive franchise for operating streetcars on the Steel Bridge then under construction. They inaugurated service soon after the new crossing, a swing bridge, was completed in July 1888. Horsecars were used while the new span was modified for use by the latest transportation technology. The present Steel Bridge is a lift bridge that replaced its predecessor in 1912.

On November 1, 1889, the first electric streetcars began running between Portland and Albina via the original Steel Bridge, a double-deck swing bridge that opened the year before. The first months of trolley operation were a time of unbridled enthusiasm. Lines of all types—electric, steam, and horse—now radiated from Portland. Most routes on the East Side were operated by the Willamette Bridge Railway.

The Portland & Albina Line ran 1.4 miles, from what is now NW Glisan Street between 2nd and 3rd Avenues, to N Interstate and Russell streets in Albina. Since the railway company did not yet have a franchise for operation in the city of Portland, trolleys ran from a shelter on the west approach to the bridge.

A number of significant route changes were made to the original Albina Line during the 1890s. Within days, its eastern terminus was extended northward to N Commercial Avenue, where construction was underway on a connecting steam motor line to St. Johns. On January 17, 1891, tracks were completed between N Williams and Hancock streets, and N McMillan and Russell streets, creating a loop through Albina.

The biggest change for the first Albina Line took place after the Willamette Bridge Railway merged with the Waverly and Woodstock Electric Railway and the Transcontinental Street Railway to form the City & Suburban Railway in June 1891. The City & Suburban split the Albina route into separate Upper and Lower Albina lines.

In October 1899, the Lower Albina Line trolleys stopped climbing steep N Commercial

Avenue in favor of new tracks on N Mississippi Avenue. The transfer point for St. Johns passengers was then relocated from N Commercial Avenue and Stanton Street to a new station eighteen blocks farther north on N Commercial Avenue and Killingsworth Street.

By August 1903, Portland had a second Albina Line. The City & Suburban Railway briefly faced competition from a Portland Railway Company line running from NE Russell Street and Union Avenue (renamed Martin Luther King, Jr., Boulevard in 1989) to N Maryland and Prescott streets in the Overlook neighborhood. The intention was for this route to eventually extend to St. Johns; however, a few months after the later Albina Line opened, another merger would see it repurposed as the Russell–Shaver stub line by the new Portland Consolidated Railway Company.

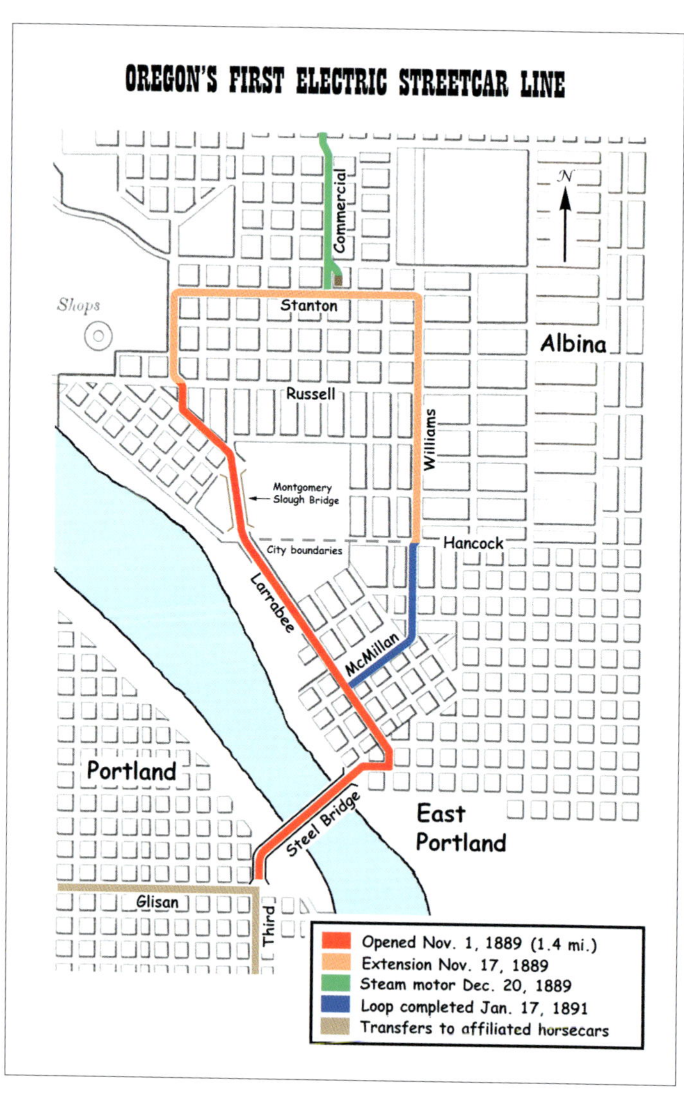

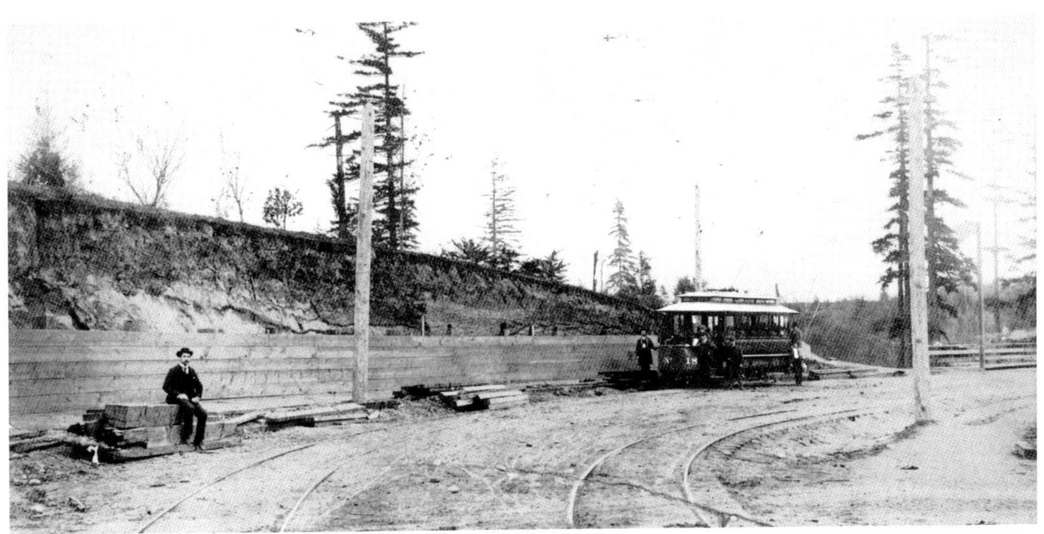

The Willamette Bridge Railway began operating the first electric streetcars across the Steel Bridge to Albina in November 1889. Car 18 is three blocks from the original Portland & Albina Line terminal in this view looking south on Goldsmith Street toward the Montgomery Slough Bridge. The inscription reads "Showing double curve leading off Albina Bridge on the electric railway between Portland & Albina." (*Photograph courtesy Norm Gholston*).

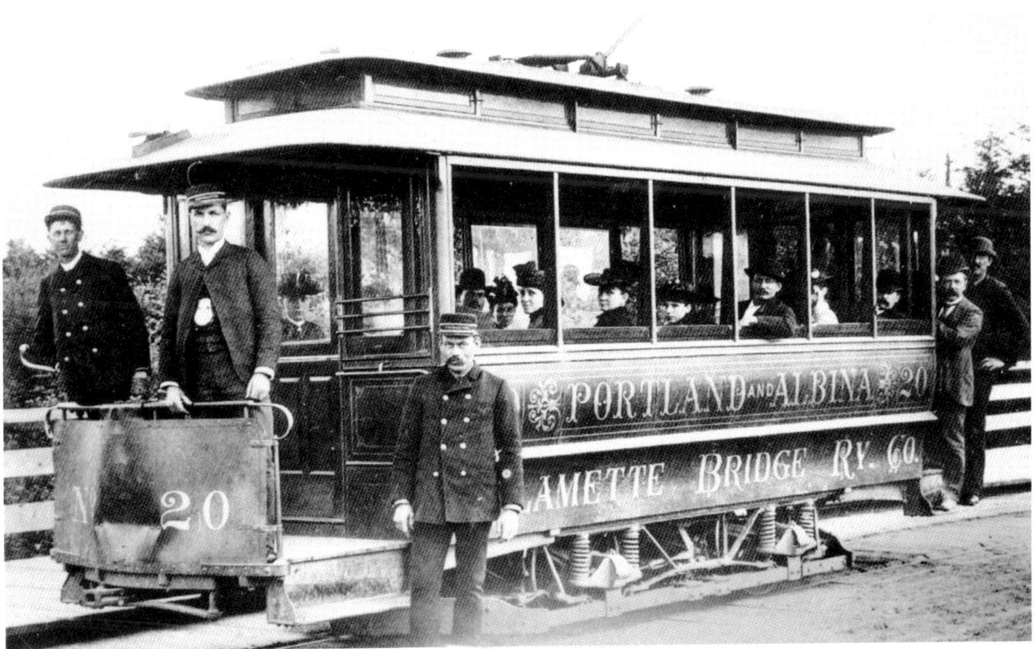

Motorman Jack Workman has brought one of the first electric streetcars in Portland to an unscheduled photograph stop on the bridge over Montgomery Slough near present-day N Interstate Avenue and Tillamook Street. No. 20 was built by the Pullman Palace Car Company in 1889. The dented dashboard resulted from the kick of a horse used to tow the car during a breakdown.

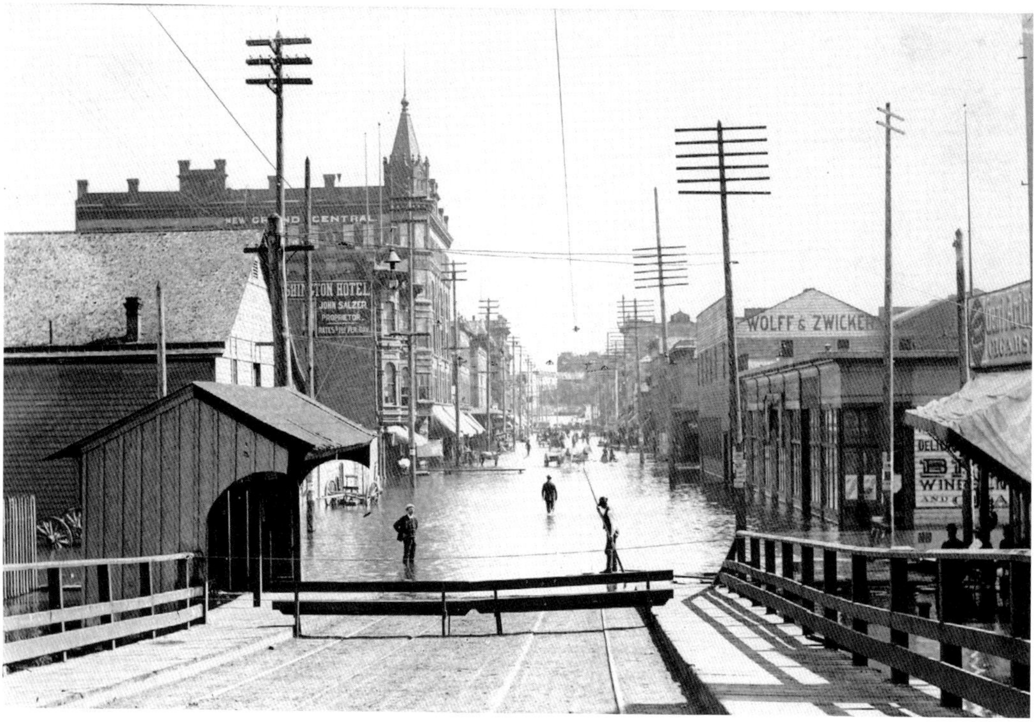

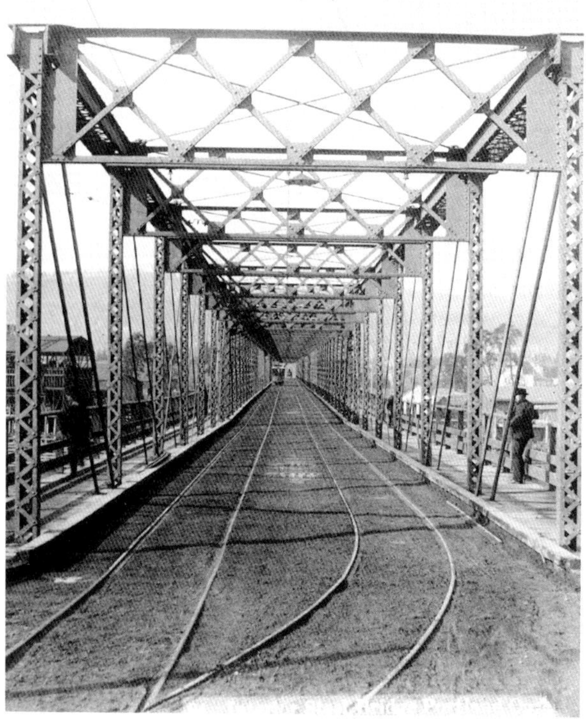

Above: This photograph, probably taken during the historic 1894 flood, looks south from the Steel Bridge ramp at the intersection of NW 3rd Avenue and Glisan Street. The shelter at left served as the western terminus of the Portland & Albina Line. Locating the station at the western end of the bridge was an accommodation since the Willamette Bridge Railway did not have a franchise to operate inside the Portland city limits. (*Oregon Historical Society 46930*)

Left: This stereopticon view was taken from the east end of the Steel Bridge looking west as an eastbound City & Suburban Railway open platform streetcar approaches. Although the original Steel Bridge was a swing bridge, it carried railroad traffic on the lower level with pedestrians and vehicles on the top like its modern successor.

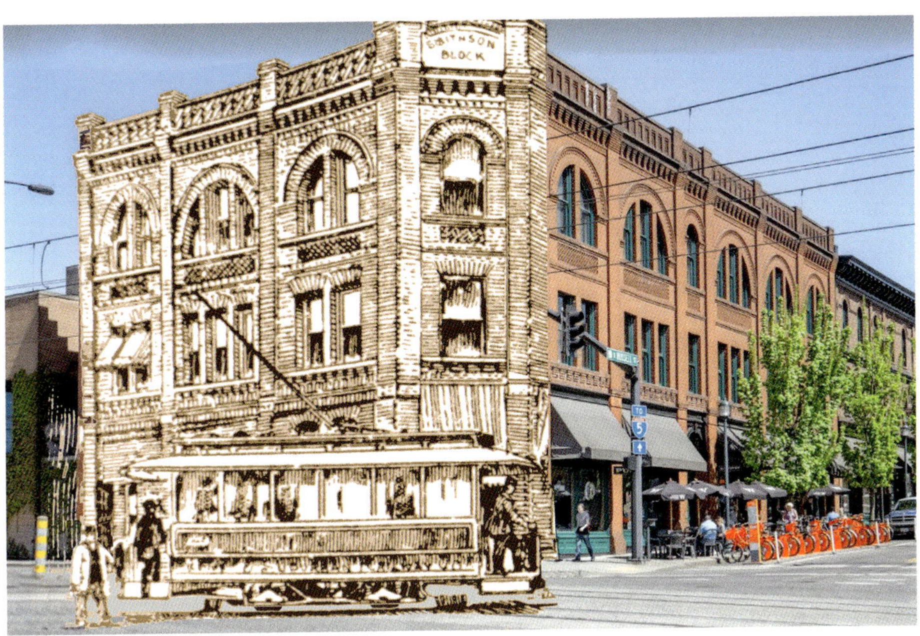

A City & Suburban Railway streetcar has been overlaid on a modern scene in a then-and-now view at the corner of N Interstate Avenue and Russell Street. The engraved image is from 1894's *The Oregonian's Handbook of the Pacific Northwest.* The three-story brick Smithson Block was erected in 1892 on the western edge of the historic Albina business district fostered by the building of the streetcar line.

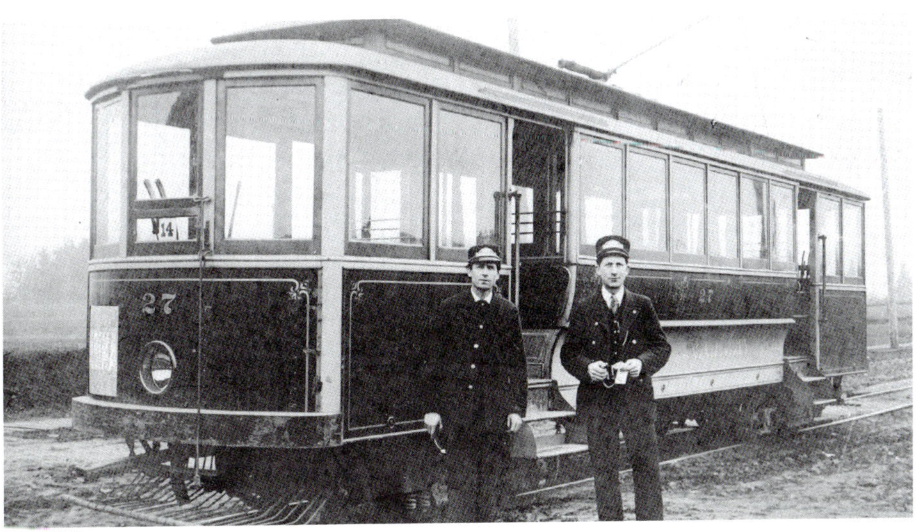

Car 27, seen on Portland's other Albina Line, was the first of eight "Fuller Standard" streetcars created in 1902 by adding large vestibules to 1890-vintage Pullmans. The Fuller cars were the brainchild of Portland Railway President F. I. Fuller, who had them built locally in response to a shortage of available trolleys from national car builders. They were manufactured at the new Washington Street Carbarn. (*Photograph courtesy Mark Moore*)

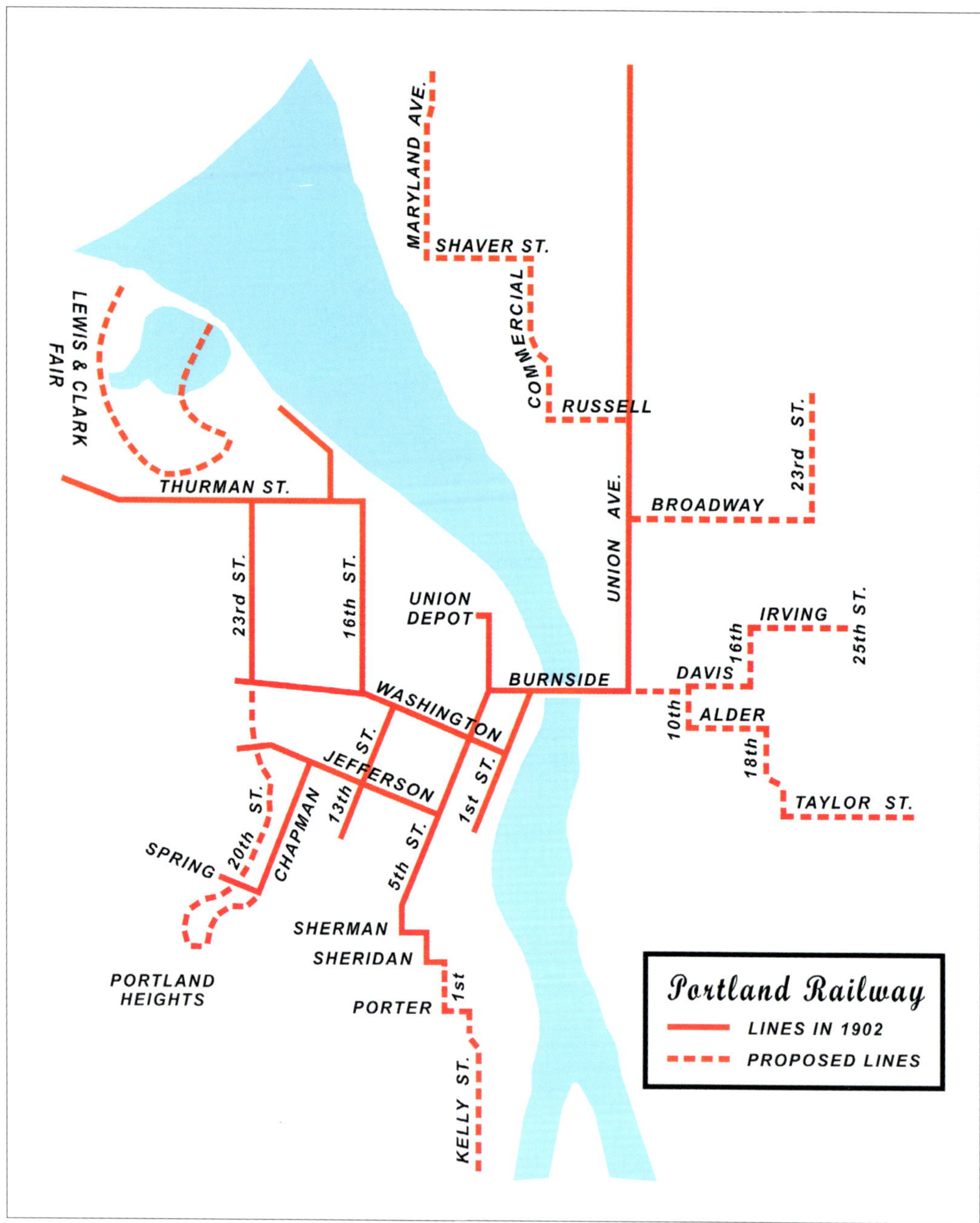

In this April 20, 1902, *Street Railway Review* map, the Portland Railway Company's proposed Albina Line is the branch running from NE Russell Street and Union Avenue to N Maryland Avenue. This second Albina Line was intended to eventually reach St. Johns. However, by the time the first Portland Railway merged into the Portland Consolidated Railway in 1904, the route had become the Russell–Shaver stub line.

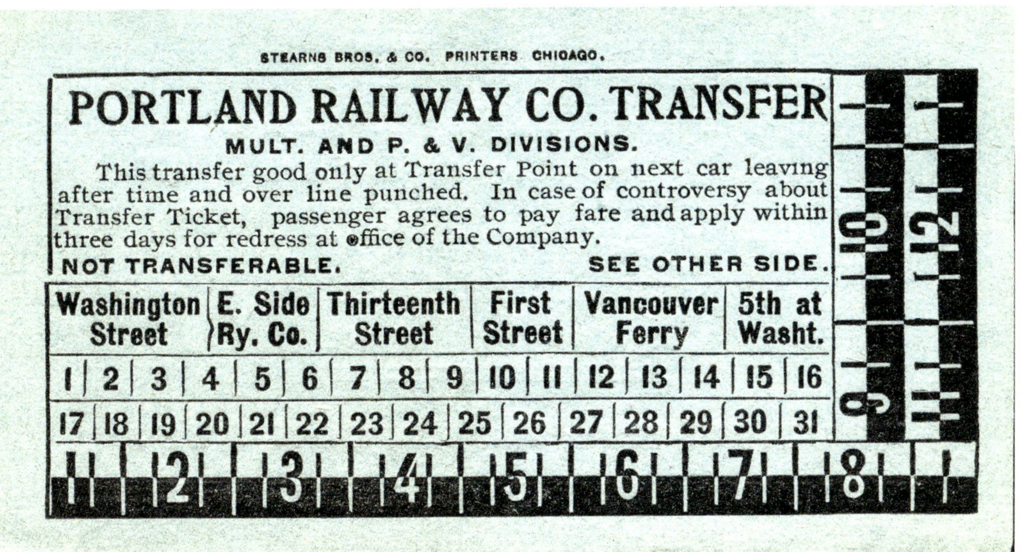

STEARNS BROS. & CO. PRINTERS CHICAGO.

PORTLAND RAILWAY CO. TRANSFER

MULT. AND P. & V. DIVISIONS.

This transfer good only at Transfer Point on next car leaving after time and over line punched. In case of controversy about Transfer Ticket, passenger agrees to pay fare and apply within three days for redress at office of the Company.

NOT TRANSFERABLE. **SEE OTHER SIDE.**

Washington Street	E. Side Ry. Co.	Thirteenth Street	First Street	Vancouver Ferry	5th at Washt.

1	2	3	4	5	6	7	8	9	10	11	12	13	14	15	16
17	18	19	20	21	22	23	24	25	26	27	28	29	30	31	

1 2 3 4 5 6 7 8 9 10 11 12

The first Portland Railway Company had two divisions, as can be seen on this turn-of-the-nineteenth-century transfer. The west side of the Willamette River was served by the Multnomah Division and the east side by the Portland and Vancouver Division. These divisions reflected the names of two previous railway companies that were merged into Portland Railway in 1892: the Multnomah Railway Company and the Portland & Vancouver Railway Company.

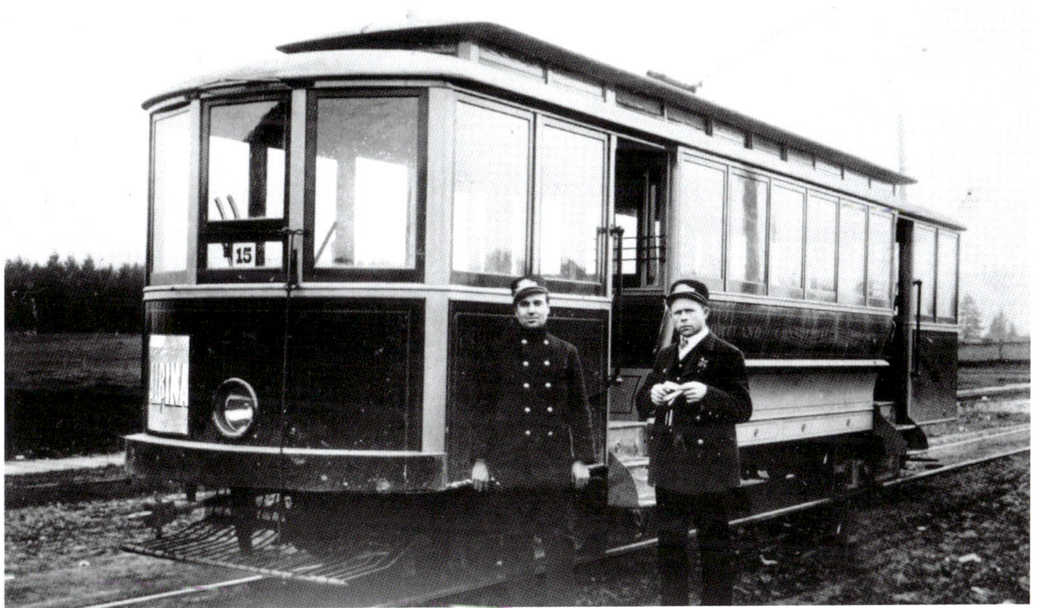

No. 28 was another of the first eight Fuller Standard cars. It is seen here in 1904 during the Portland Consolidated Railway period. The land behind the streetcar is open pasture and forest, so this is likely along N Shaver Street. The Fuller double-purchase-lever handbrake seen in the window was of a type confused for a cablecar grip in an early inventory since they are remarkably similar in appearance.

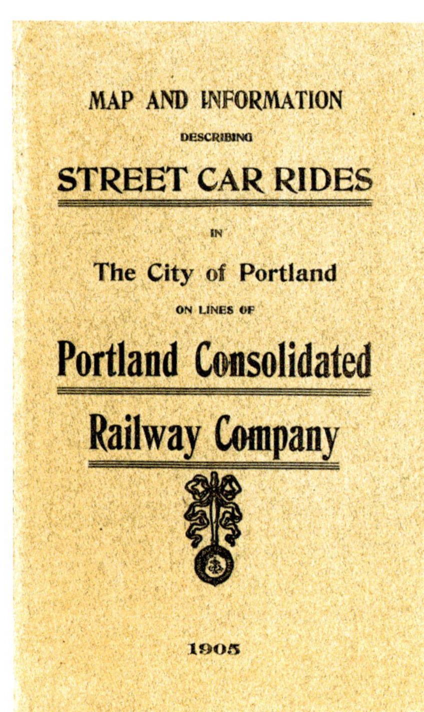

MAP AND INFORMATION
DESCRIBING
STREET CAR RIDES
IN
The City of Portland
ON LINES OF
Portland Consolidated
Railway Company

1905

Left: The Portland Consolidated Railway Company was formed on October 18, 1904, to take over the properties of the City & Suburban Railway, the first Portland Railway Company, and the Portland & Fairview Railroad Company. By the time its property was transferred to the second Portland Railway Company on November 1, 1905, it was operating twenty-eight streetcar lines. This brochure promoted "scenic rides" to Vancouver, Portland Heights, Willamette Heights, Mt. Tabor, City Park, St. Johns, Riverview Cemetery, and Montavilla.

Below: This picture of former Portland Railway Company No. 35 was taken outside the Ankeny Carbarn during the PRL&P years. Although long after the Albina Line had become the Russell–Shaver stub, No. 309 is included here because it clearly shows how the first Fuller series was created by extending the bodies of old Multnomah Street Railway Pullmans to create double-truck, three-compartment cars. Kerns School is in the background.

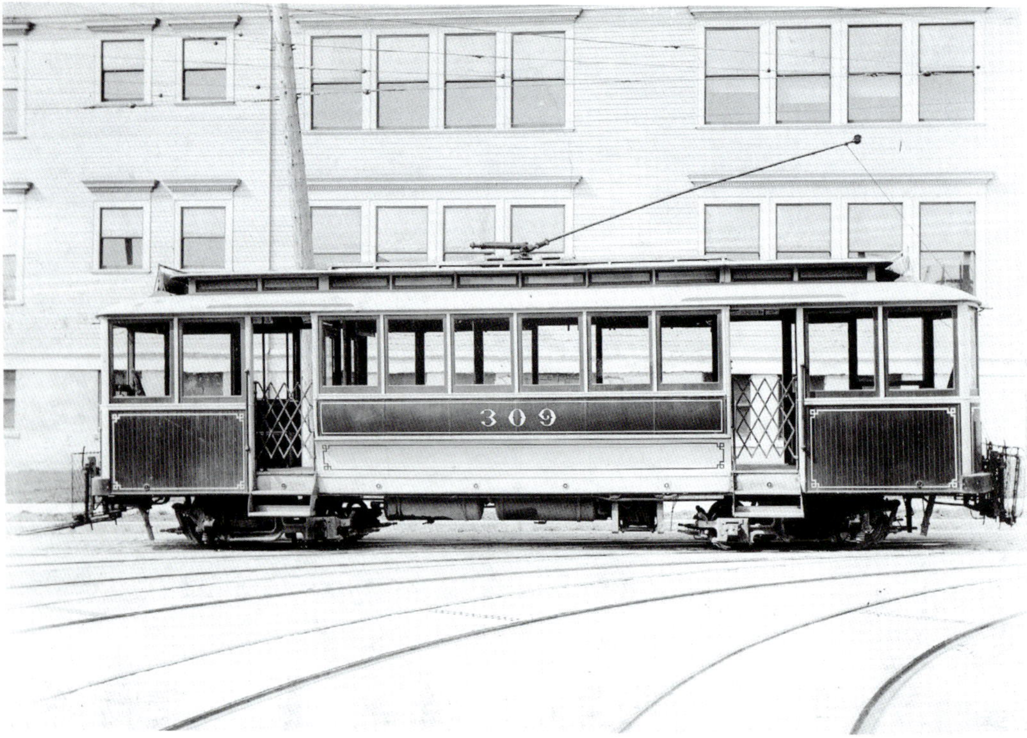

2

The St. Johns Motor Line

By December 20, 1889, Portland & Albina Line streetcars were carrying destination signs for St. Johns, yet passengers boarding the new trolleys on the west end of the Steel Bridge were not heading directly out the Portland Peninsula. Those wanting to reach St. Johns would need to transfer to the trains of the new St. Johns Motor Line on N Stanton Street and Commercial Avenue for an additional 6-mile journey.

Since the Peninsula was sparsely populated, the Willamette Bridge Railway Company determined that it could not yet support an electric railway. Instead, they built a less expensive steam "dummy" railroad. A dummy was a small locomotive enclosed in a wooden body that resembled a streetcar. Steam dummies were considered to be less frightening to passing horses and carriages because their noise was muffled and escaping steam was hidden from view. It was hoped they would also be more acceptable than traditional locomotives on city streets. As evident from the line's name, dummies were known as "motors."

The St. Johns Motor Line was the third steam street railway in Portland. The Willamette Bridge Railway Company had experience with this type of operation, having built the first steam motor line in the state to Mt. Tabor on July 9, 1888. Within four years, Portland could boast of having seven steam dummy lines, the most of any U.S. city.

The first trip over the St. Johns Motor Line took place in conjunction with the opening of the Portland & Albina electric line on November 1, 1889. At that time, the steam railroad was not complete so the dignitaries aboard a coach borrowed from the Mt. Tabor Line only made it as far as the P. T. Smith farm, 1 mile south of the town of St. Johns. The extension to N Jersey (now Lombard) Street and Philadelphia Avenue in the center of St. Johns was completed on May 12, 1890.

During the initial weeks of operation, the northern terminal for Portland & Albina Line trolleys was four blocks north of the Montgomery Slough Bridge at N Patton (renamed Interstate in 1916) and Russell streets. As the electrified line was extended, construction of the St. Johns Motor Line also progressed. By December 20, 1889, steam trains met trolleys at the long tunnel-like Willamette Bridge Railway carbarn on N Stanton Street and Commercial Avenue.

In 1901, the difficult 8 percent grade on N Commercial Avenue was abandoned in favor of new track on N Williams Avenue. The Upper Albina Line trolleys now operated north on Williams to N Killingsworth and then west to N Commercial Avenue. A new Piedmont transfer station had been built there, and the steam line cut back to that point.

Although the St. Johns Motor Line was built as a temporary expedient, it was not electrified until 1903 by which time it had become the last steam dummy railroad in Portland. At first, trolley operation to St. Johns was hampered by inadequate electric power and storage batteries were placed in the new Piedmont Carbarn to alleviate the problem. Unfortunately, the need to transfer was not yet over. Disappointed passengers were required to use the Piedmont Transfer Station until 1905 because the big interurban-style streetcars built for the St. Johns Line could not run downtown until tracks could be adjusted and bridges strengthened.

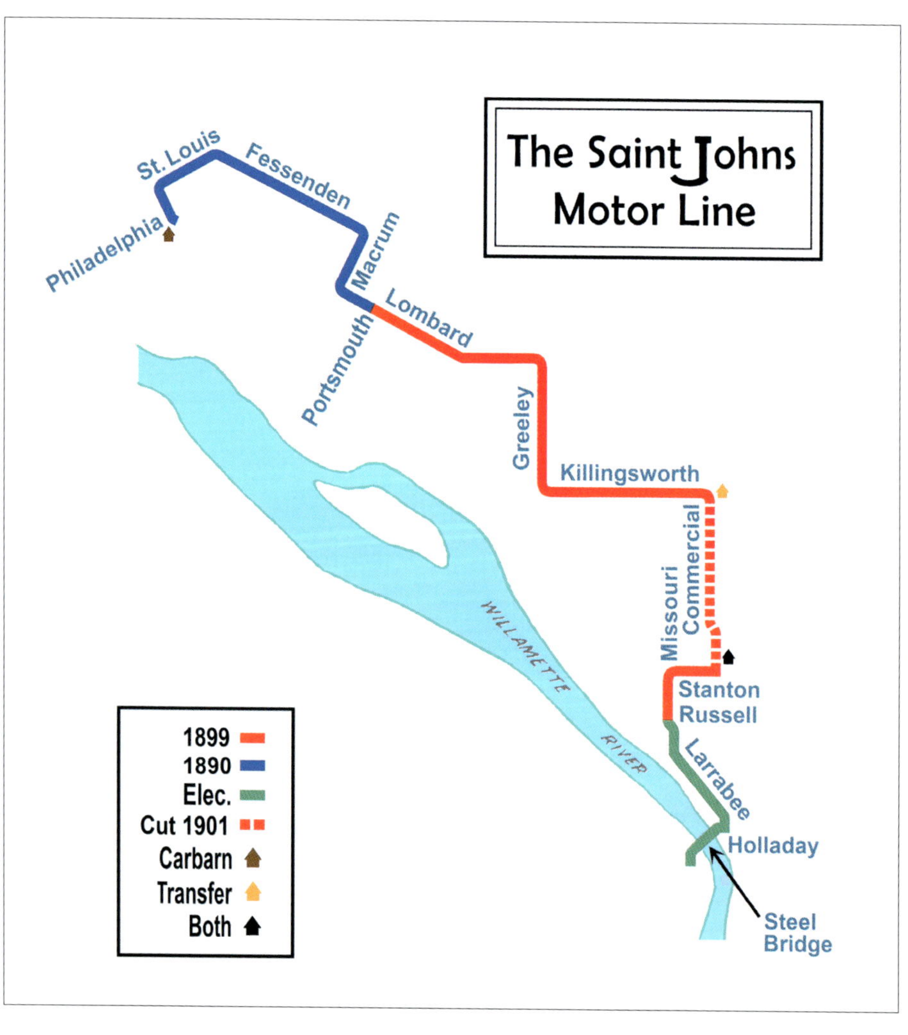

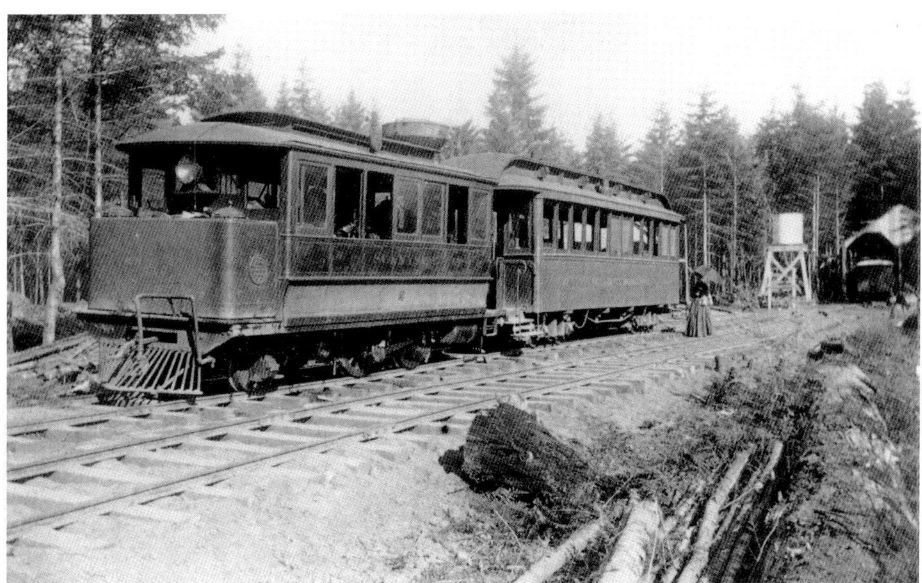

As evidenced by the name on the side of the locomotive, the Willamette Bridge Railway borrowed Baldwin dummy No. 2 and Pullman coach 10 from the Sunnyside Line in Southeast Portland. They made the first trial run over the as-yet-uncompleted St. Johns Motor Company line on November 1, 1889. The train is seen here in front of the engine shed near what is now SE 69th Avenue and Belmont Street.

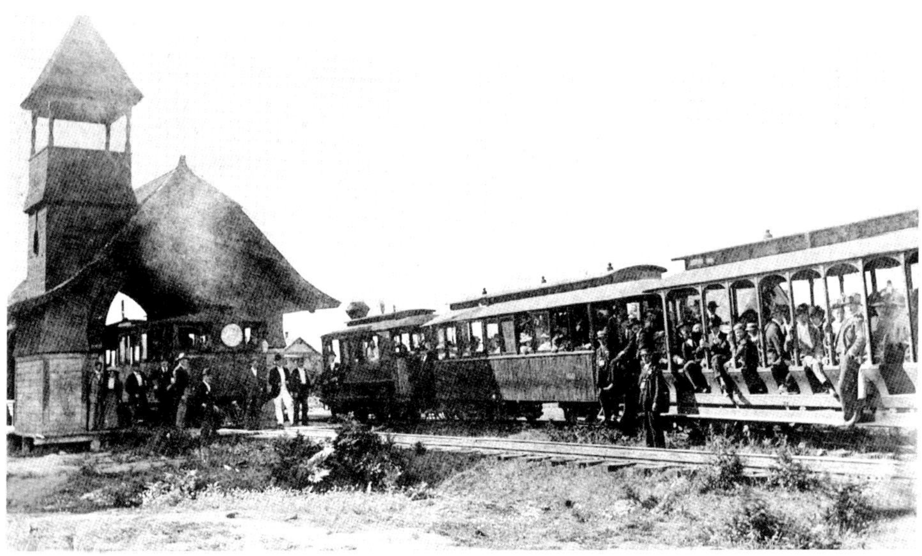

Inbound and outbound trains meet at Portsmouth Station in a photograph labeled "First run." That would make this November 4, 1889, when regular operation commenced on the St. Johns Motor Line. Portsmouth Station was the western terminus of the line until May 12, 1890. Motors 2 and 3, closed trailer 100, and an eight-bench open trailer would have made up a preponderance of Willamette Bridge Railway steam railroad equipment at the time.

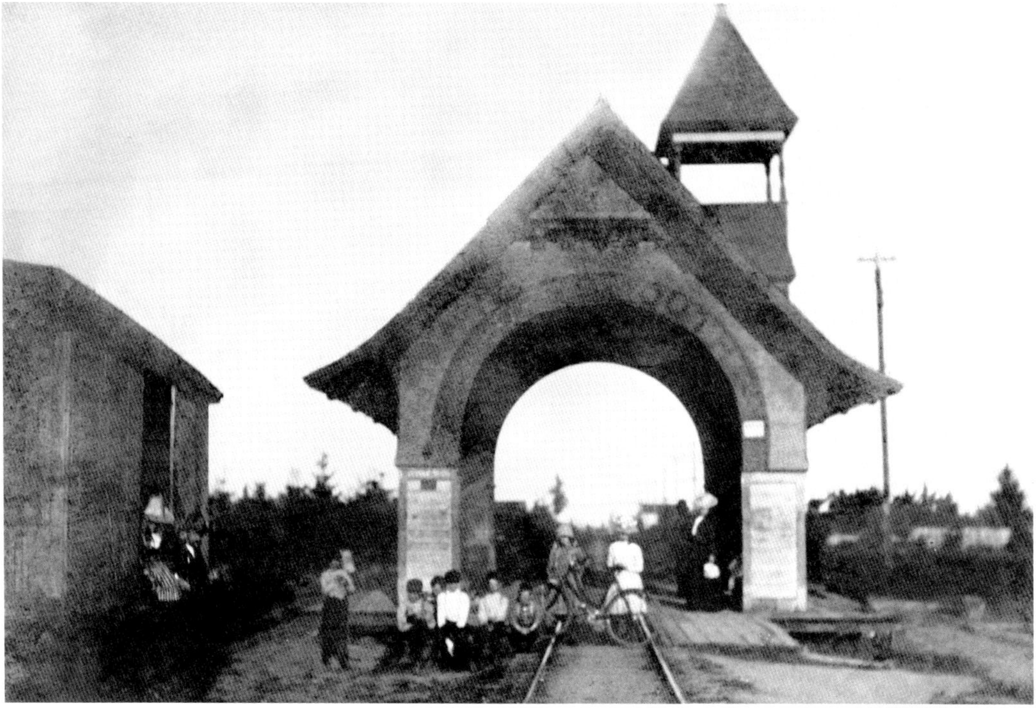

The picturesque Portsmouth Station on N Lombard Avenue at Portsmouth Street may not have been overly busy during the steam railroad days, since the children posing on the track do not seem to be concerned about the possible arrival of a train. The boxcar at left served as a shelter for waiting passengers. (*Photograph courtesy Don Nelson*)

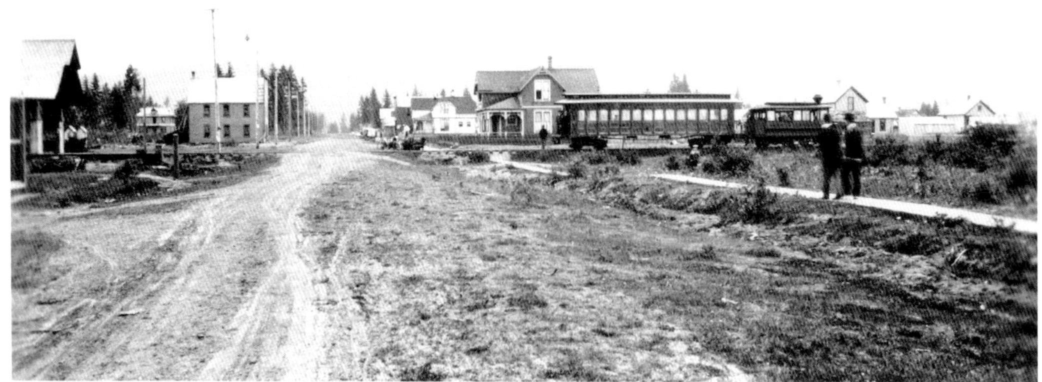

A St. Johns Motor Line train has just crossed the muddy intersection of N Lombard Street and Portsmouth Avenue near Portsmouth Station. The little dummy is hauling a trailer built in Portland by the Columbia Car & Tool Company. It is a Heacock and Lovejoy convertible whose removable side panels were designed to allow use in all types of weather.

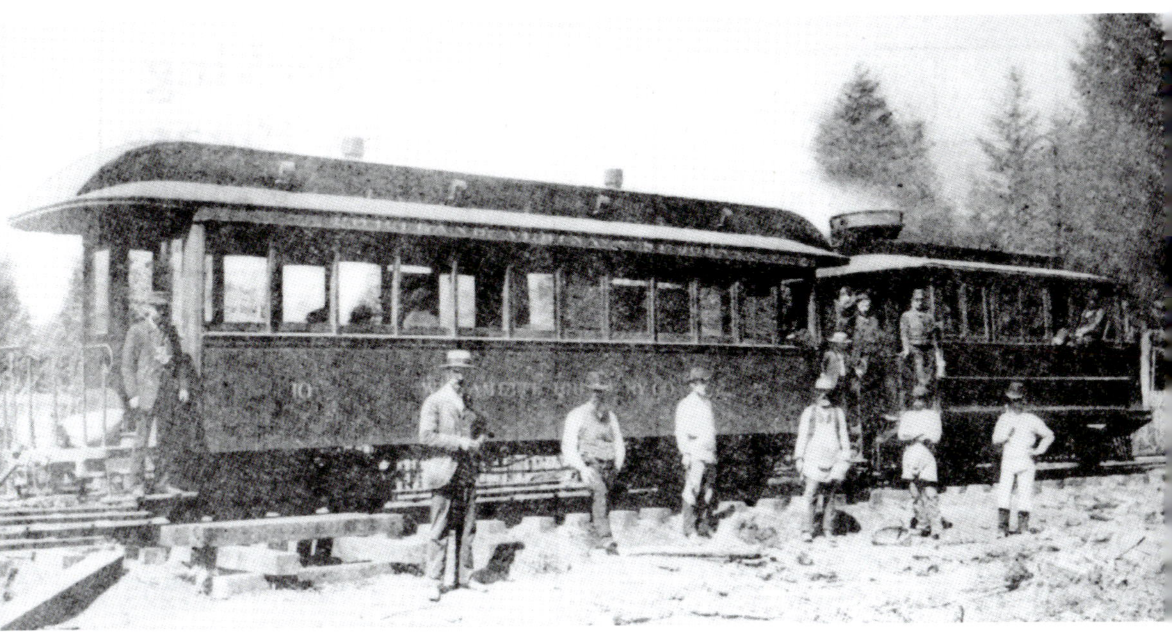

Dignitaries and workmen were on hand on May 12, 1890, when the first train entered the city of St. Johns. Willamette Bridge Railway coach 10 again took the honors, although this time with dummy No. 3. The letterboard on the Pullman coach reads "Portland Albina & St. Johns," the three cities that were finally linked by a transit company. (*The Peninsula magazine*)

AUG. 3

WILLAMETTE BRIDGE RAILWAY CO.

ST. JOHNS MOTOR LINE.

TRANSFER SLIP.

From St. Johns Motor Line to Electric Car Going West.

This slip will not be honored unless presented at junction of Elliott and Hawley Sts., Albina Line, and is good only on this date and for trip indicated by punched mark in margin.

A M
6:15
8:50
10:15
11;10
P M
1:25
2:25
3:25
4:50
5

In March 1890, the Willamette Bridge Railway Company reached an agreement with the Metropolitan Railway Company for passengers crossing the Steel Bridge to transfer to lines in the city of Portland without paying an additional fare. It was now possible to travel from St. Johns to South Portland for a single 5-cent fare. This transfer slip was punched during the evening rush hour on August 3 of that year.

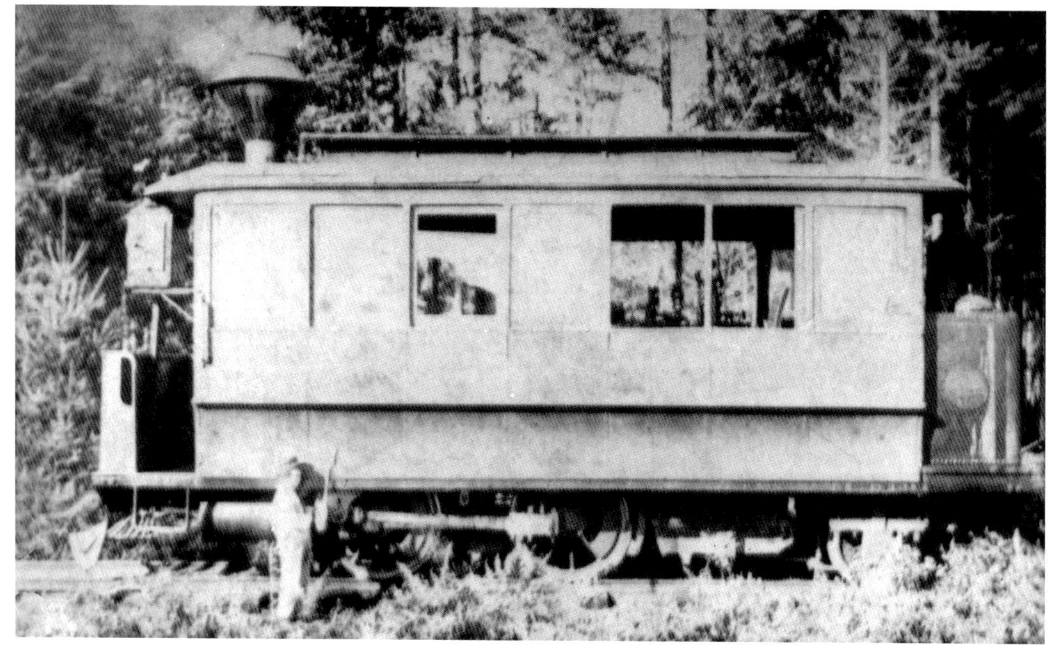

A young lad is helping "oil around" a St. Johns Motor Line engine—an important task during the steam era when the moving parts on a locomotive needed frequent lubrication. This is either dummy No. 2 or 3, built by the Baldwin Locomotive Works in 1889. It was an 0-4-0 T tank engine, which means it carried wood and water onboard and did not require a tender.

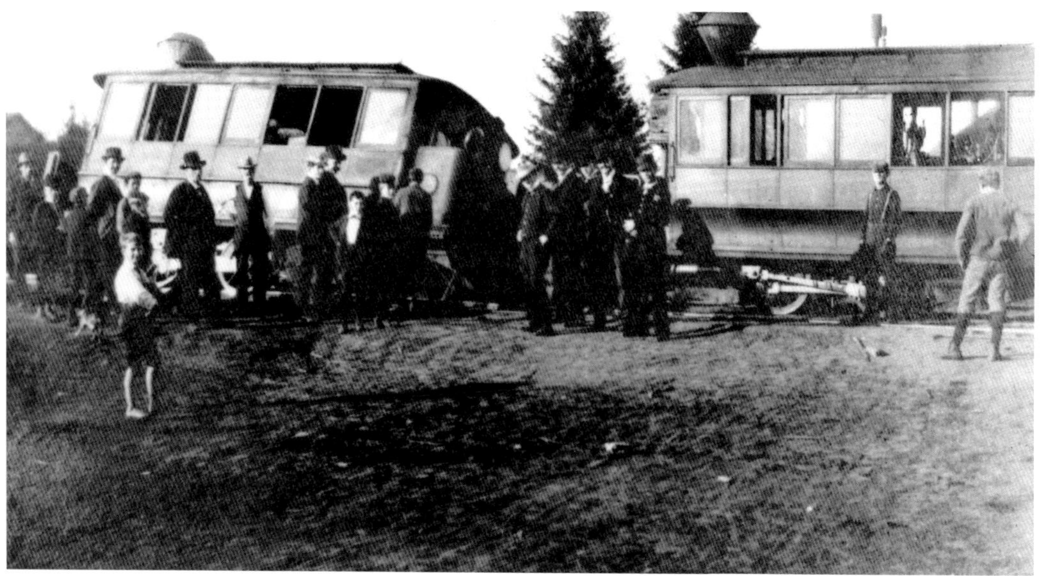

This is not the scene of a locomotive collision. Motor No. 3 is simply helping get No. 2 back on the track after a derailment while passengers and neighbors watch. At center, a group of policemen are posing for the fireman from No. 3 as he sets up a photograph.

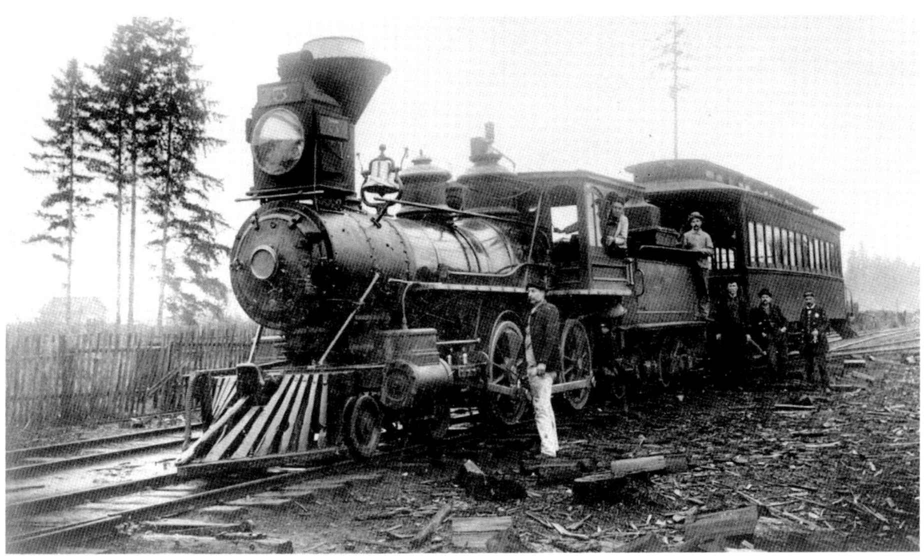

The St. Johns Motor Line had one engine that was a traditional 4-4-0 locomotive rather than a "motor." No. 5 was acquired from the Kansas Central Railroad on December 3, 1890, in order to free up the heavy 2-3-0 dummy No. 4 for use on the Mt. Tabor Line. It is seen here in St. Johns with engineer Frank Smith and Conductor Tom Monahan.

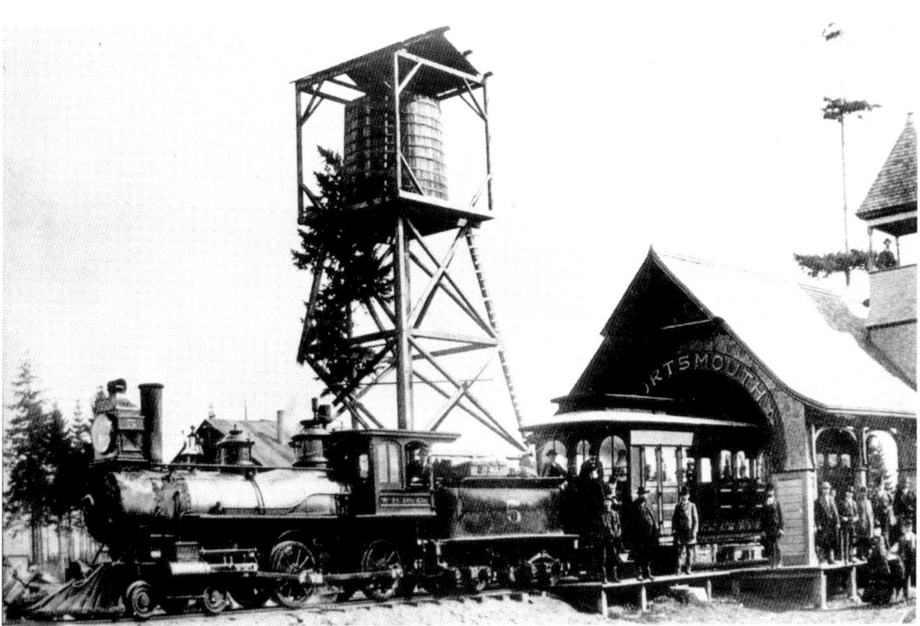

Locomotive No. 5 is ready to depart the ornate Portsmouth Station with a Heacock and Lovejoy trailer. These convertible trailers were manufactured at the Columbia Car and Tool Company to a design by M. E. Heacock, who came to Portland with a streetcar construction order from the Stockton Combine Harvester and Agricultural Works in California. He set up shop in the Metropolitan Railway carbarn on SW 2nd Avenue and Montgomery Street.

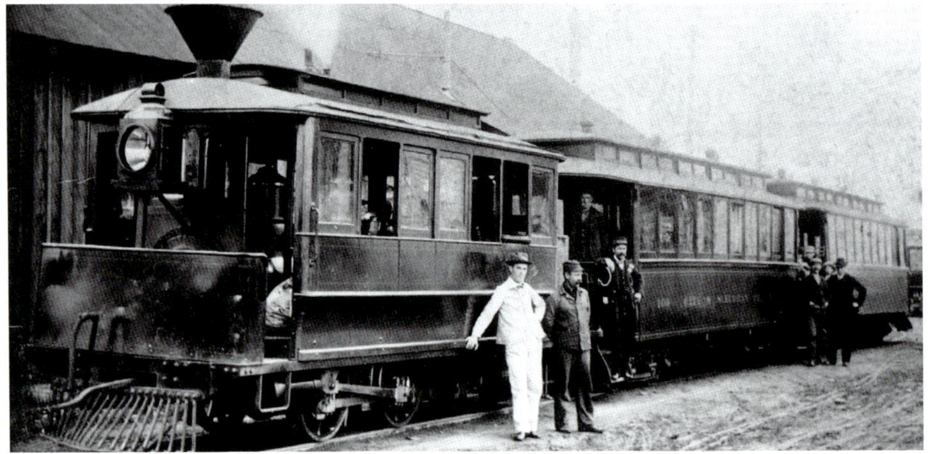

The last addition to St. Johns line motive power came after the City & Suburban Railway took over in 1891. Baldwin No. 7 had been built in 1889 and bought secondhand by the short-lived Portland, Mt. Tabor & Eastern RR as their No. 1. It is seen with Pullman No. 109 and another coach next to the St. Johns Carbarn on N Commercial Avenue and Stanton Street in Albina. (*Photograph courtesy Norm Gholston*)

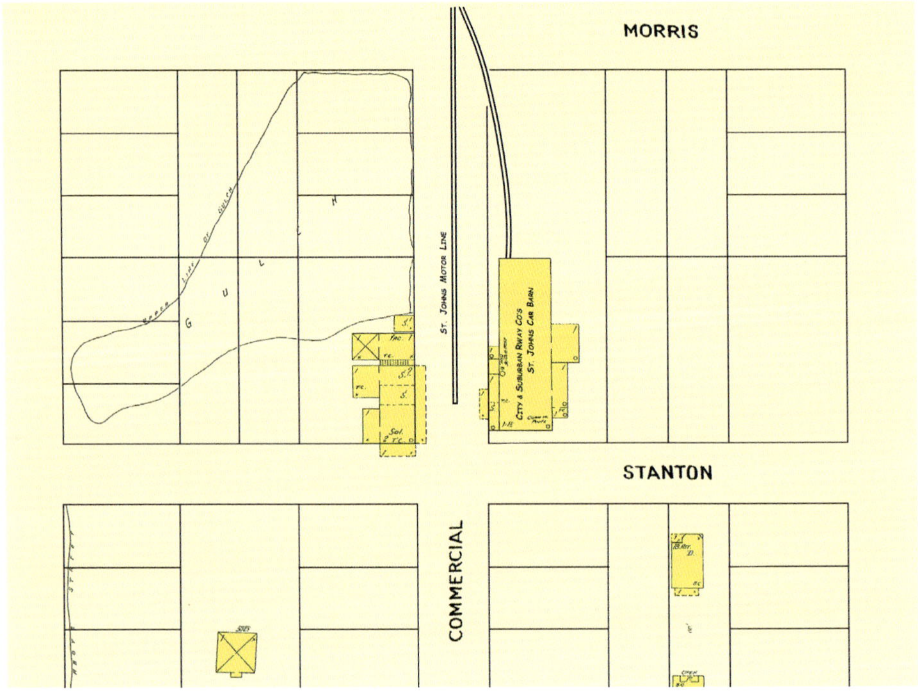

The City & Suburban Railway Company's tunnel-like St Johns Carbarn and adjacent St. Johns Motor Line tracks appeared on this 1901 Sanborn Fire Insurance Map two years before the steam dummy trains were replaced by electric streetcars. The route of the Portland & Albina trolley line is not shown. Note the large gully across from the station.

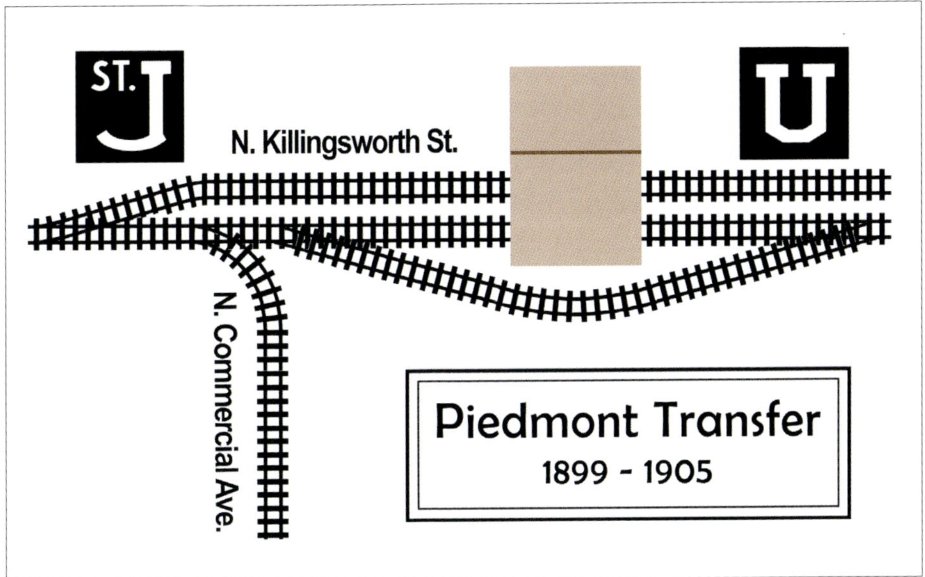

This author's conception is based upon an examination of photographs taken at the Piedmont Transfer Station, which suggest that it featured a bypass track in addition to dual tracks that passed through the shed. In later years, a wye would be added to these tracks so that the streetcars built for use on the St. Johns Line could be turned around. They were of a long interurban design that precluded their use in downtown Portland.

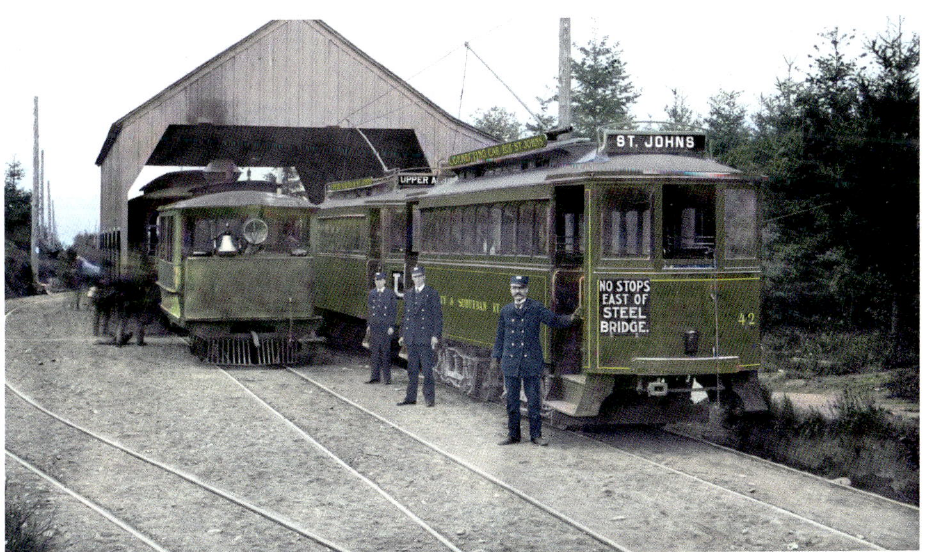

City & Suburban Railway St. Johns Line No. 42 and a matching Upper Albina Line spliced horsecar are seen meeting a steam dummy train at the new Piedmont Transfer station on N Moore Avenue and Killingsworth Street. Upon completion of new tracks on Williams Avenue in 1901, Upper Albina trolleys began operating to this new terminal. Note that passengers transferring from St. Johns trains could not disembark on the east side of town.

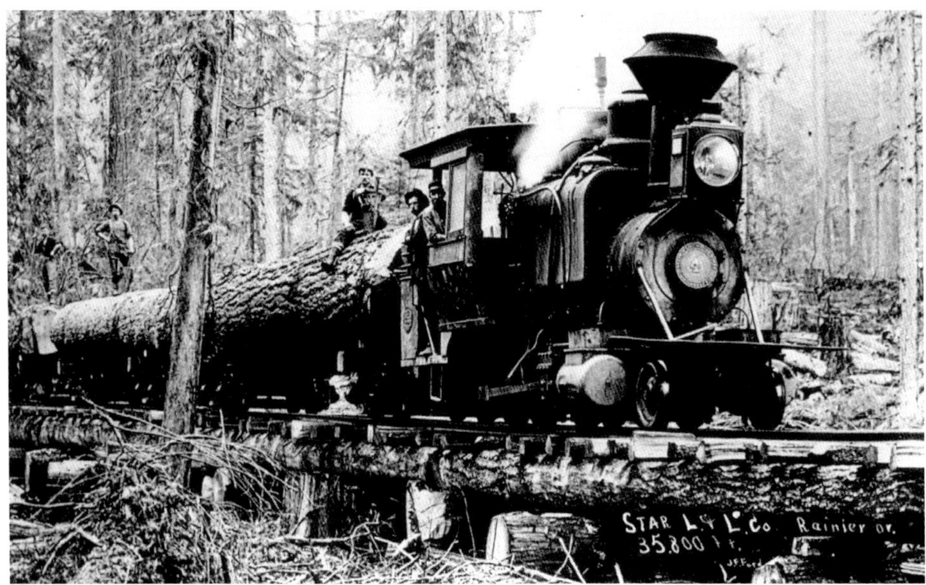

As streetcar lines converted to electric operation, old steam motors were often sold for use on logging railroads. Such was the case with City & Suburban Railway No. 4, which was sold to the Star Logging & Lumber Company. The pretentious dummy body is gone in this postcard scene, showing the little Baldwin hauling old growth timber to the south bank of the Columbia River. Note the makeshift trestle built from logs.

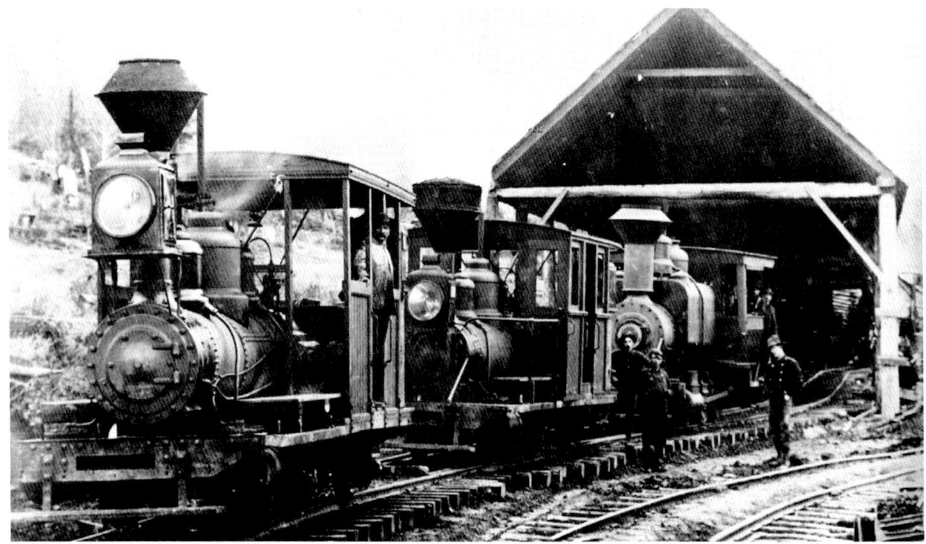

When the curtain came down on steam dummy streetcars, three former Willamette Bridge Railway motors went to the Star Lumber Company (later Yeon & Pelton Company and then Portland Lumber Company) whose logging railroad hauled timber in the rugged hills near Rainier, Oregon. Locomotives 3, 2, and 4 are seen in front of the shed where loads were prepared for lowering down a steep log chute on the south bank of the Columbia River.

3

The Lower Albina and Mississippi Avenue Line

The Lower Albina Line was an outgrowth of Portland's first electric streetcar line, which was opened by the Willamette Bridge Railway Company on November 1, 1889. The company had obtained franchises on both Mississippi and Williams Avenues in Albina in 1891 prior to merging into the City & Suburban Railway Company; however, the laying of rail beyond N Stanton Street did not begin for several years. Work was postponed by the need for extensive filling and grading on steep terrain as well as a lack of funding following the financial Panic of 1893.

Soon after its formation, the City & Suburban Railway Company split the Portland & Albina Line into two separate lines named for the Upper and Lower areas of Albina they served. The two lines operated across the original Steel Bridge from SW 3rd Avenue and Morrison Street in downtown Portland to the St. Johns Motor Line terminal on N Stanton Street and Commercial Avenue. Later, Upper Albina trolleys would follow a different route to the East Side via N McMillan Street and Williams Avenue.

Work on extending the Lower Albina Line finally commenced during the spring of 1899 when track was completed between N Stanton and Beech streets on N Mississippi Avenue. Track on N Commercial Avenue would be removed, and St. Johns Line streetcars on the sister Upper Albina Line rerouted to a new transfer station under construction on N Killingsworth Street. Meanwhile, the Lower Albina Line was extended, reaching N Shaver in 1902 and N Prescott in 1904.

When the new Portland Consolidated Railway Company was formed in 1904, the two Albina branches were renamed. The Lower Albina Line was now the Mississippi Avenue Line. The new designation "Mississippi Av." appeared on rollsigns, although the "L" dash signs would remain in use for several years to avoid confusion.

In 1905, the Mississippi Avenue Line reached a more permanent terminus on N Killingsworth Street and Albina Avenue. The railway company had moved the route over to Albina Avenue five blocks south of Killingsworth to avoid a property assessment.

A stub service began operating north from N Albina Avenue and Killingsworth Street to the town of Kenton in 1909. Regular Mississippi Avenue cars continued to terminate on N Killingsworth Street until October 13, 1912, when the Mississippi and Kenton lines were combined, and the northern terminus moved to N Denver Avenue and Kilpatrick Street. After this, the line remained essentially the same on the east side although bridge access and downtown termini changed several times.

The first streetcars used on the Upper Albina/Mississippi Avenue run were City & Suburban Standards renumbered into the 100-146 series. Later, PRL&P introduced the Fuller 300s and, after 1912, PAYE cars (mainly 521 class). Around 1935, the 800-class Broadways made their appearance. After the Mississippi Avenue streetcar line was discontinued on September 14, 1940, trolleybuses took over twice. The Mississippi Avenue trolleybus line operated from February 6, 1949, to January 28, 1958, and again from February 25 to October 23, 1958.

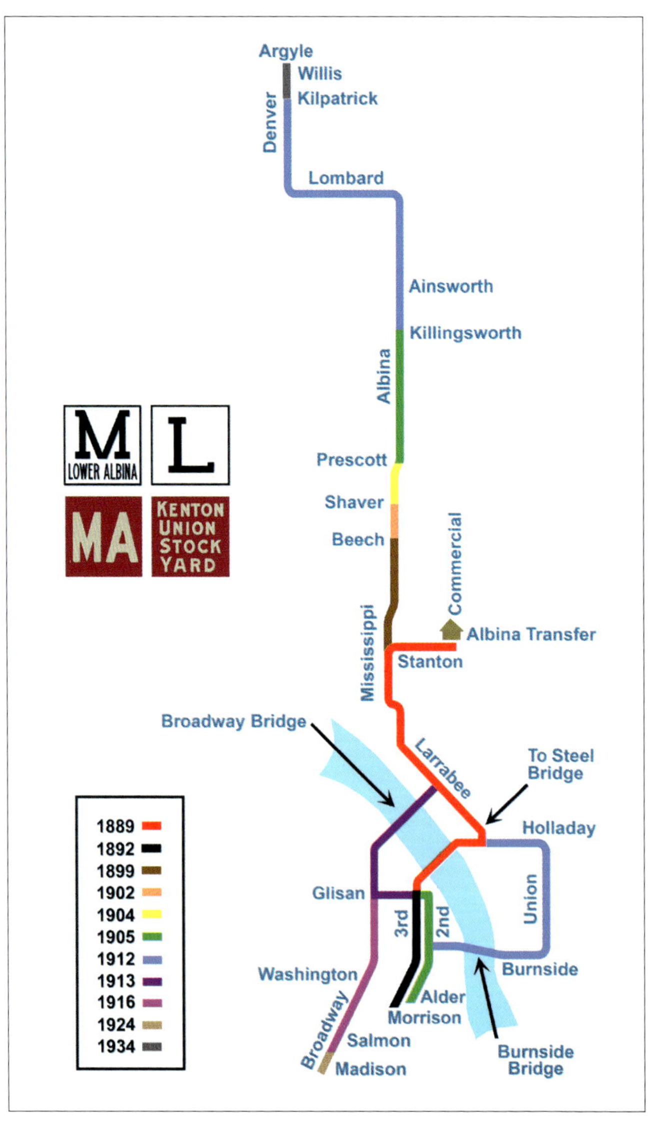

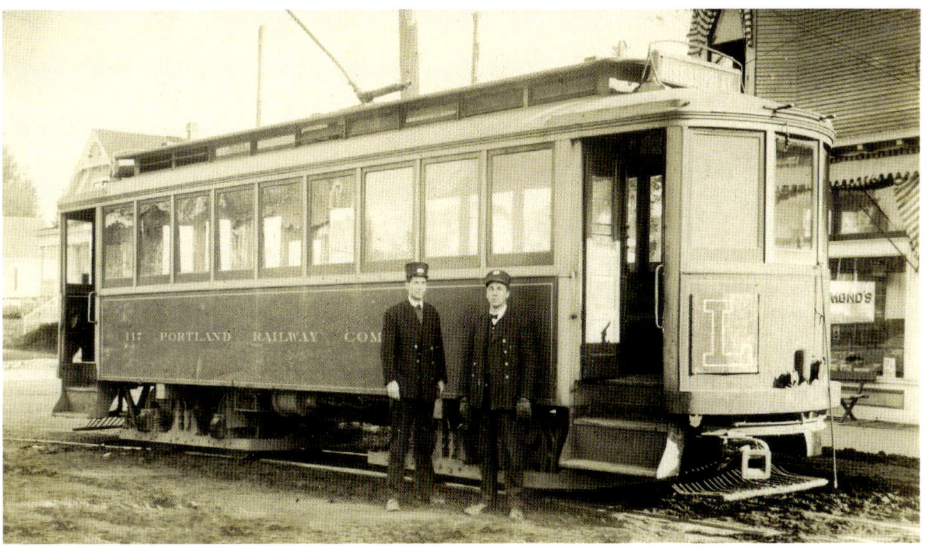

Among the first double-truck (eight wheel), closed platform streetcars assigned to the Lower Albina Line was No. 117, which is seen around 1905 at the outer terminal on N Killingsworth Street and Albina Avenue. The car was a City & Suburban "Standard" built in the Savier Street shops in 1901.

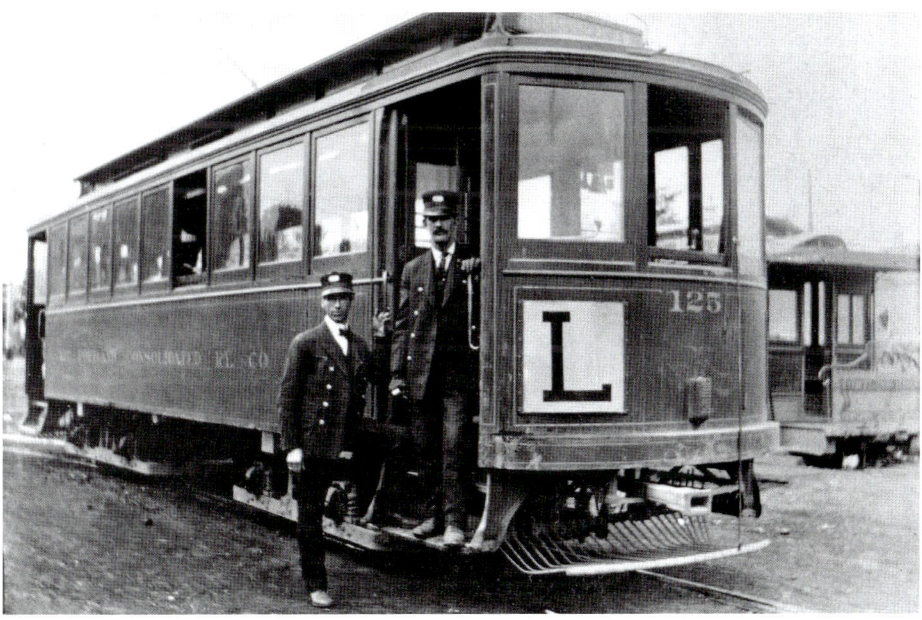

No. 125 is probably waiting at the N Killingsworth Street and Albina Avenue terminal shortly after it opened in 1905, because a former cable car is serving as a waiting station in the background. The last cable line was discontinued that year (and no cable car ever ran in North Portland). The trolley, still lettered for the Portland Consolidated Railway, is another of the locally built C & S Standards.

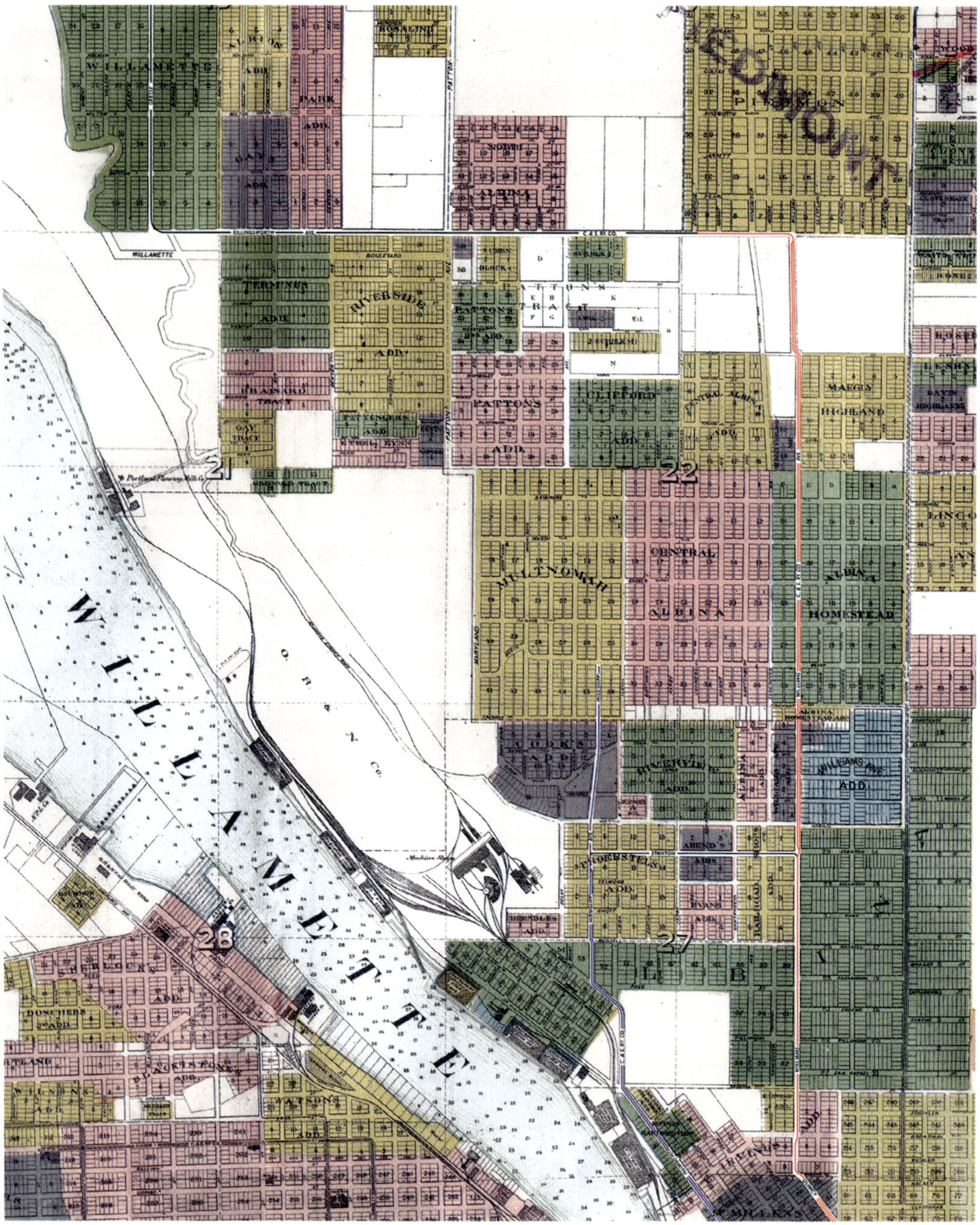

City & Suburban Railway lines in North Portland are highlighted in this detail from the 1901 J. Thornburn Ross real estate map of Portland. The map promoted Piedmont as "The Heart of the Peninsula (with) Double-Tracked Electric Trunk Lines." The Lower Albina Line is blue and the Upper Albina line is red. The 1899 Lower Albina Line outer terminal has reached N Beech Street, while the Upper Albina route extends to the new transfer point with St. Johns Motor Line trains on N Killingsworth Avenue. (*Courtesy Dan Haneckow*)

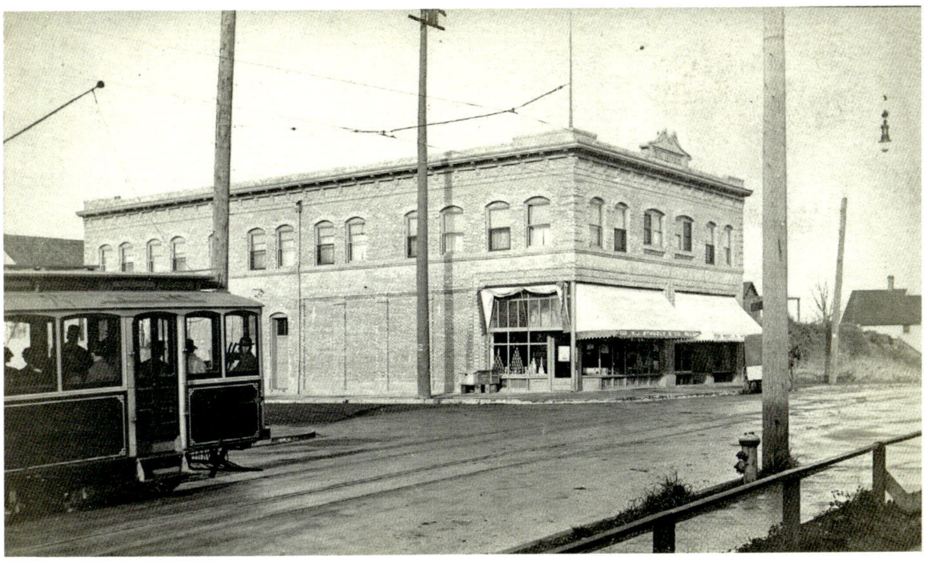

City & Suburban Railway rival Portland Railway also built its own "Standard" cars in response to the national shortage of electric streetcars. One of the 311 series Fuller Standards is seen rolling southward when the 1910-vintage building in the background on N Mississippi Avenue at Skidmore Street was new. The attractive structure survives today. (*Photograph Courtesy Mark Moore*)

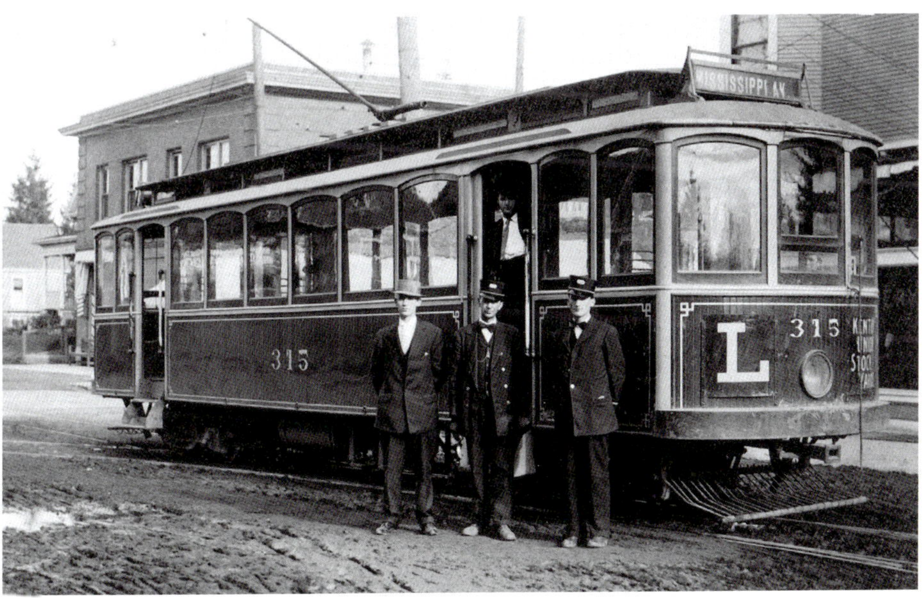

No. 315 and crew are at the muddy intersection of N Albina Avenue and Killingsworth Street in the early 1910s. The car is a second series Fuller Standard built at the Washington Street shops in 1901. The three-compartment Fuller cars are mainly remembered because smoking was allowed in their large vestibules, a feature attributed to cigar smoking company president Franklin Fuller, for whom they were named. (*Photograph Courtesy Mark Moore*)

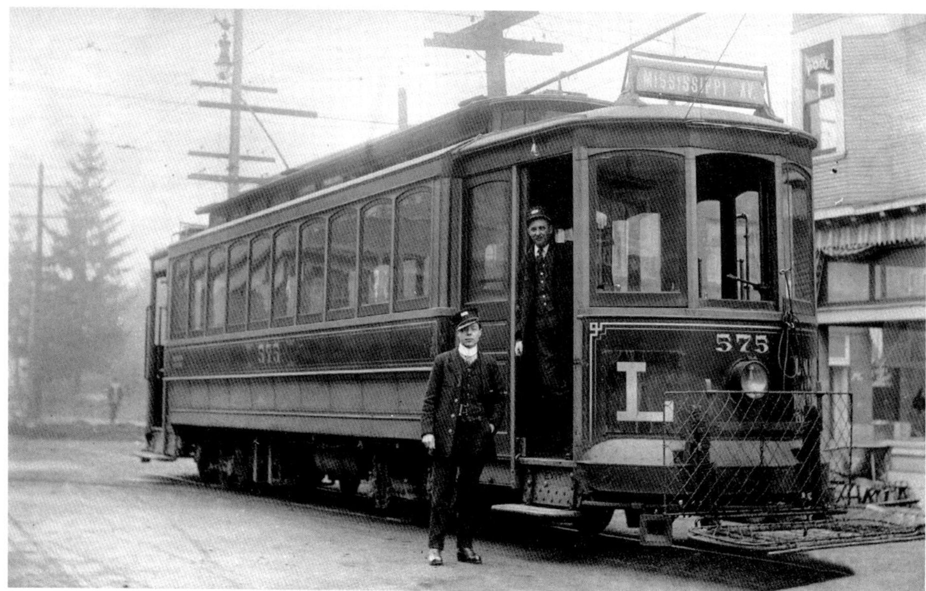

Pay-as-you-enter (PAYE) cars have arrived as evidenced by car 575 seen here at the N Albina Avenue and Killingsworth Street terminus after installation of city-mandated Nelson Safety Fenders during 1912–13. No. 575 was one of a group of large PAYE cars built by the American Car Company of St. Louis in 1910. Conductor Harold Bird is wearing his cap at a jaunty angle.

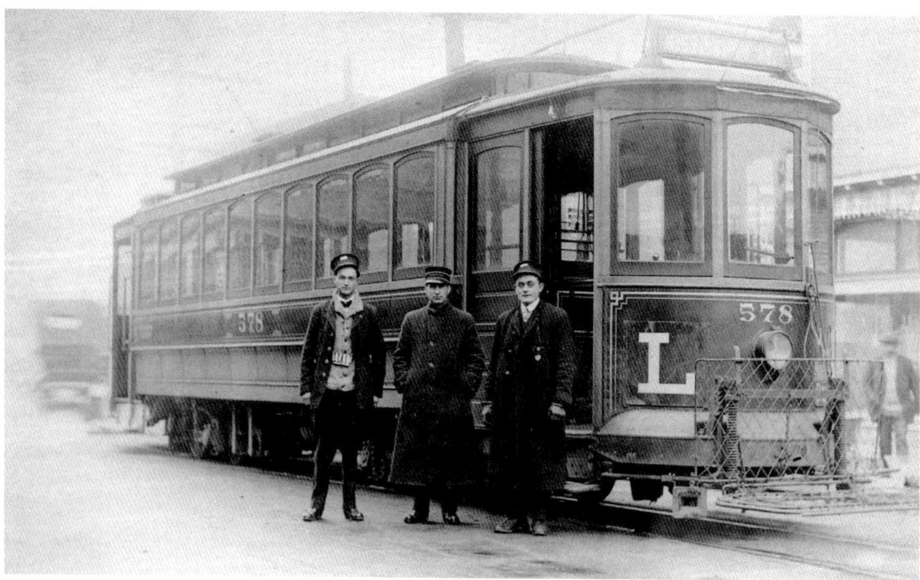

The crew of Lower Albina car 578 are dressed for winter in this *c.* 1913 picture at the N Killingsworth end of the line. Conductor Lewis White is dressed in a heavy sweater and motorman William Stunkard and inspector Perry Palmer wear long uniform coats. All are paying no heed to the automobile that has just passed by.

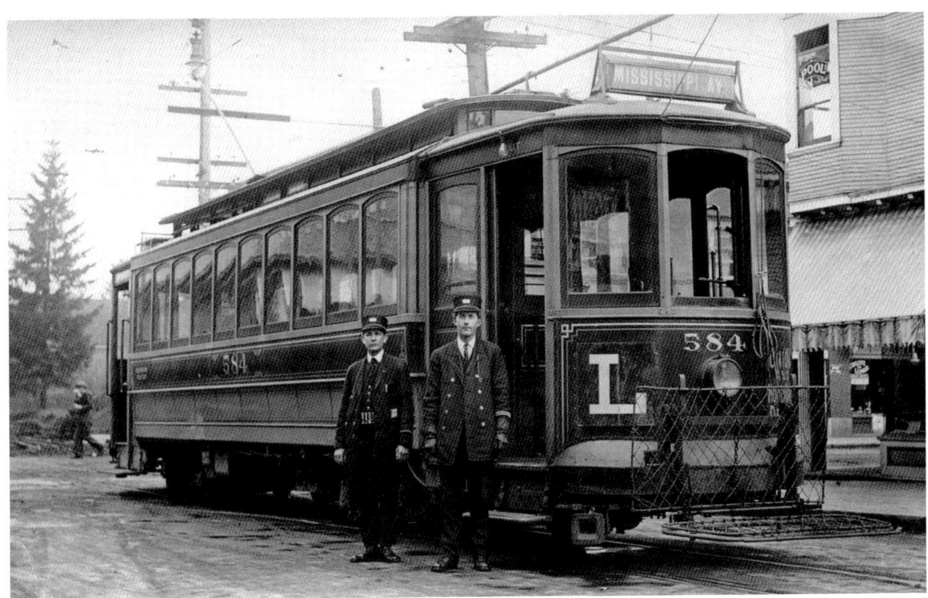

Conductor James Lemarr and motorman Stull must be proud of car 584, whose ornate decoration is easy to see in this close-up. The 143 classic trolleys in this series, with omnibus-sided wooden bodies, PAYE vestibules, clerestory roofs, and maximum traction trucks would become the quintessential Portland streetcar. The bay-windowed store at right, which also served as a waiting station, still exists today.

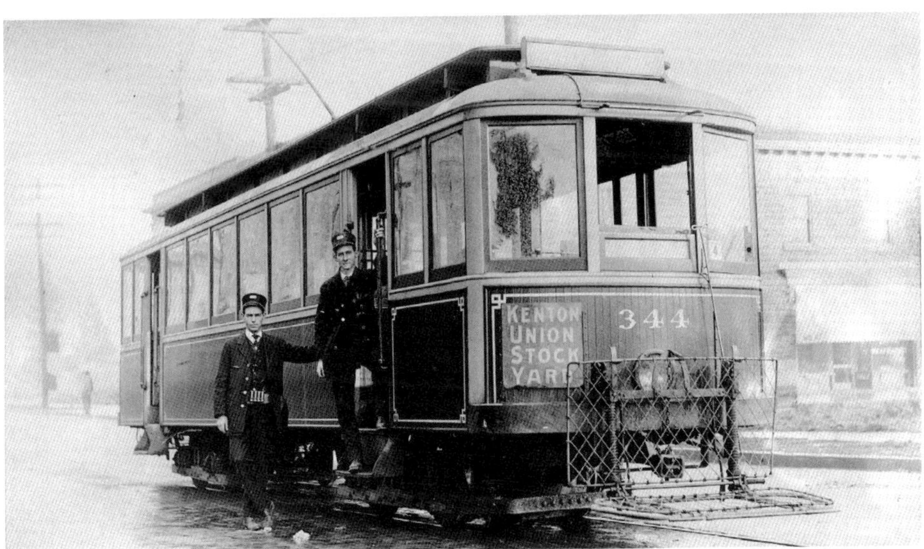

After PRL&P took over part of the Kenton Traction Company Line in October 1912, Mississippi Avenue Line cars began carrying dash signs for Kenton Union Stock Yard (soon changed to Kenton Union Stock Yards). The new outer terminal became N Denver Avenue and Kilpatrick Street in the company town of Kenton, where we see conductor Benjamin Brainard and motorman Brown posing with Fuller car 344.

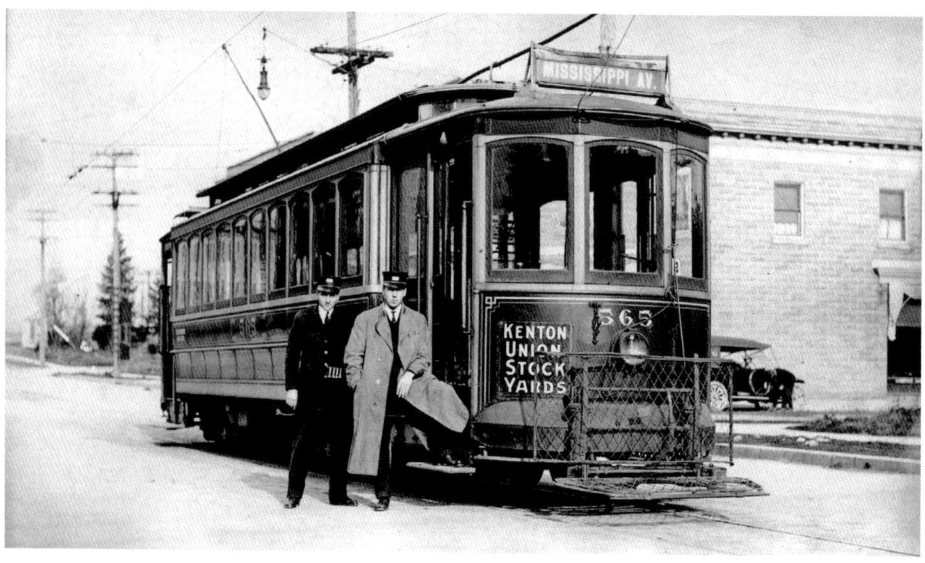

Car 565 and crew are "watching the birdie" at the northern Mississippi Avenue Line terminal. Although conductor Robert Groskopf is wearing his regular uniform on this sunny winter day, motorman Harry Otterstrom is draped in an unusual long coat. In the background a motorist is bending over the hood of an open touring car. The building his auto is parked next to is still in use today.

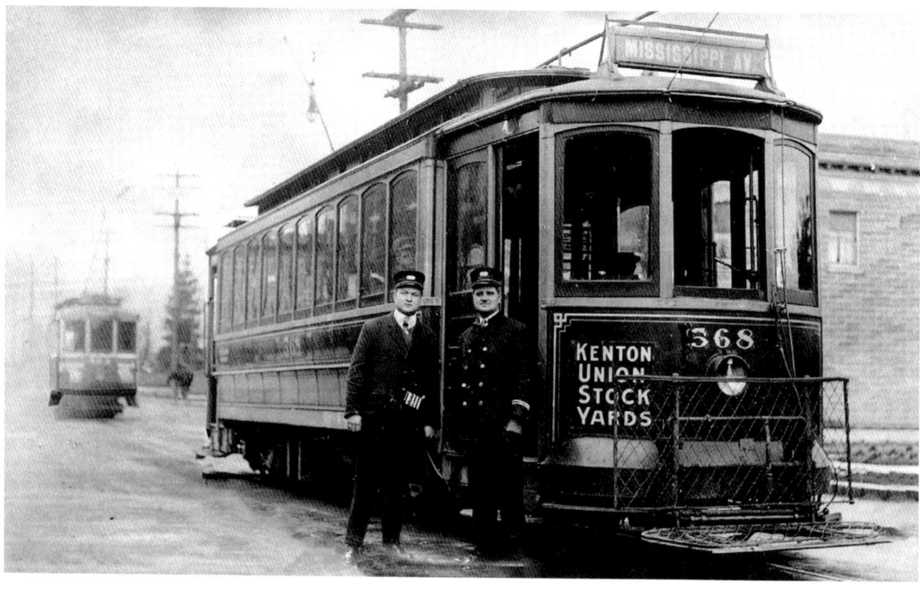

Mississippi Avenue car 568, with conductor Carl Keller and motorman George Foss, is ready to depart the northern terminal in 1913 after having met the 100-class C & S Standard seen in the background. The 100s were leased to the Kenton Traction Company. In 1920, Keller had a medical emergency while working and suffered a fatal accident when he fell from his streetcar.

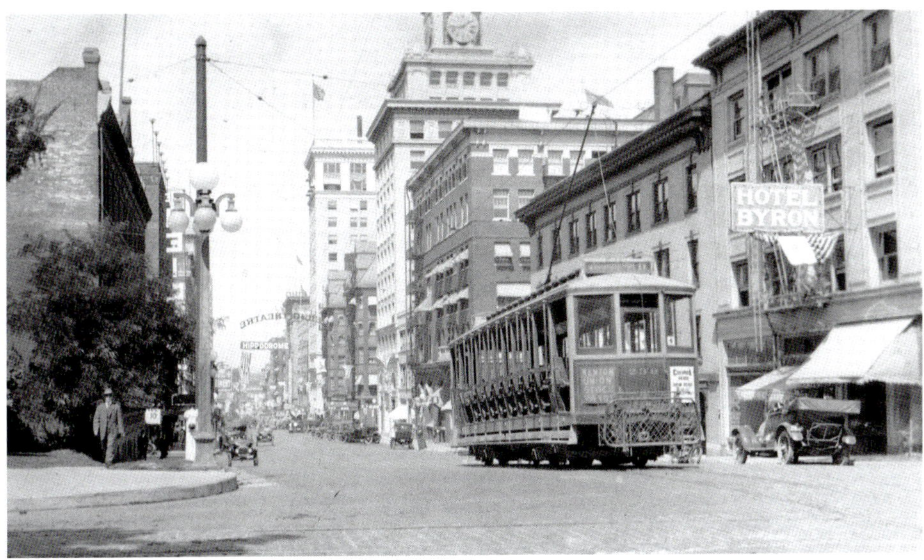

No. 239 is departing the 1916 downtown Mississippi Avenue Line terminus on SW Broadway Avenue at Salmon Street. The YMCA, Jackson Tower, and Portland Hotel are visible in the background next to banners for the Heilig and Hippodrome theaters. This open car, built by the C&S in 1903, was out of service with most of its sisters by 1919, when management decided operation of these fair weather "open breezers" was not cost-effective.

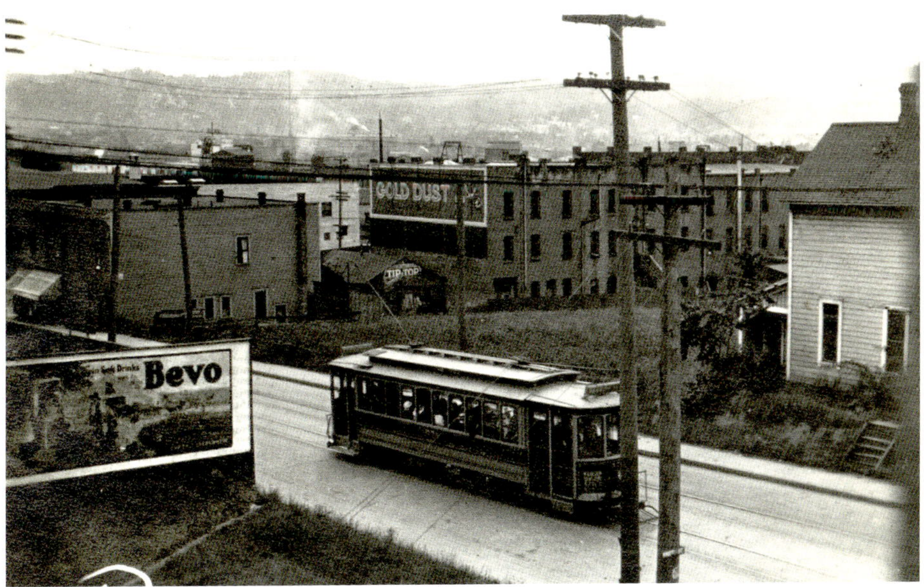

No. 573 is outbound on N Mississippi Avenue near Knott Street in a 1916 view looking south and west toward the Willamette River and West Hills. The bustling Lower Albina industrial district is behind the streetcar. The billboard at left advertises Bevo, a non-alcoholic malt beverage brewed by Anheuser-Busch that was popular during Prohibition. The other billboard is for Gold Dust all-purpose laundry powder. (*Photograph courtesy Don Nelson*)

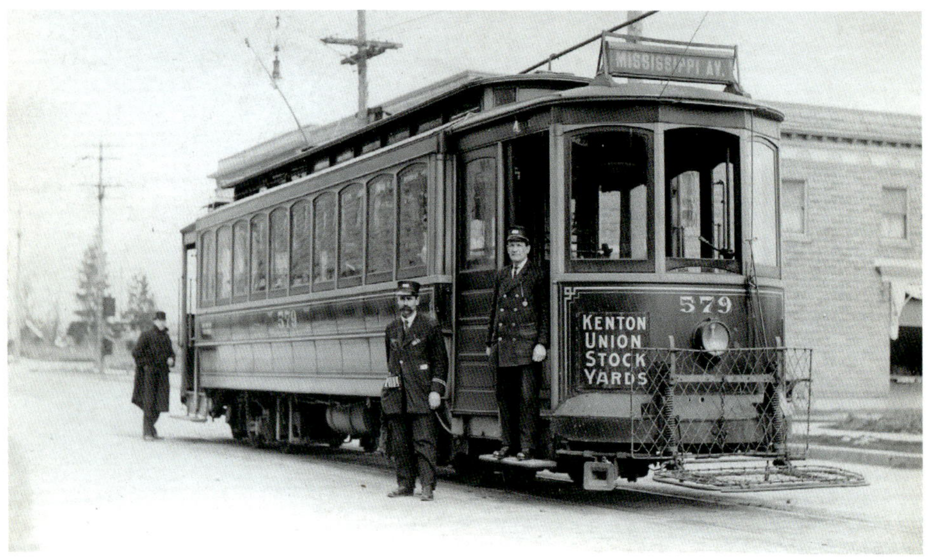

Mustachioed conductor Curtis Damon and motorman Peter Kugel have their picture taken at the northern end of the Mississippi Avenue Line while a passenger approaches at the rear. On the telephone pole behind him is what appears to be a telephone box for reporting to the dispatcher at the Piedmont Carbarn.

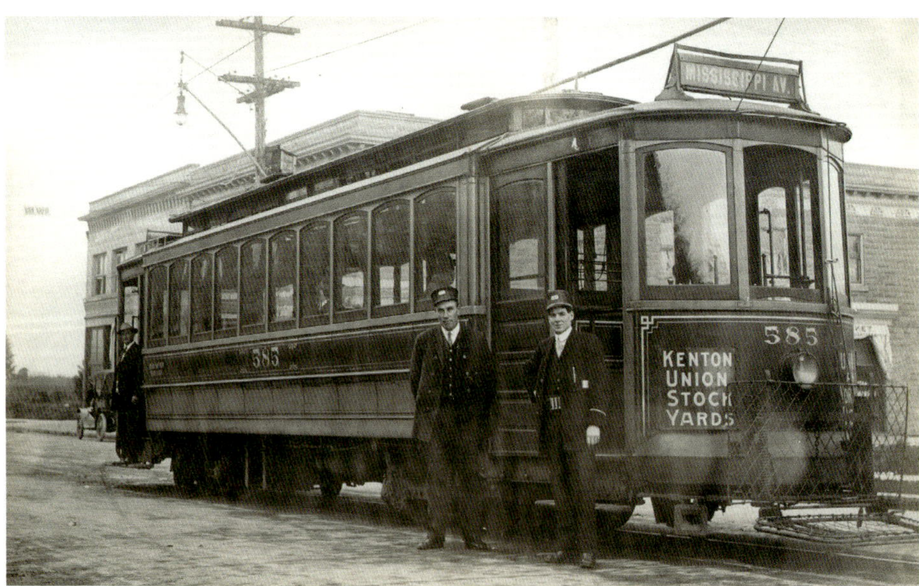

A passenger watches from the rear steps while motorman Andrew Swanson and conductor Alex McNeil pose with Mississippi Avenue car 585 at N Denver Avenue and Kilpatrick Street. Beyond the street light, a "Breaker" sign warns motormen to pass under section insulators with power off so as not to trip a circuit breaker. Breakers were used to activate automatic track switches or separate sections of 600-volt overhead wire, as perhaps between the PRL&P and Kenton Traction Company systems.

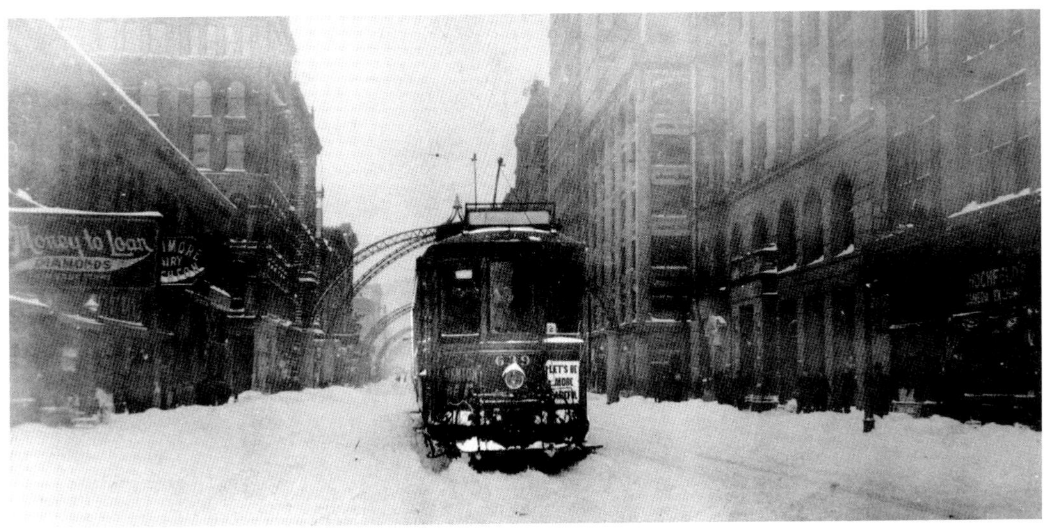

Mississippi Avenue No. 639 has stalled on SW Third Avenue between Stark and Washington streets in downtown Portland during a rerouting caused by the Big Snow of 1916. Third Avenue was known as "The Great Light Way" after boosters installed a series of illuminated arches above each intersection from W Burnside to SW Yamhill streets in June 1914 in an effort to keep shoppers from gravitating to the new commercial district along SW Broadway.

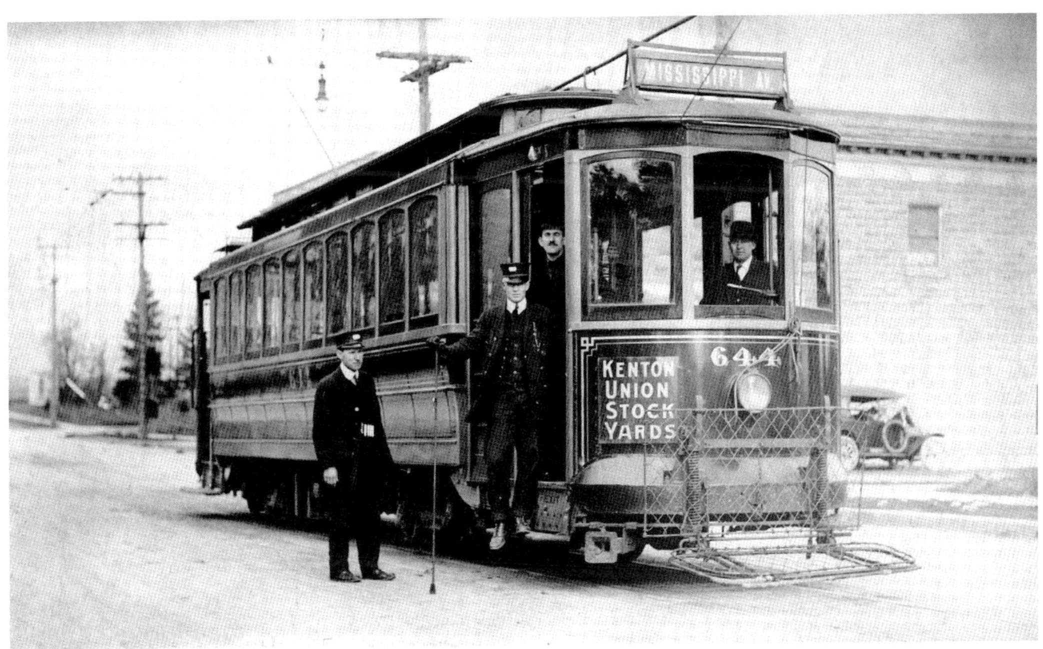

As Mississippi Avenue car 644 prepares to head back to Portland, conductor Robert Clemmitt has changed the poles and motorman Crabtree is holding the tall metal switch iron used to set the switch for the southbound section of dual track between N Argyle and Winchell Streets on N Denver Avenue.

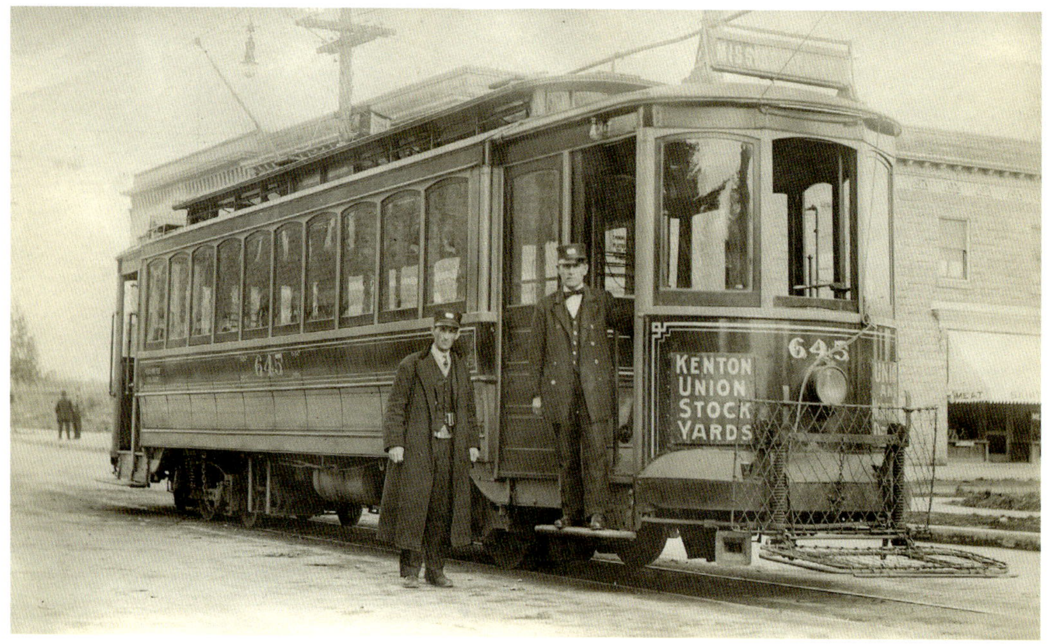

Mississippi Avenue car 645, with conductor Williams and motorman "Otto" Ottosen, is laying over at the end of the line. No. 645 displays a "Union and North Bank Depots" sign on the right side of the dash, referring to the two train stations the line passed close to in Northwest Portland. The awning over the store in the background identifies it as the Sanitary Meat Company.

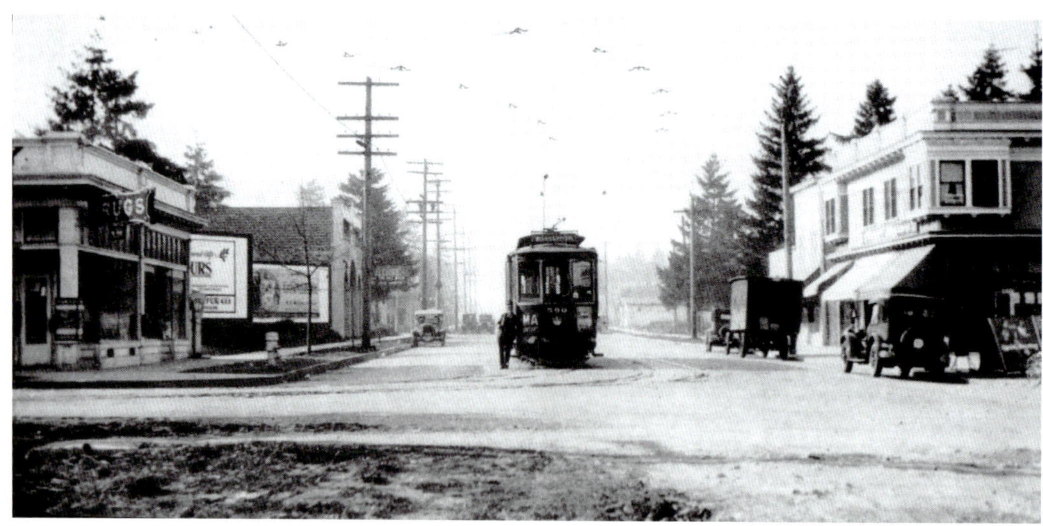

The Mississippi Avenue Line had three outer terminals during the 1920s. No. 590 is at the alternate terminal on N Albina Avenue and Lombard Street. The next Mississippi Avenue Line trolley will go through to Denver Avenue and Argyle Street in Kenton. Rush hour "trippers" (short run cars) turned back farther south at N Albina Avenue and Ainsworth Street. Corner drug stores like the one at left were once common in Portland. Lombard Street was home to five.

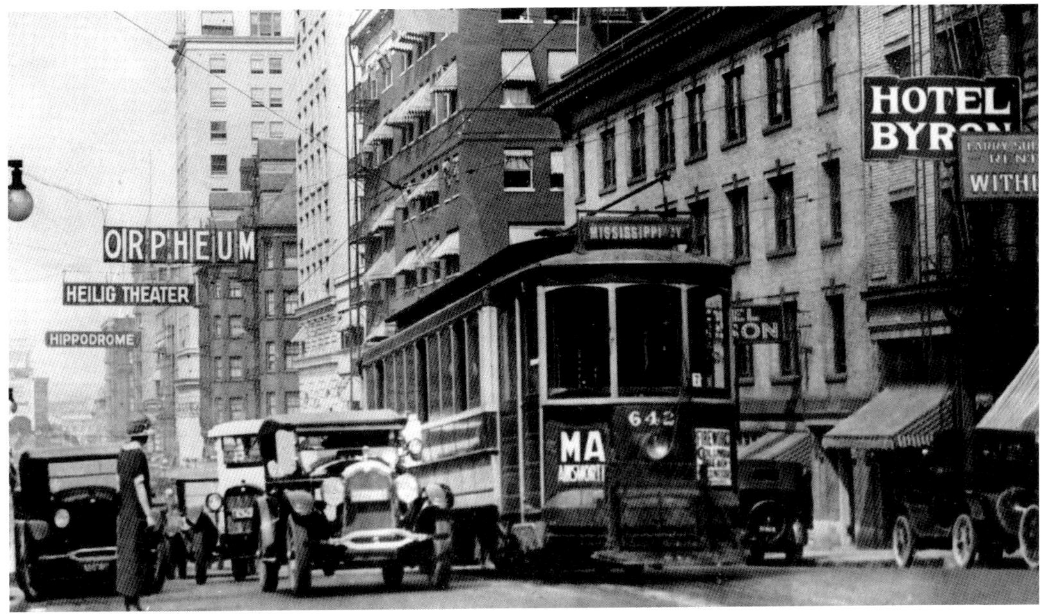

By 1916, Mississippi Avenue streetcars ran through Portland's prestigious shopping and theater district to a terminus on SW Broadway and Salmon Street. Car 642 is southbound approaching this terminal in 1925. In the background, banners for the Orpheum, Heilig, and Hippodrome theaters hang above the street in front of the YMCA, Portland Hotel, and Jackson Tower. Narrow-gauge cars in this series bore the highest numbers prior to the arrival of the Broadways in 1932.

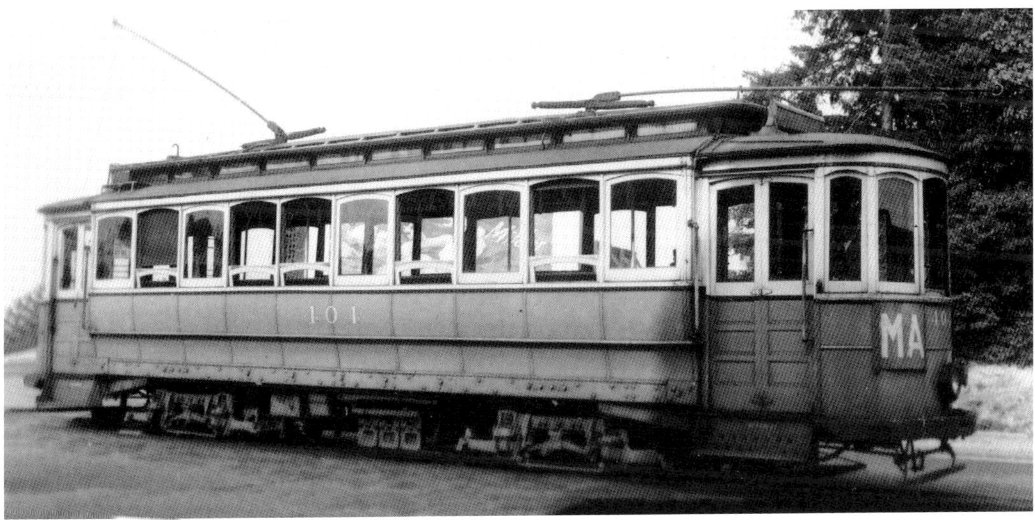

In the later years, 400-class cars operating out of Piedmont Carbarn were used mainly on the Alberta and Williams Avenue lines, but as this view attests, they could also be assigned to the Mississippi Avenue run. No. 404 is wearing the green and cream Portland Traction Company livery chosen by school students in a 1930s contest, a popular color scheme that ignored the dictum that paint should be used to protect from the elements rather than for aesthetic considerations.

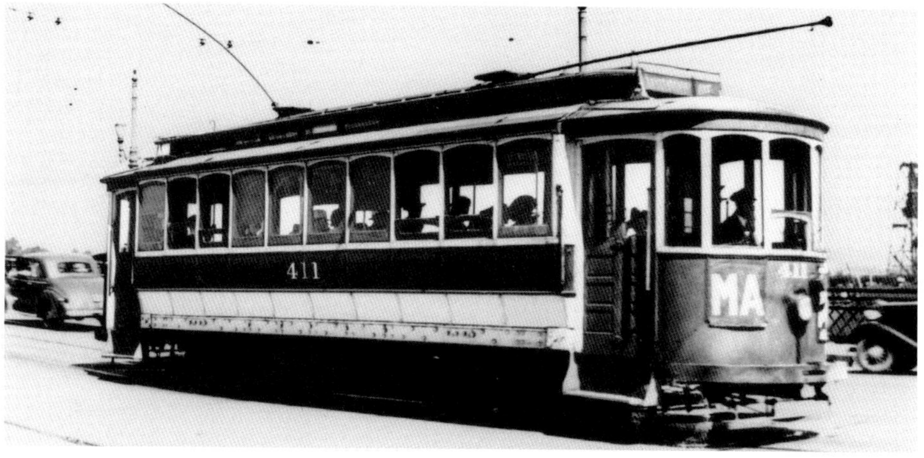

Mississippi Avenue Line car 411 is westbound on the Broadway Bridge on July 3, 1939. As can be seen, Portland trolleys had returned to using the traditional colors of dark red and cream, but with no pin-striping. The 400-439 American Car Company series were the only narrow-gauge trolleys equipped for multiple-unit (MU) operation, which allowed the motorman on the front car to control the speed and braking of both cars in a train.

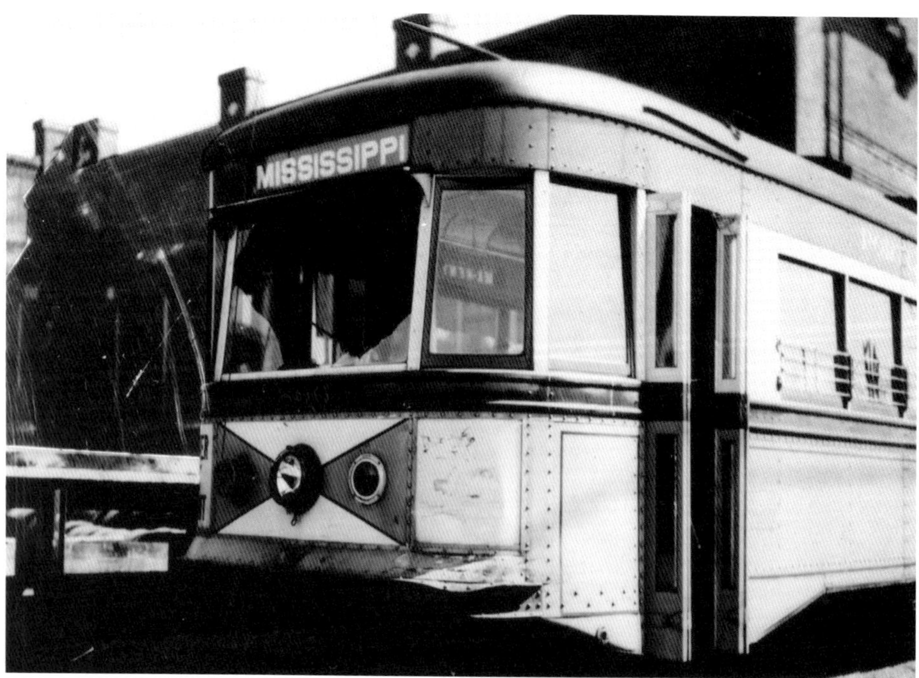

When Portland Traction Company's newest streetcars, "The Broadways," arrived in 1932, they bore a stunning new livery featuring gray bodies, ivory window trim, and green and black belt lines. They also sported pin striping and diamond patterned ends. This elaborate paint appears little damaged by the collision with an automobile that No. 806 suffered on April 16, 1934. It is pictured undergoing repair at the Center Street Shops on SE 17th Avenue and Center Street.

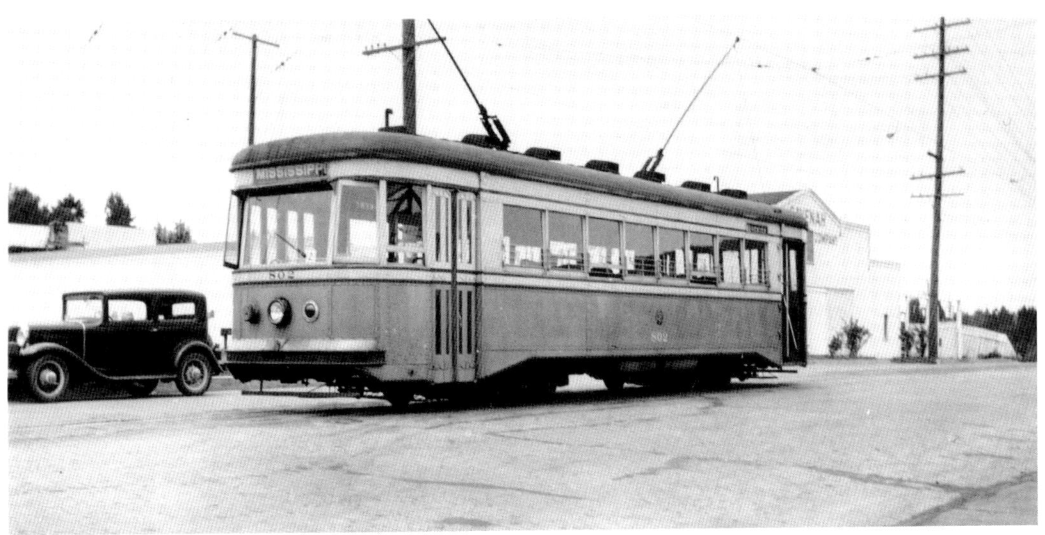

By the late 1930s, the Broadway cars had been assigned to the Alberta and Mississippi Avenue lines in addition to their namesake Broadway Line run. That is the case with No. 802, seen changing ends on N Denver Avenue and Argyle Street. Note that the original fancy color scheme has been somewhat simplified; the streamliner is still gray and ivory, but end diamonds are gone as is the dark green belt line. The sides still bear a PTC monogram.

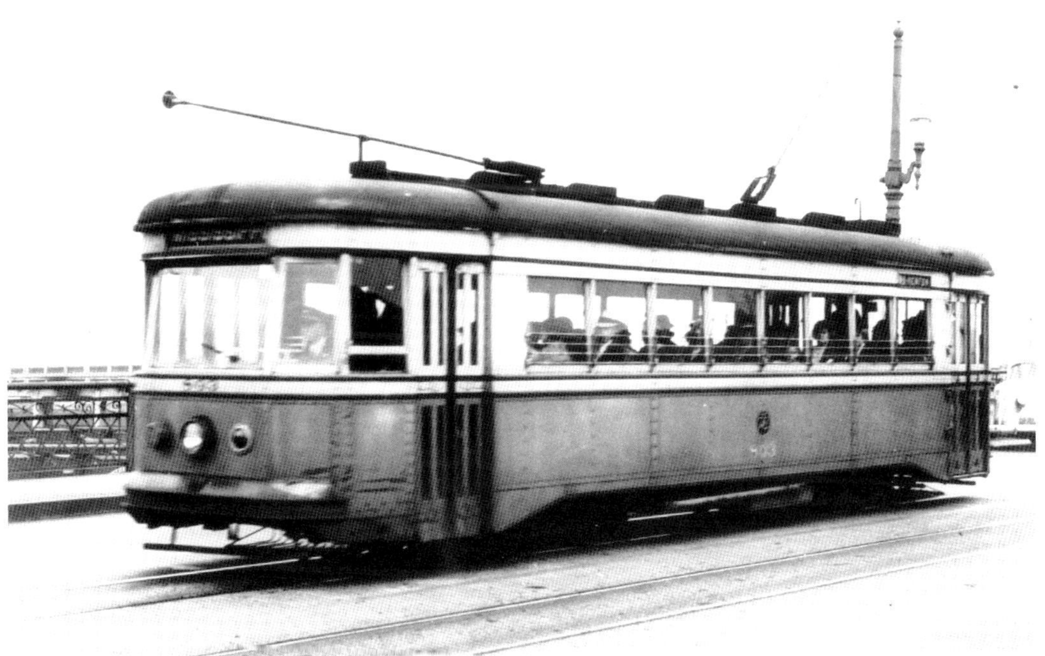

Mississippi Avenue car 803 is accelerating as it heads outbound on the Broadway Bridge with a rush-hour passenger load. The Broadway car is still wearing its gray and ivory in this blurry late 1930s snapshot. The Yamhill Street ramp, most of which has been removed today, is visible in the left background.

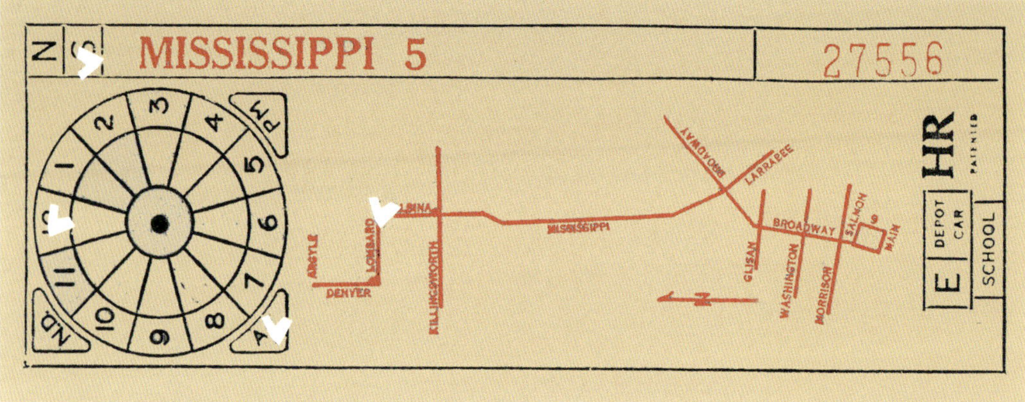

On August 30, 1936, the Portland Traction Company introduced a system of "wheel transfers." The new transfers were less cluttered since they featured a clock dial for recording boarding time and line maps replaced the previous zone blocks and names. The Mississippi Line transfer above appears to have been used on an owl car because it is punched for a southbound passenger boarding at N Lombard Street and Albina Avenue around midnight.

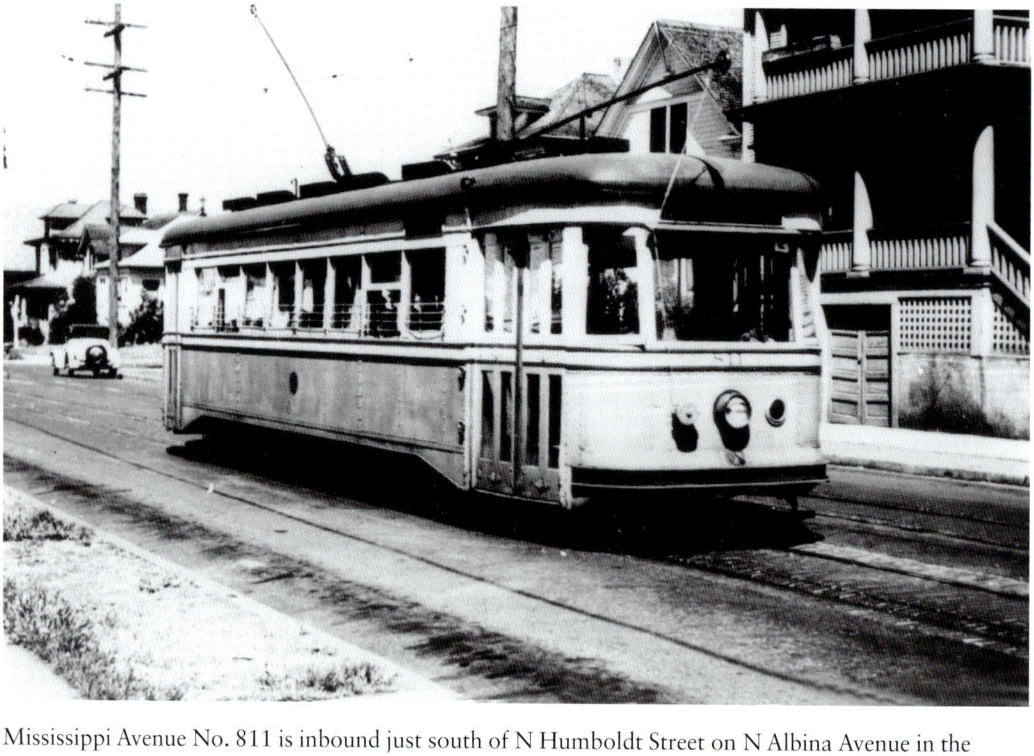

Mississippi Avenue No. 811 is inbound just south of N Humboldt Street on N Albina Avenue in the 1930s. Most of the homes in the background, including the four-unit-flat at right, are still standing. Like most Brill Master Units, the Broadway Cars were of standard gauge dimensions but equipped with narrow gauge trucks for operation in Portland. Portland Traction Company avoided using them on lines with tight curves because of their wide bodies.

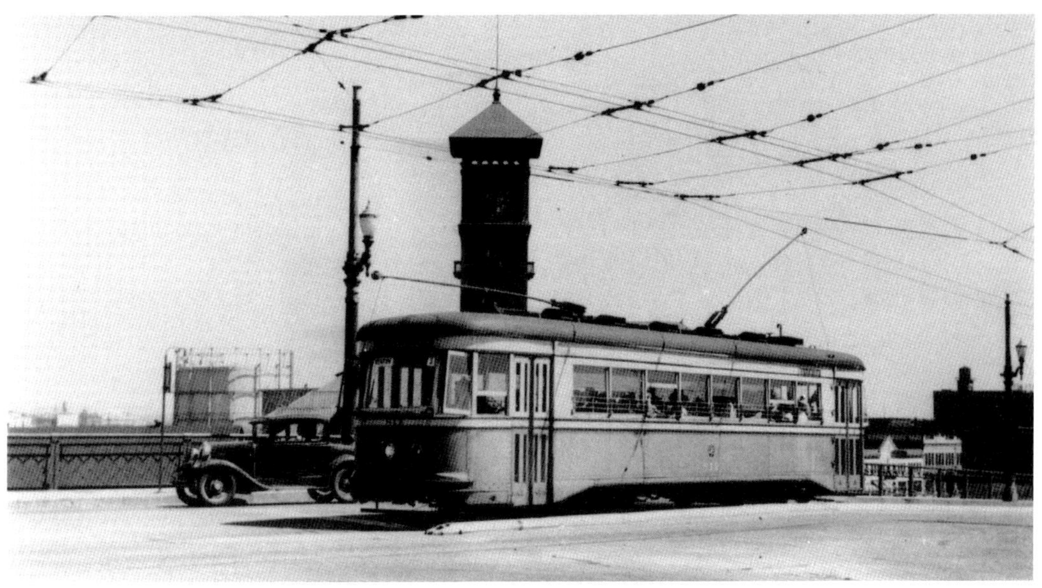

No. 812 growls up the ramp to the Broadway Bridge on a warm, sunny afternoon. The clock on the Union Station tower in the background reads 2:30. Next door to the station is the natural gas storage tank at NW Front Avenue and Glisan Street built by Northwest Natural Gas Company predecessor Portland Gas & Coke Company.

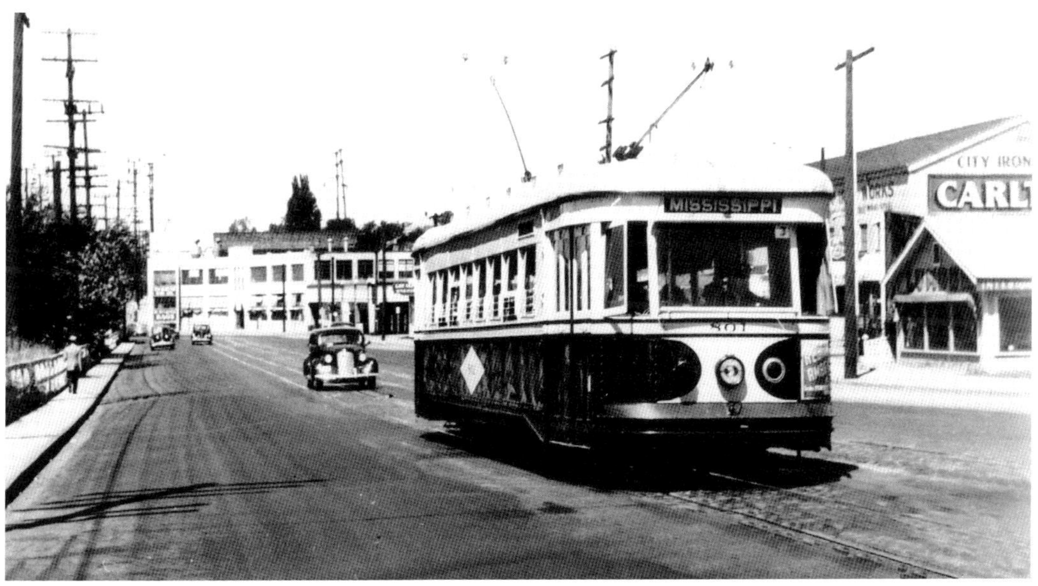

Car 801 displays new colors as it hums south on N Interstate Avenue near Tillamook Street. The early 1940s paint scheme uses traditional red and cream coloring, but with scalloped end decoration and fleet numbers framed in diamonds on each side. Two of the structures in the background—the Gotham Building at left, and the warehouse housing Carlton Ransom Lumber Company at right—remain in place today. Compare this with the pictures on pages 76 and 116.

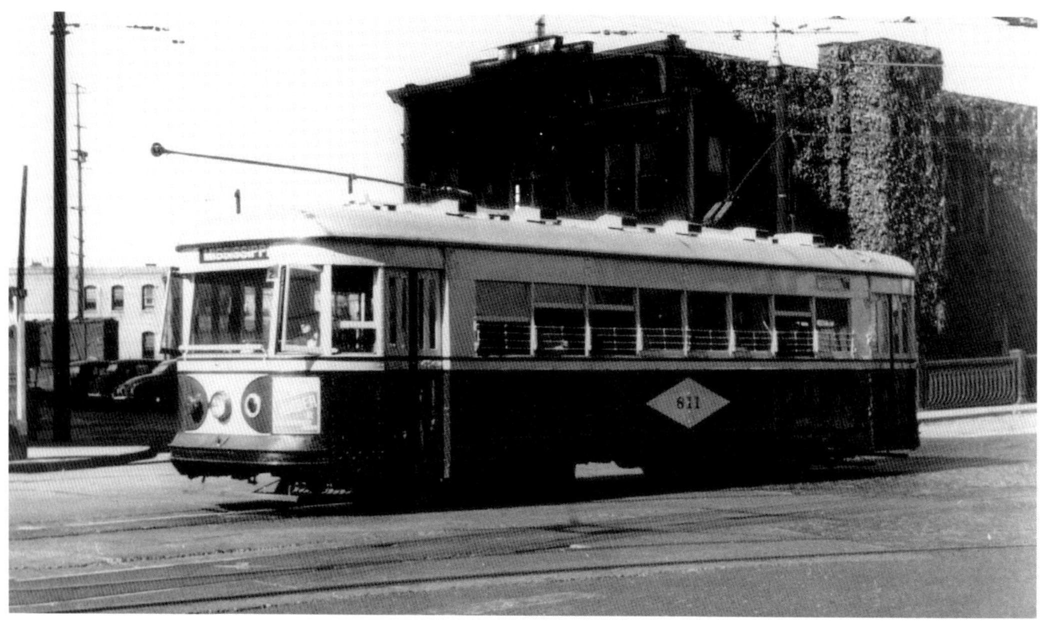

Inbound Mississippi Avenue car 812 has been rerouted from its usual Broadway Bridge path in this scene on the west Steel Bridge ramp at NW 3rd and Glisan. In the background obscured by afternoon shadow is Firehouse No. 2, which was built 1913. Although it is now condemned, this abandoned station is scheduled for demolition in 2022.

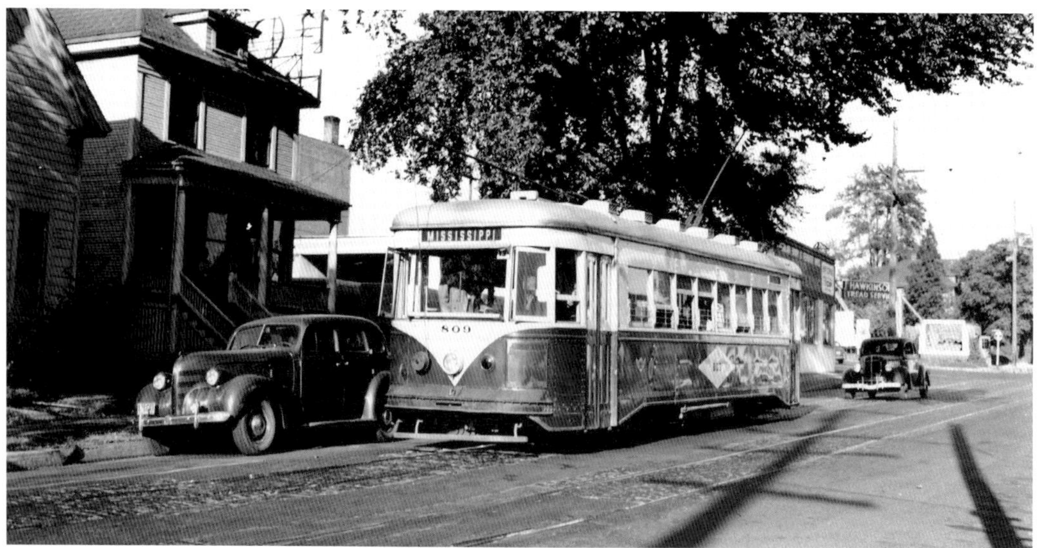

This may be one of the last pictures taken of a Mississippi Avenue Line streetcar. No. 809 is said to be an inbound tripper from the Ankeny Carbarn, but it is wearing the penultimate Portland Traction Company colors of red and cream with winged PTC logos on the sides and V-shaped end decoration, which dates from the late 1940s. If it is really from the Ankeny barn (instead of Piedmont), then the location is probably SE Ankeny Street.

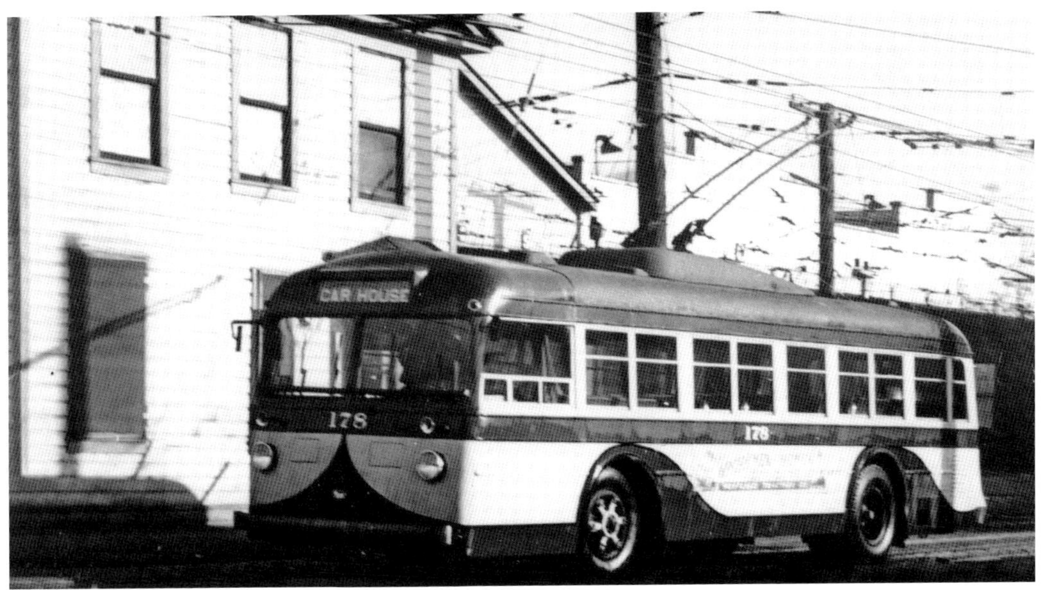

As part of the 1936 franchise renewal, Portland Traction Company agreed to modernize its system by replacing nearly half its aging streetcar fleet with trolleybuses. Its first 120 from the Mack Truck Company made up the largest order for trolley coaches placed up to that time. Ten electric bus lines were built, four of which operated out of the Piedmont Division, including Mississippi Avenue, Williams Avenue, St. Johns, and Interstate Avenue.

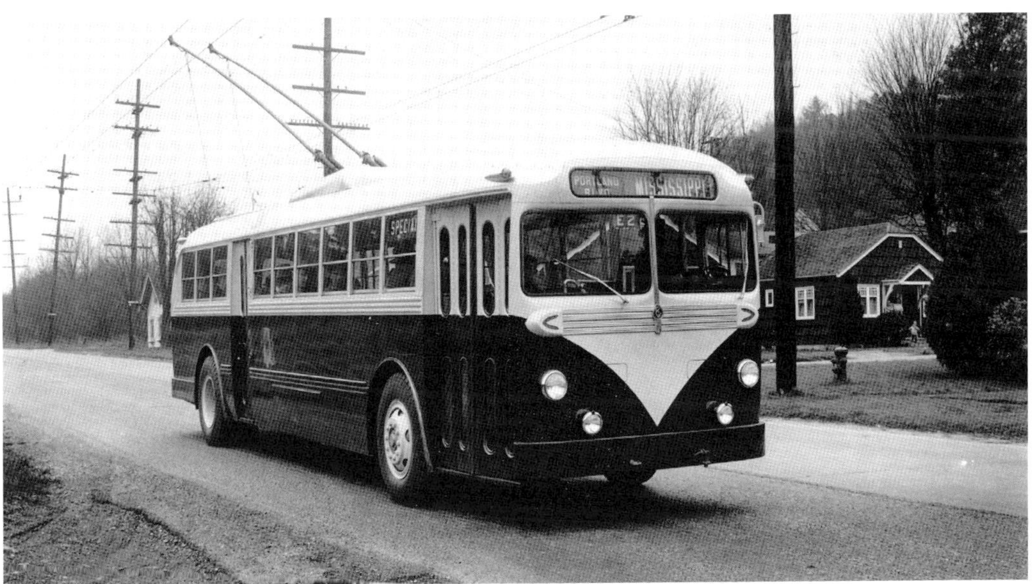

Portland Traction was the only company to operate trolleybuses produced by Seattle-based Kenworth Motor Truck Company. No. 400, the first of fifty trolley coaches built for Portland in 1947–48, is shown during a demonstration run. Although it is displaying a Mississippi rollsign, the picture was taken while southbound on Fauntleroy Way SW in Seattle. (*Photograph courtesy Bill Volkmer*)

4

The Upper Albina and Williams Avenue Line

Before merging with the new City & Suburban Railway Company on September 4, 1891, the Willamette Bridge Railway had obtained franchises from the city of Albina for extending the Lower Albina and Upper Albina lines out to N Mississippi and Williams avenues. New rail was installed on what was then E 3rd Street at the bottom of the Portland & Albina Line loop in July 1892. In 1896, while difficult terrain and the financial Panic of 1893 continued to delay work on its sister line, the Upper Albina gained an improved connection to the Steel Bridge and the Upper and Lower Albina routes separated. The Upper Albina Line was moved three blocks farther east on N Holladay and followed Quincy Street through the diagonal streets in McMillen's Addition. In 1900, new tracks were laid along N Williams Avenue to N Killingsworth Street, then west to the new Piedmont Transfer Station on N Commercial Avenue, where Upper Albina Line trolleys met St. Johns Motor Line steam trains.

After the merger of the City & Suburban and Portland railways in April 1904, the new Portland Consolidated Railway Company renamed its Upper and Lower Albina branches. The Upper Albina Line became the Williams Avenue Line, which more accurately reflected the area covered by its expansion. However, to avoid confusion, the "U" dash signs continued to be used for a few more years in addition to rooftop rollsigns reading "Williams Av."

In 1909, the Mississippi Avenue Line's outer terminal was changed to NE Union Avenue and N Killingsworth Street, then in 1926, it was moved to N Greeley Avenue and Killingsworth Street. Also in 1926, the line was extended on the west side to include the old 16th Street Line route to NW 21st Avenue and Reed Street.

The first streetcars in Oregon were original equipment for the Upper Albina Line, including single-truck Pullmans, City & Suburban 100-class Standards, and spliced horsecars later renumbered into the 151 series. During the PRL&P years the 300-class Fuller Cars saw service on Williams Avenue runs, although the low 400s were the trolleys most often seen. The newest streetcars to appear on the Williams Avenue Line were Birney Safety Cars added during the 1920s. Tighter curves may have precluded assignment of the streamlined Broadway cars on Williams Avenue service.

Streetcars ceased to operate on the Williams Avenue Line when it was converted to electric trolley coach service on February 21, 1937. Trolleybuses were replaced by motor buses on Feb. 17, 1952.

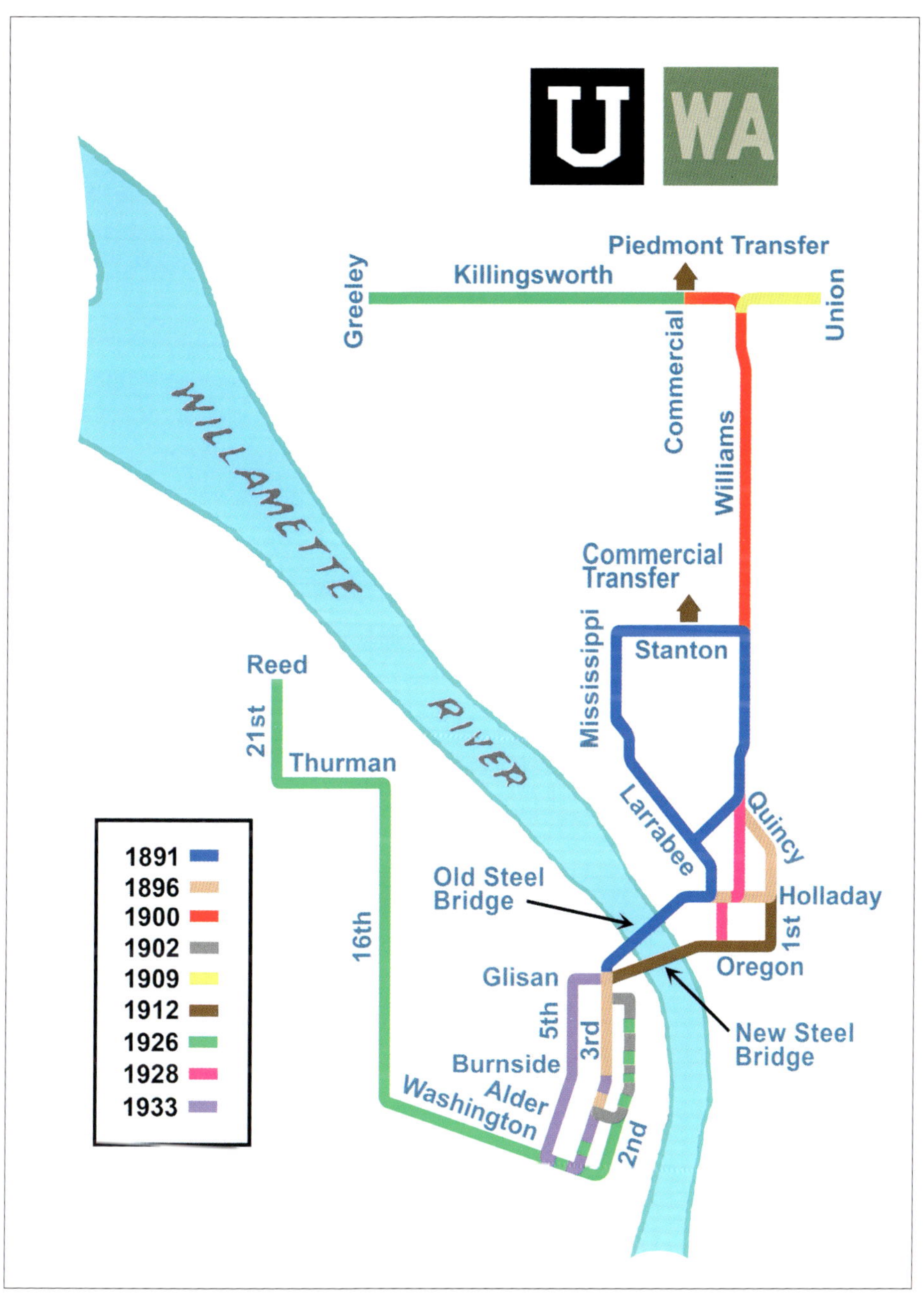

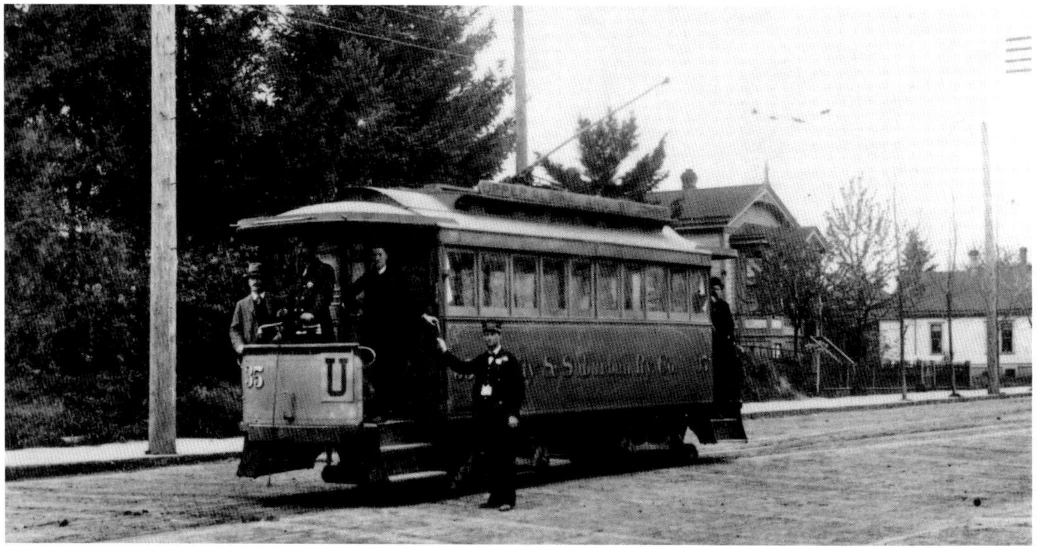

During the 1890s, Upper Albina Line trippers appear to have had a terminal on Williams Avenue at Page Street, where we see City & Suburban No. 35. It was the first of the of fifteen trolleys built in 1892 by splicing together the bodies of two horsecars to create a larger double-truck streetcar. This was a practical solution during a time when national car builders could not keep up with demand.

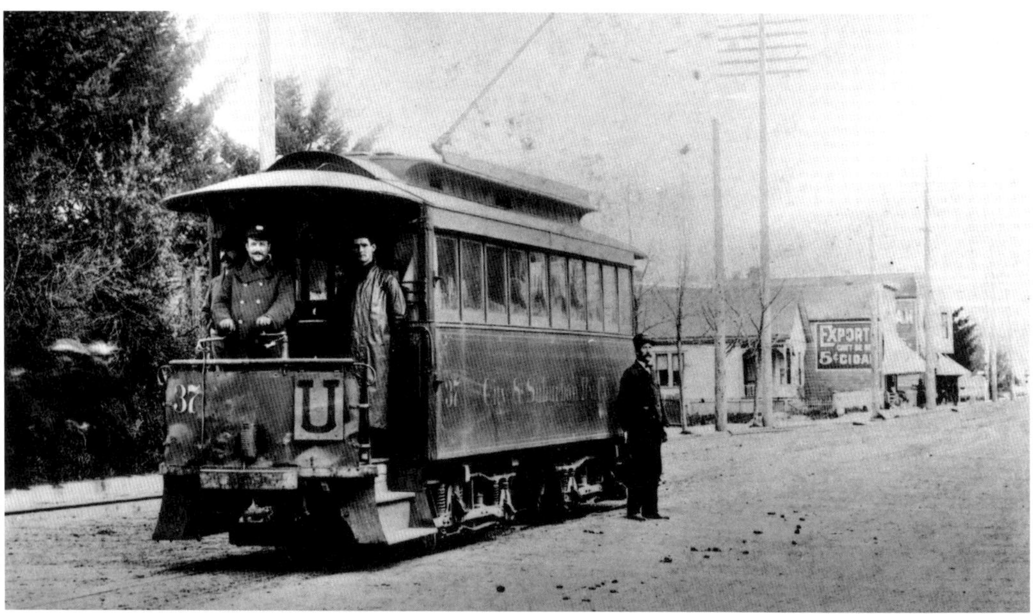

The earliest streetcars naturally had low numbers. Turtle-back-roofed No. 37 was one of the spliced horsecars that replaced the single truck Pullmans that had inaugurated electric streetcar service between Portland and Albina. It is seen here on N Williams Avenue around 1900 with a letterboard that reads "Upper Albina and St Johns." The man in the rain slicker is Frank Love, brother of the motorman Charles Love.

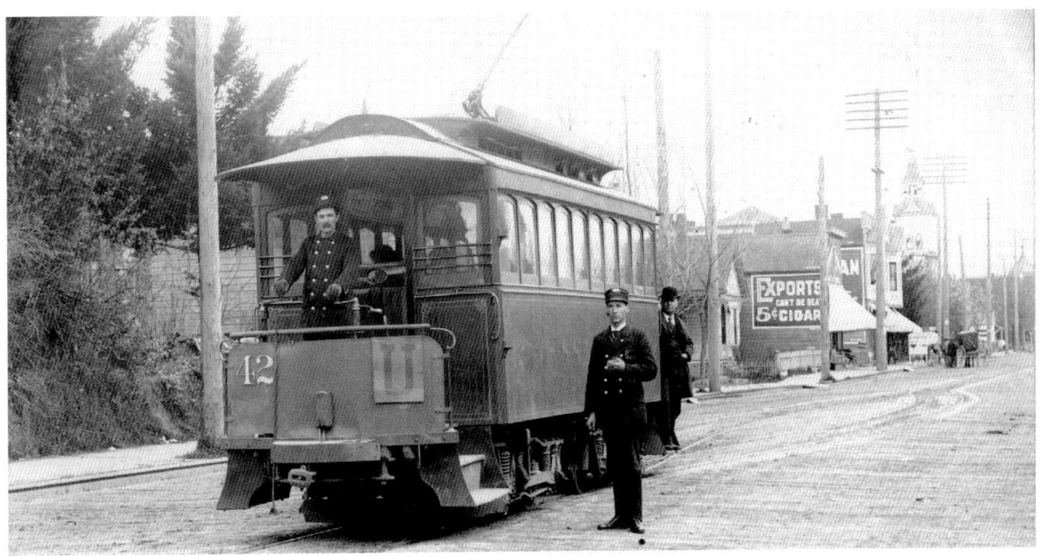

This postcard looking northward from the passing tracks at N Page Street clearly shows buildings along N Williams Avenue in the Upper Albina commercial district. Behind car 42 awnings jut from a cluster of shops. Beyond them, the bell tower of Williams Avenue School, built in 1889, soars skyward, and at far right, the round cupola of the 1890 Hill Block peeks from the trees.

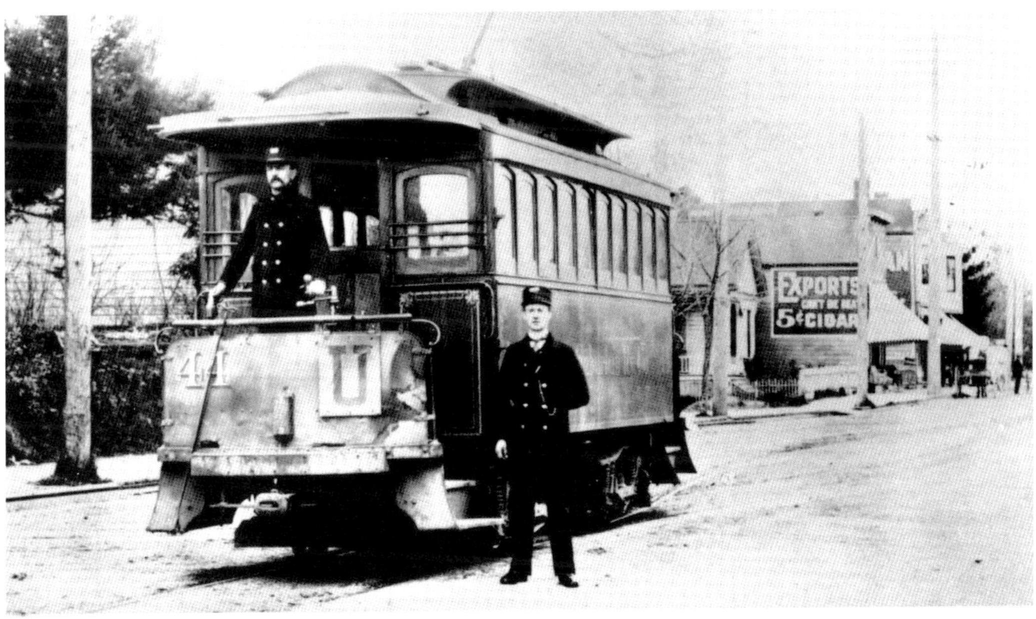

Upper Albina Line car 44 looks a bit worse for wear in another scene taken at the stop on N Williams Avenue at Page Street. The carmen look sharp in their neat uniforms, but both the dash board and destination sign on No. 42 are dented. At least the switch iron and headlight mount appear to be unscathed. Conductor Charlie Pye stands ready while his unidentified motorman grips the controller and brake handles.

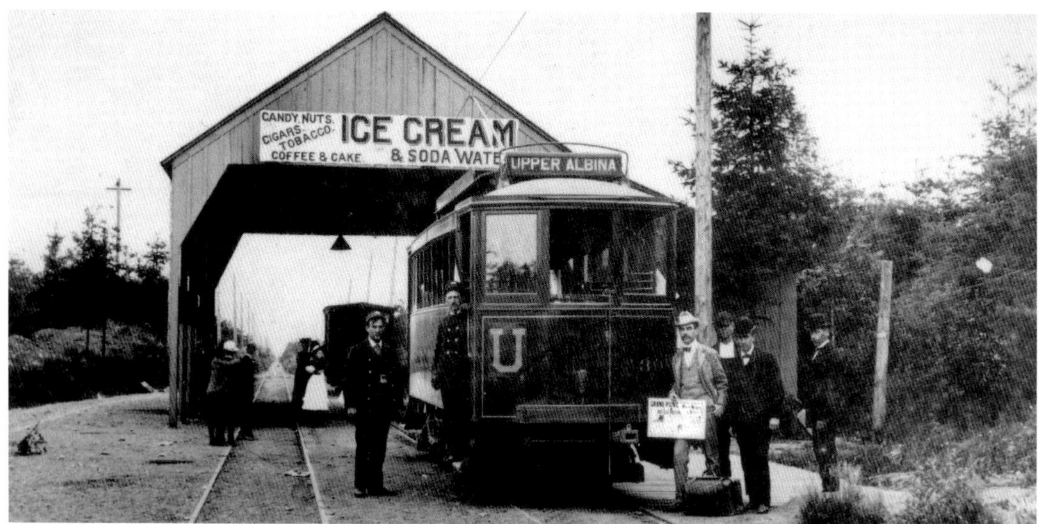

C&S opened the Piedmont Transfer Station on N Killingsworth Street and Commercial Avenue in 1900. Passengers could transfer here between the Upper Albina Line and St. Johns Motor Line. No. 39 is waiting while a group of women and children pose for a photograph in the shade of the station. The man in the light-colored suit is holding a sign for a "Grand Picnic and Log Rolling" excursion and a large banner above the station advertises ice cream and refreshments.

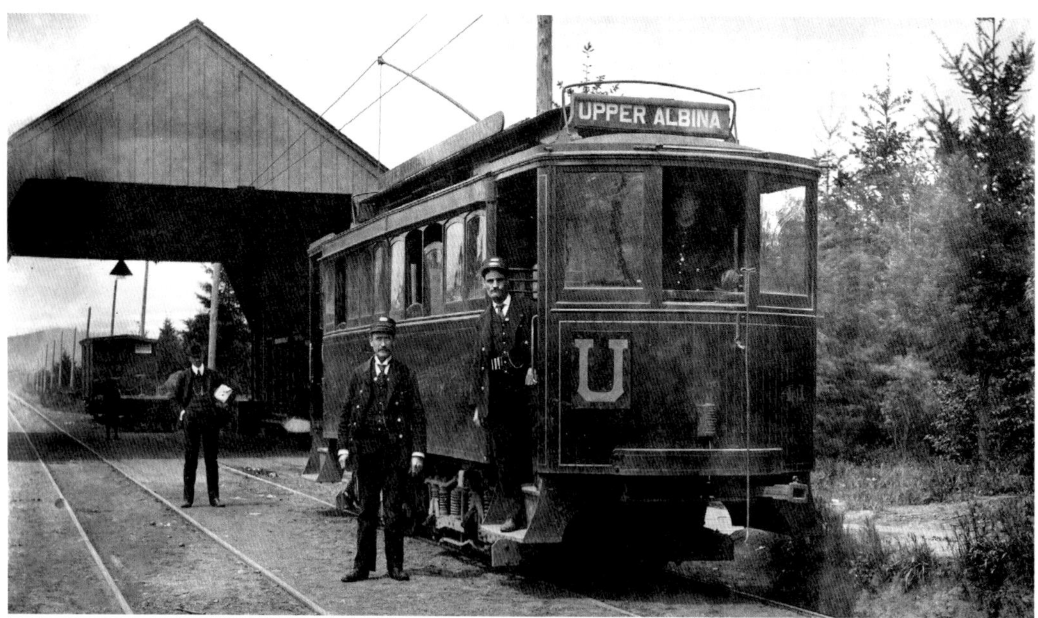

Upper Albina Line car 41 is at the Piedmont Transfer Station in a view looking west on N Killingsworth Street between N Commercial and Moore avenues. Both the crew and the passenger holding a package in the background are wearing high-starched collars. Before long, these locally built cars would be relegated to service on shorter lines. By 1910, rosters listed them as having been "junked." Note the seam between the two former horsecar bodies above the windows.

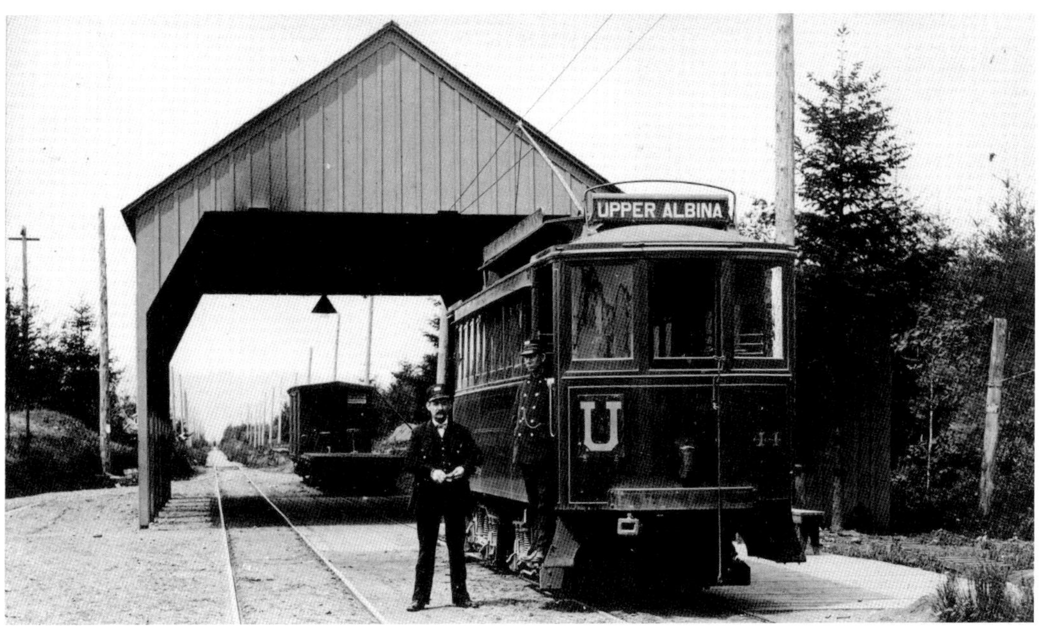

The conductor of Upper Albina No. 44 is ready with a pad of transfers in a picture taken around 1902 at the Piedmont Transfer Station. He does not have long to wait, since the smoke from an approaching steam dummy can be seen in the distance. Note that trolleys always seem to have used the righthand tracks and steam trains the left.

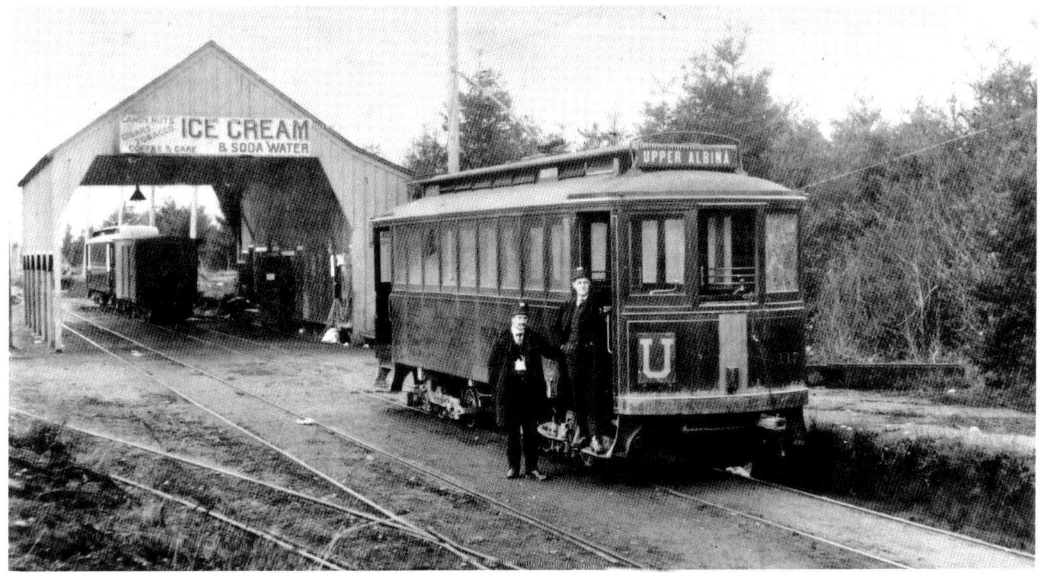

Time is running out for the Piedmont Transfer Station in this picture because C&S Standard No. 117 is waiting for a trolley, not a steam train. The St. Johns Motor Line ceased operation in 1903, but because the interurban cars built for the St. Johns Line during 1902–04 were too big to run into Portland, Piedmont Station continued in use as a transfer point between large and small streetcars until 1905.

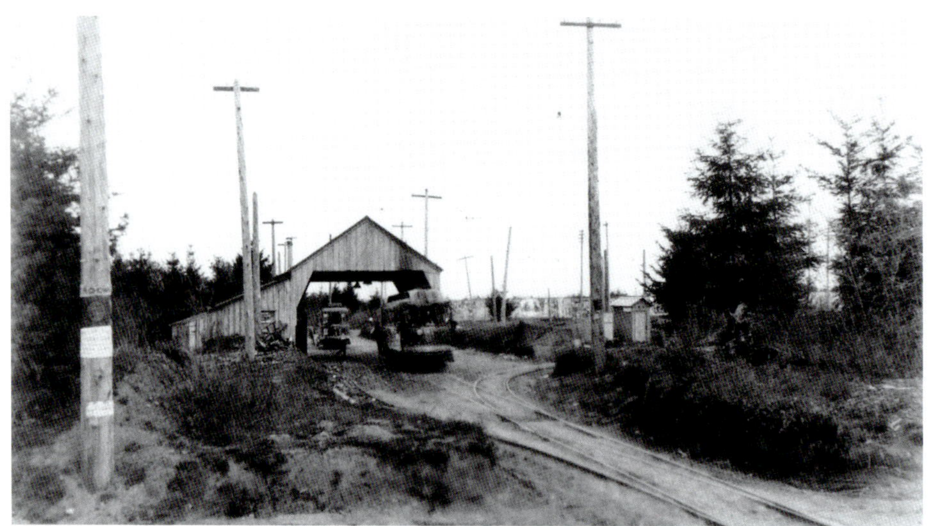

In a rare view looking eastward at the Piedmont Transfer Station, an Upper Albina Line C&S standard, numbered into the 151-165 series by the Portland Consolidated Railway, meets one of the large new 600 series St. Johns Line interurbans. Note the outhouse at the right next to the tracks to Commercial Avenue formerly used by the steam trains.

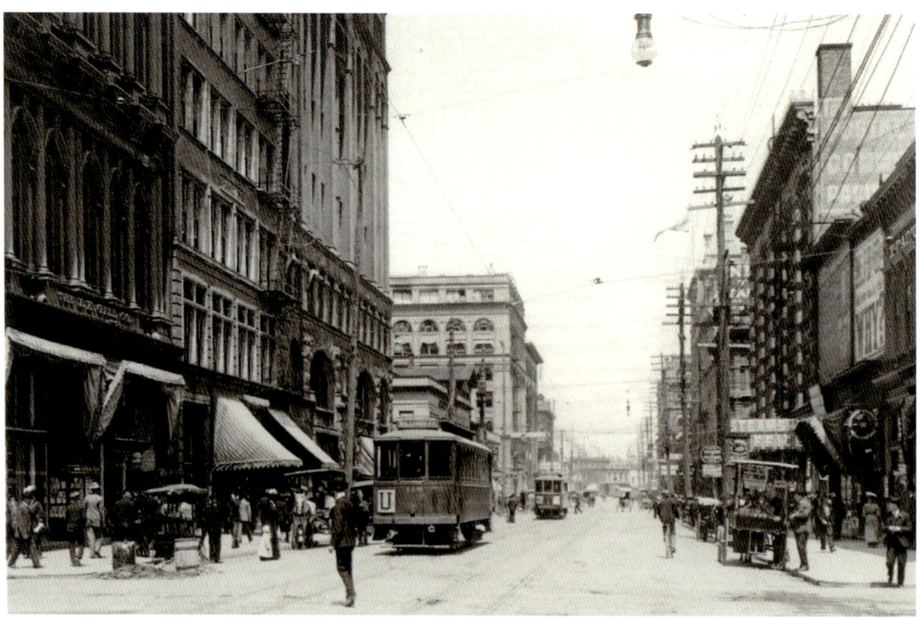

Southbound Portland Consolidated Railway No. 118 has just crossed the intersection of SW 3rd Avenue and Washington Street around 1904. Until the 1930s, the route through downtown Portland for Williams Avenue Line streetcars was along SW 3rd Avenue. Several of the buildings in this scene remain today, including the Dekum Building at left and the Postal Building at right. However, the Chamber of Commerce Building in the center background is gone. (*Photograph courtesy Old Oregon Photos*)

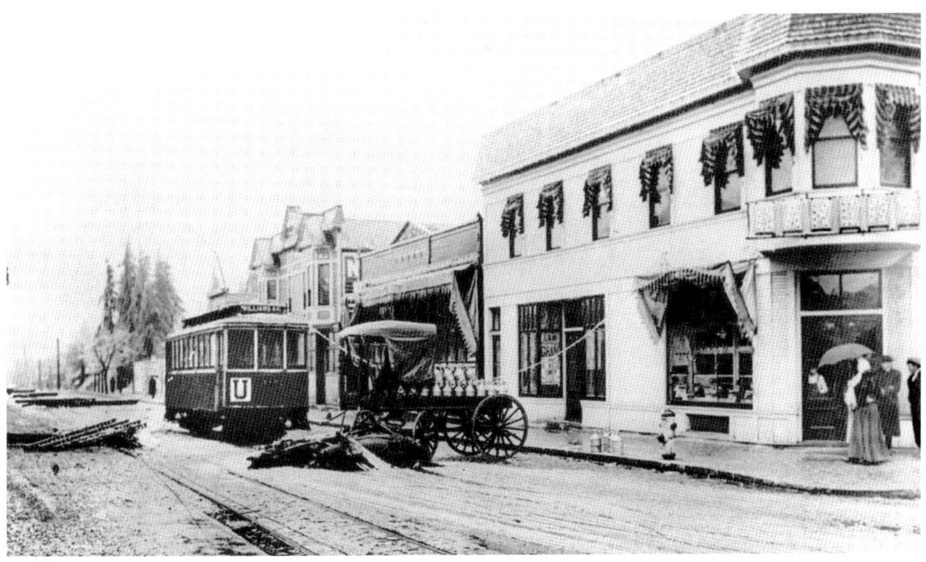

On January 29, 1907, a silver thaw brought down wires and poles along N Williams Avenue from N Hancock Street to N Going Street, cutting telephone and electric service and paralyzing streetcars. Upper Albina car 117 was halted when the overhead trolley wires fell across it. Although the streetcar and its passengers were not hurt, two dairy wagon horses were instantly killed by the 600-volt current.

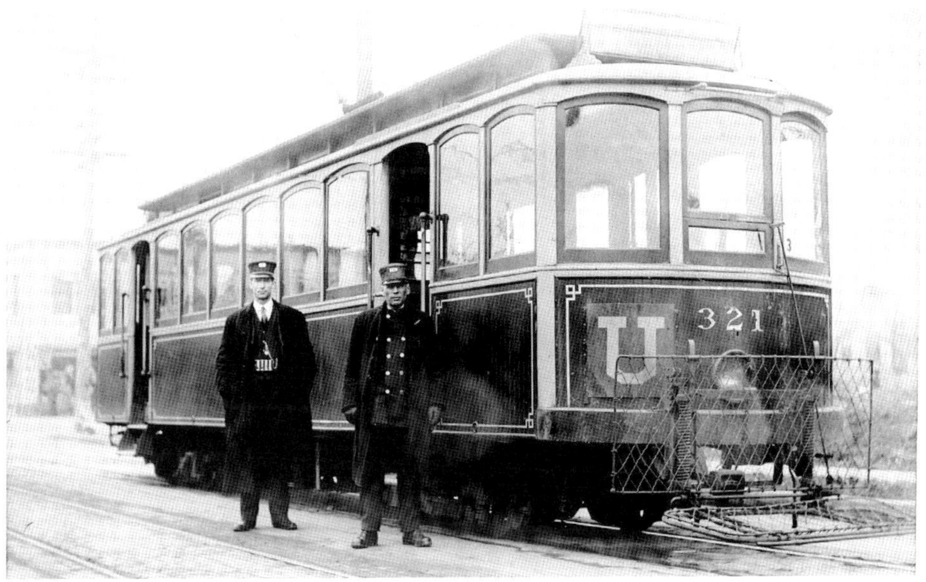

PRL&P car 321 and crew are one block east of the Piedmont Carbarn on N Killingsworth Street near Albina Avenue. Inbound and outbound Williams Avenue cars waited at this point for passengers wishing to transfer from St. Johns Line trolleys. The picture dates from the mid-1910s after installation of Nelson Safety Fenders. Note that the dash sign still bears the Upper Albina "U," while Williams Avenue appears on the rollsign.

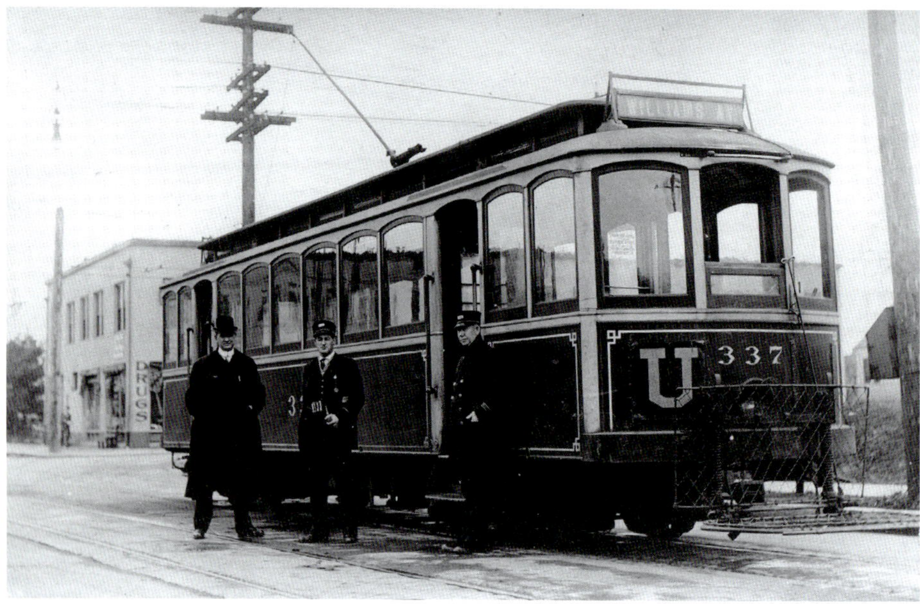

An executive is posing with conductor Earl Holliday and motorman Davis while car 337 waits on N Killingsworth Street and Albina Avenue. It is heading east to the new terminus at N Killingsworth and Union Avenue, which remained the outer end of the Williams Avenue line until 1926. A carman can be seen walking past Killingsworth Avenue Drug in the background.

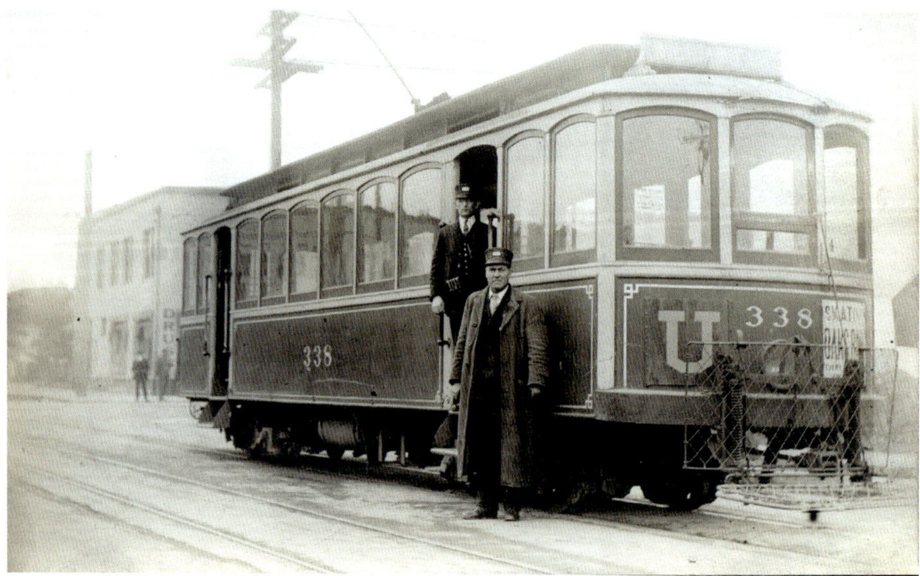

Conductor Albert Schaefer is standing in the doorway of Mississippi Avenue Line Fuller car No. 338 above gruff-looking motorman Homer Ogle on N Killingsworth Street at Albina Avenue. A call box can be seen at the right edge of the picture. These were placed at important junctions and termini so that crewmen could call the dispatcher at divisional headquarters.

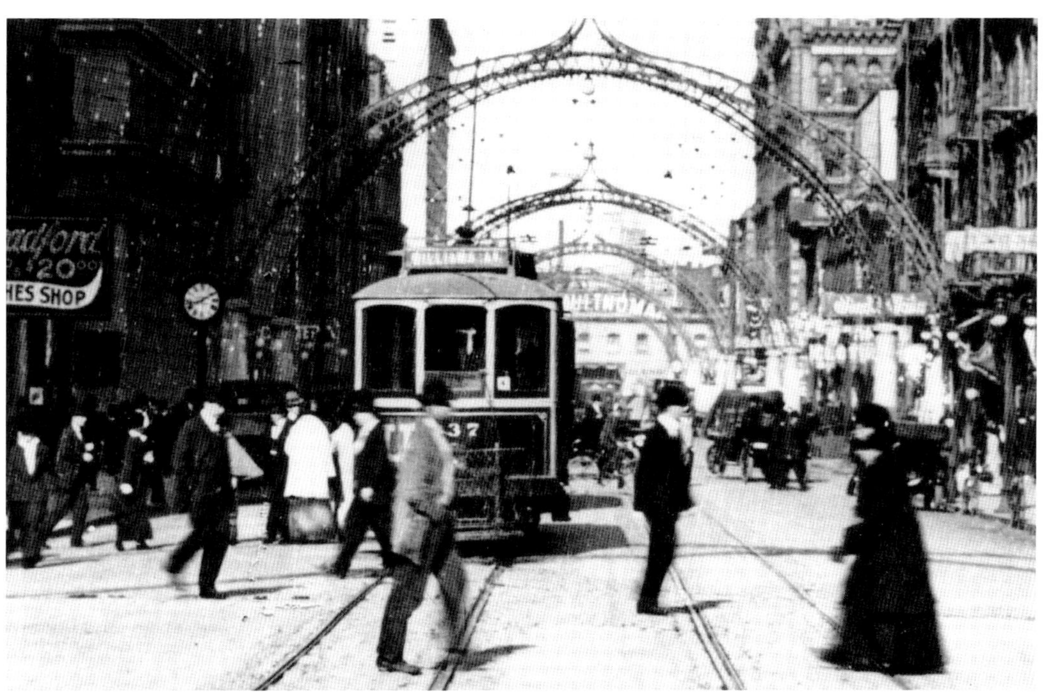

Above: In this bustling mid-1910s scene in downtown Portland afternoon shoppers, office workers, bicyclists, and a few automobiles, crowd the street as Williams Avenue car 337 changes ends beneath the archways of SW 3rd Avenue's "Great Light Way." Southwest 3rd Avenue and Alder Street was the southern terminus of the line until 1926. The over-the-street sign in the background was for the Multnomah Hotel.

Right: Outbound Williams Avenue Line No. 467 is seen passing inbound Irvington-Jefferson car 577 on the Steel Bridge in an eastward-looking view taken about 1915. The 466-class cars were the first new PAYE (pay as you enter) trolleys purchased by PRL&P and were in use from 1908 until 1948.

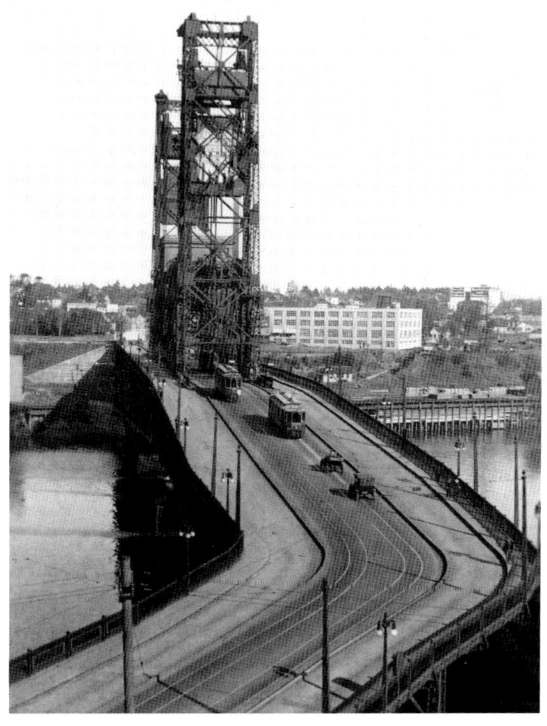

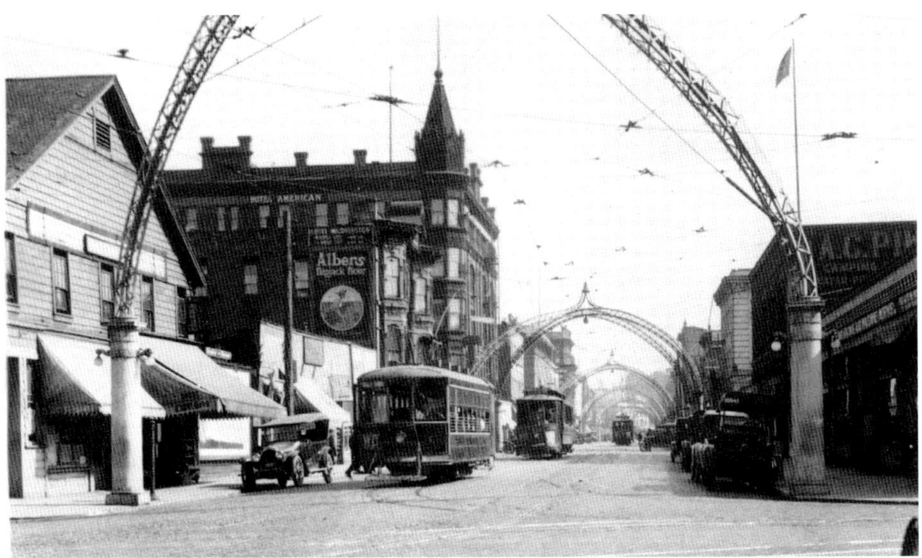

In 1919, PRL&P began operating Birney Safety cars on the Williams Avenue Line. No. 1 is seen on NW 3rd Avenue at Glisan Street in 1921. These little single-truck trolleys were called safety cars because of features that included "dead man" control, which halted the car if the controller or foot pedal were released. Portland's Birneys were leased from the Emergency Fleet Corporation during World War I and purchased in 1922. (*Photograph courtesy Don Nelson*)

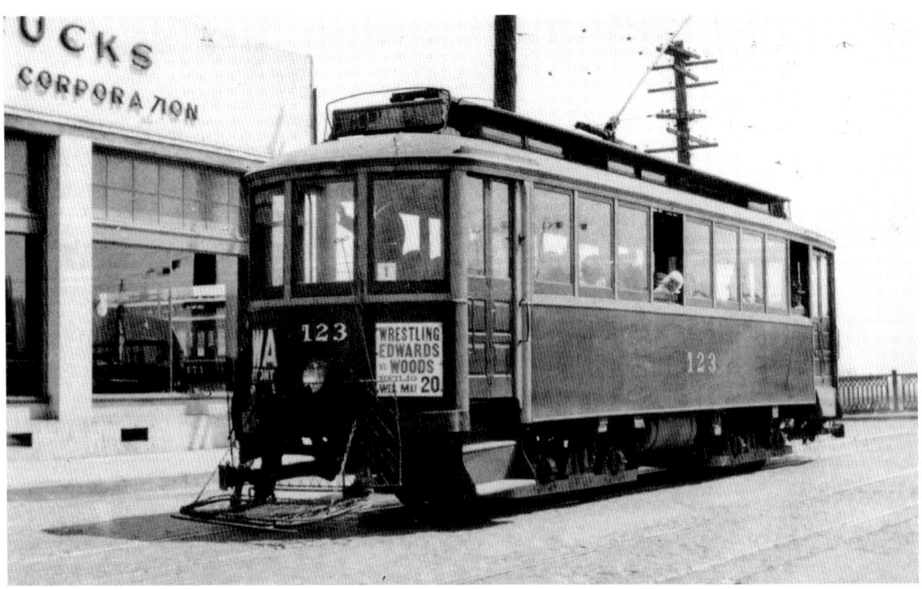

Car 123 is about to turn north onto N Adams Avenue from Oregon Street to access the new "Williams Avenue Cut-off" between N Cherry Street and Holladay Avenue, which opened in 1928. The east ramp to the Steel Bridge is in the background. When retired in 1933, No. 123 was the last remaining City & Suburban Standard. Today, Adams is a street absorbed by a parking lot near the Moda Center.

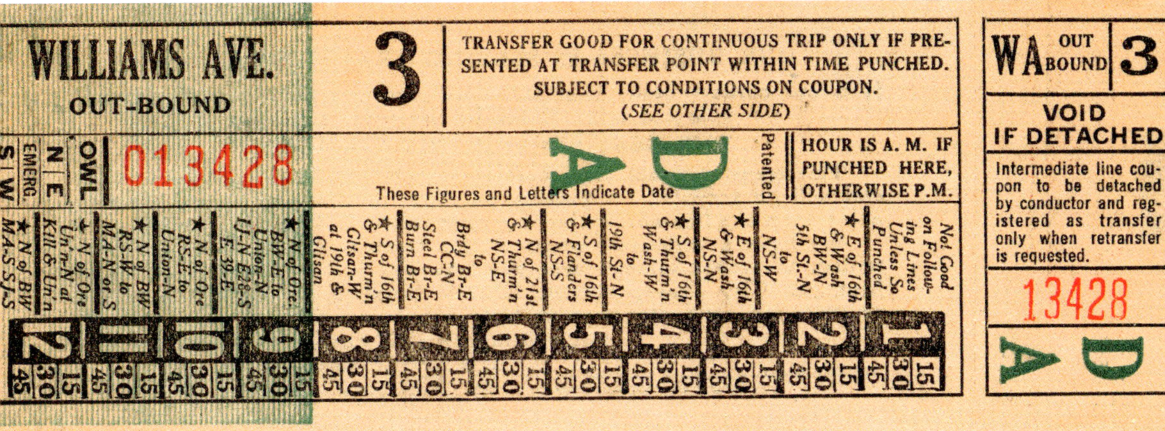

WILLIAMS AVE.
OUT-BOUND

3

TRANSFER GOOD FOR CONTINUOUS TRIP ONLY IF PRESENTED AT TRANSFER POINT WITHIN TIME PUNCHED. SUBJECT TO CONDITIONS ON COUPON. (*SEE OTHER SIDE*)

OWL | N E | EMERG. | S W

013428

A D

These Figures and Letters Indicate Date

Patented

HOUR IS A. M. IF PUNCHED HERE, OTHERWISE P.M.

Not Good on Following Lines Unless So Punched
★ E of 16th & Wash 5th St-N BW-N
★ E of 16th & Wash NS-N to NS-W
★ S of 16th & Thurm'n Wash-W to 19th St-N
★ S of 16th & Flanders NS-S
★ N of 21st & Thurm'n NS-E to Brdy Br-E CC-N Steel Br-E Burn Br-E
★ S of 16th & Thurm'n Glisan-W at 19th & Glisan
★ N of Ore BW-E to Union-N Union-N E28-S U-N E 39-E
★ N of Ore RS-E to Union-N
★ N of BW RS-W to MA-N or S
★ N of Ore Un'n-N at Kill & Un'n
★ N of BW MA-S-SJ-S

1	2	3	4	5	6	7	8	9	10	11	12
15	15	15	15	15	15	15	15	15	15	15	15
30	30	30	30	30	30	30	30	30	30	30	30
45	45	45	45	45	45	45	45	45	45	45	45

WA OUT BOUND 3

VOID IF DETACHED

Intermediate line coupon to be detached by conductor and registered as transfer only when retransfer is requested.

13428

A D

This unused Williams Avenue outbound transfer was issued by the Portland Traction Company during the 1930s. As with most transfers, it was good only for a continuous ride in one direction and within the times indicated by a punch mark. Further conditions were listed on the back.

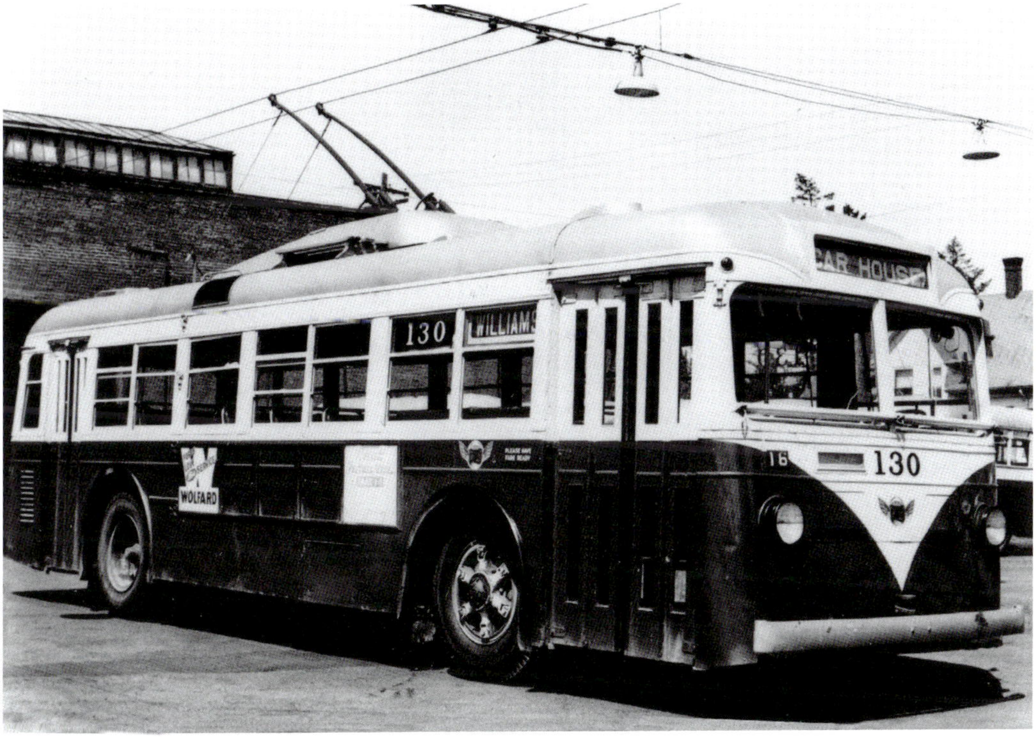

Streetcars disappeared from the Williams Avenue Line when it became Portland's fifth trolleybus line on February 21, 1937. The electric buses were part of the modernization plan agreed to in the 1936 franchise renewal. Mack trolley coach No. 130 is seen in front of the Piedmont Carbarn wearing the winged Portland Traction Company emblem on front and sides. The Williams Avenue trolleybus line was discontinued on February 16, 1952.

5

The St. Johns Line

The St. Johns Line was a paradox in that its southern terminus was part of the first electric streetcar operation in the state, while its northern terminus was served by Portland's last steam streetcars. Service over the lower portion of the St. Johns Line was begun on November 1, 1889, by electric streetcars of the Willamette Bridge Railway running from NW 3rd Avenue and Glisan Street, across the original Steel Bridge, to a transfer point at N Elliott and Hawley streets (later renamed N Stanton Street and Commercial Avenue) in the city of Albina. From here, passengers bound for St. Johns transferred to steam trains. The St. Johns Motor Line went north via Commercial Avenue, Killingsworth Street, Greeley Avenue, Lombard Street, Macrum Street (later moved to Wall), Fessenden Street, and St. Louis Street in the St. Johns retail district.

In the early years, what is now Lombard Street changed names several times along the way. In Albina, it was Pippin, in Portsmouth, Dawson, and in St. Johns, Jersey. By 1900, tracks on N Williams Avenue had been extended to a new transfer station on N Killingsworth.

In January 1903, the City & Suburban Railway inaugurated electric service from St. Johns to SW 3rd Avenue and Alder Street in downtown Portland. The route north continued along N Williams Avenue; however, passengers still had to transfer between St. Johns interurbans and city streetcars at the Piedmont Transfer Station on N Killingsworth Street. It was not until 1905 that tracks into Portland were upgraded to accommodate the large St. Johns interurbans. Improvements included rerouting via the Burnside Bridge, rebuilding the Union Avenue Bridge, and the construction of new downtown loops. At first, an inadequate supply of electric power was supplemented with storage batteries at the Piedmont Carbarn while a permanent solution was worked out with the utility company.

Several important changes were made during the 1910s. In 1911, a loop was completed at the northern end of the line with new tracks along N Lombard. Between November 1909 and September 1912, St. Johns streetcars were shifted five blocks eastward from N Williams Avenue to NE Union Avenue (now NE Martin Luther King, Jr., Blvd.). The route returned to N Williams on September 8, 1912, in order to cross the new Steel Bridge. On

September 2, 1913, the St. Johns Line was again rerouted to access the new Broadway Bridge. In 1926, time and distance were shaved from the schedule when the line started using the new Greeley cutoff. With tracks adjacent to Greeley Avenue, the line became an interesting mixture of street and private right-of-way running.

Two-car trains were the rule on the St. Johns run until 1926. In the beginning, these were the big 191-class cars with trailers. After 1908, the 466-485 series multiple-unit cars joined in. At first, only five streetcars were required to maintain service. The powerful four-motor 466-class trolleys were Portland's first PAYE cars when they arrived in 1907.

Most St. Johns Line streetcars were converted to one-man operation in 1931. Trolley coaches replaced streetcars on Portland's oldest line on April 11, 1937. The electric buses were discontinued on January 29, 1958, but were reactivated just a month later, on February 25. The reprieve was short-lived, however, and final replacement by gas buses came on October 23, 1958.

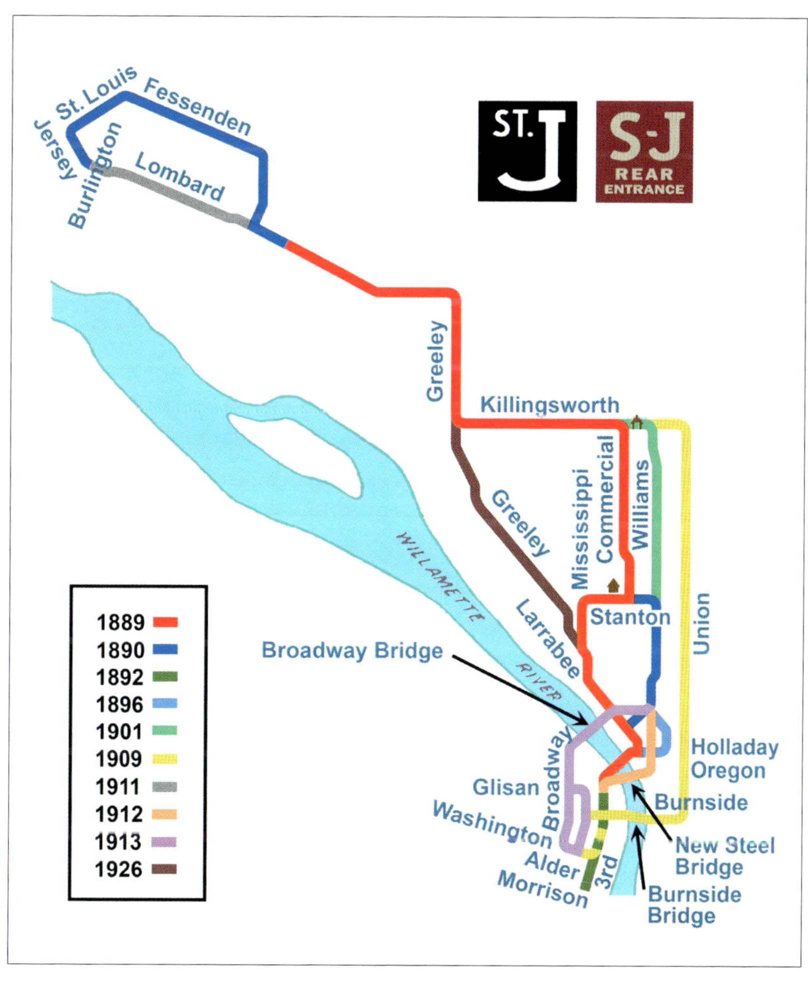

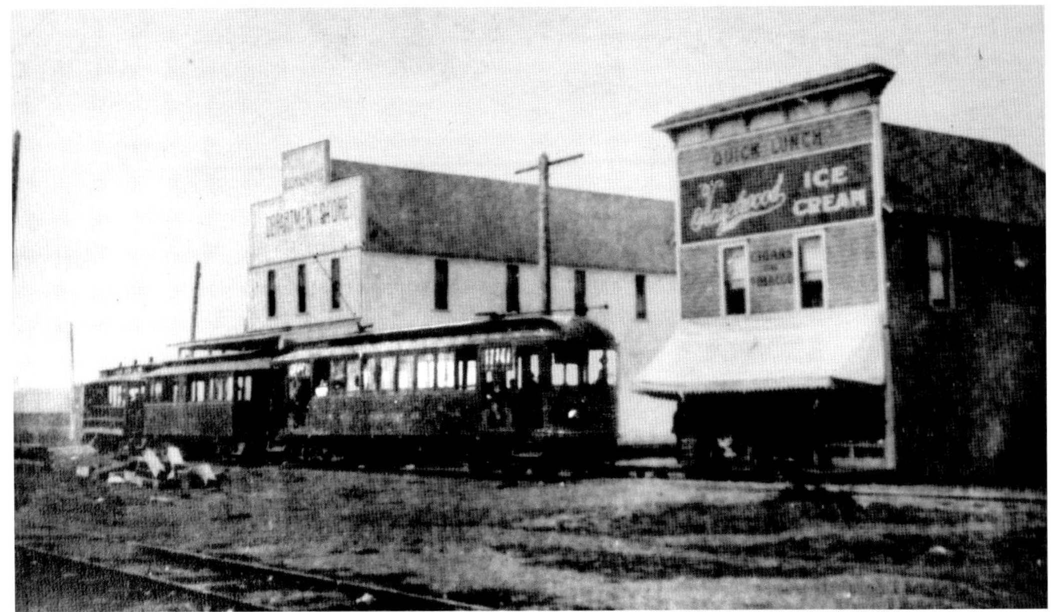

This blurry picture shows one of the first trolleys to reach St. Johns in 1903. City & Suburban Railway 198 or 199 is pulling two trailers inherited from the steam motor line. The closed trailer was built in 1893 by splicing together two horsecars. Next to the train are the St. Johns Department Store and a market offering a "Quick Lunch." The track in the foreground leads to the old engine house. Note the interurban has open vestibules.

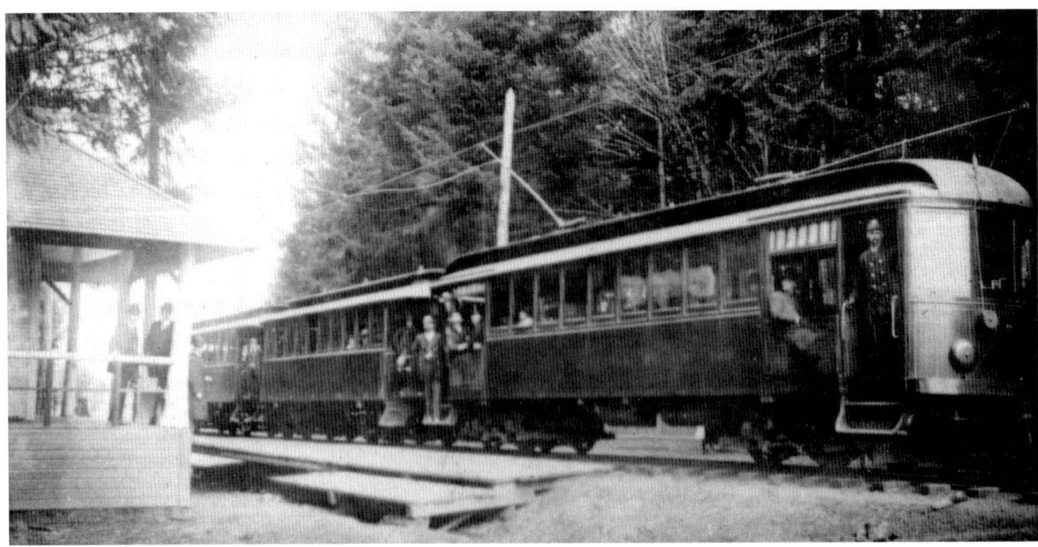

The first of the large interurban cars built for the St. Johns Line was No. 195, seen here at Cedar Park Station on N Fessenden Street *c.* 1904. The 195–199 series cars were built with open ends. However, this proved unpopular, and they were soon enclosed. No. 195 was unique in that it was the only St. Johns "convertible" since it featured side panels that could be removed in warm weather.

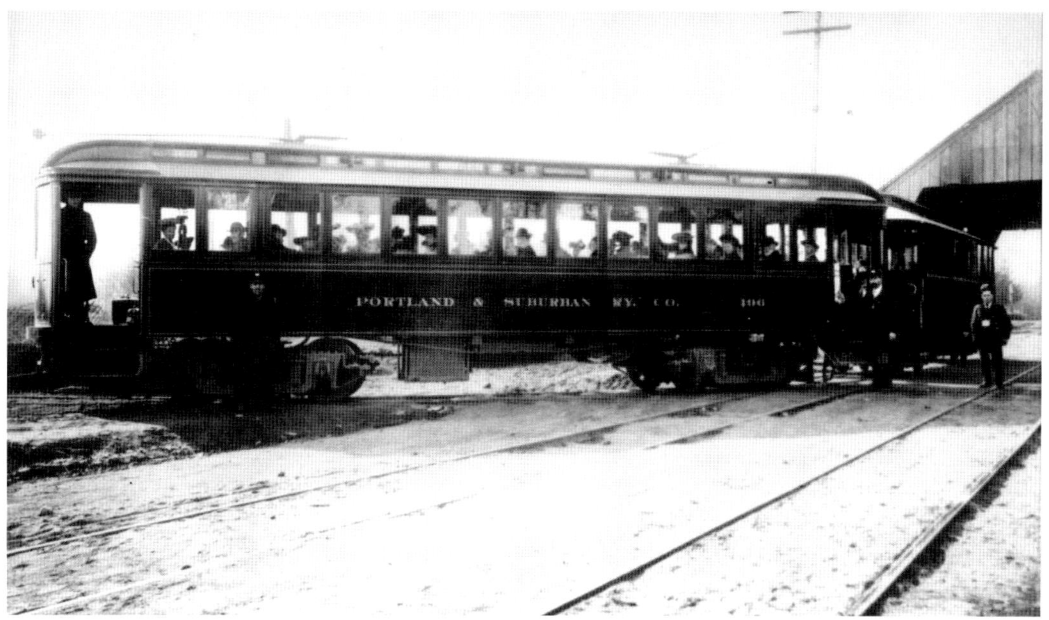

St. Johns Line car 196 and its trailer are turning on the wye at Piedmont Station in 1904. Rails laid in a "Y" shape were a less expensive solution for changing train directions at the end of a line than building loop tracks. No. 196 was one of a handful of cars lettered for the Portland & Suburban Railway before management discovered that that title was already in use by another company and changed it to the Portland Consolidated Railway Company.

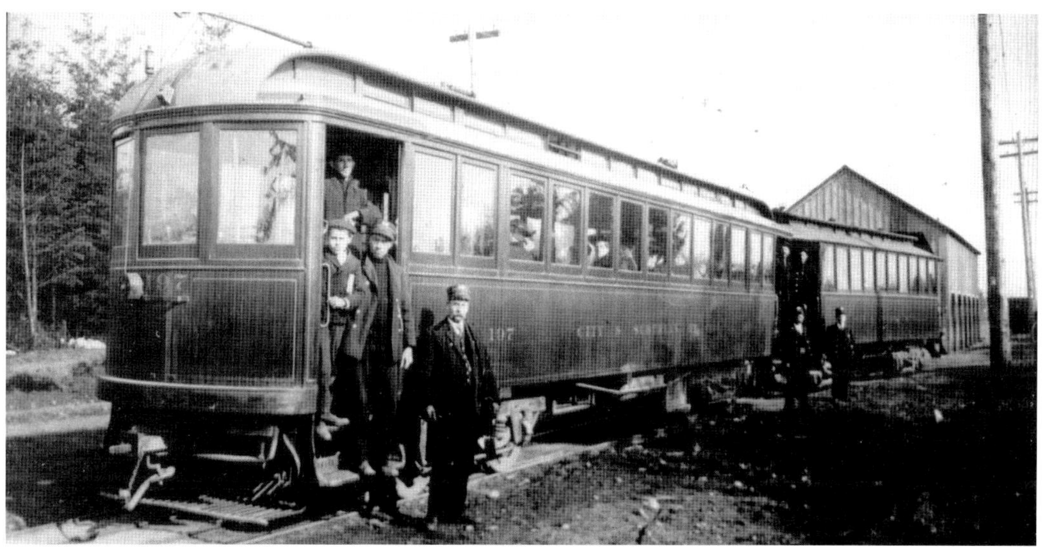

No. 197 and a trailer are seen in front of the west end of the Piedmont Transfer Station in a picture taken not long after the St. Johns Line was electrified in 1903. These large cars and their two-car trains could not run into Portland until downtown tracks could be adjusted for them. The City & Suburban Railway built five of these interurban streetcars for the St. Johns Line during 1903–04.

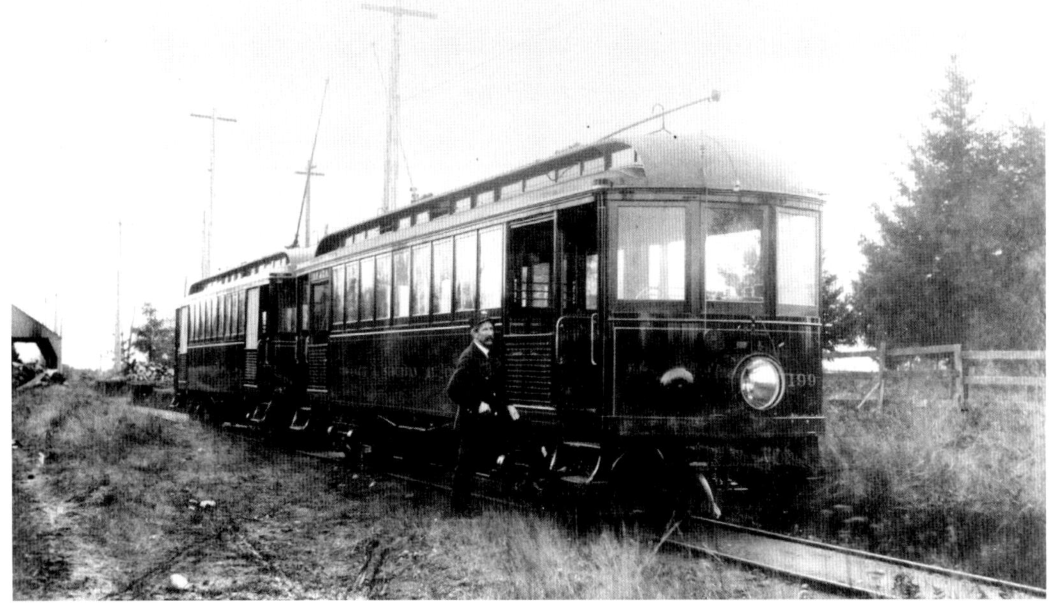

City & Suburban Railway No. 199 and sister 198 are preparing to return to St. Johns from the Piedmont Transfer Station. This pair were the only St. Johns interurbans built with open-sided vestibules equipped with roller shades. Note the large removable headlight. (*Photograph courtesy Dan Haneckow*)

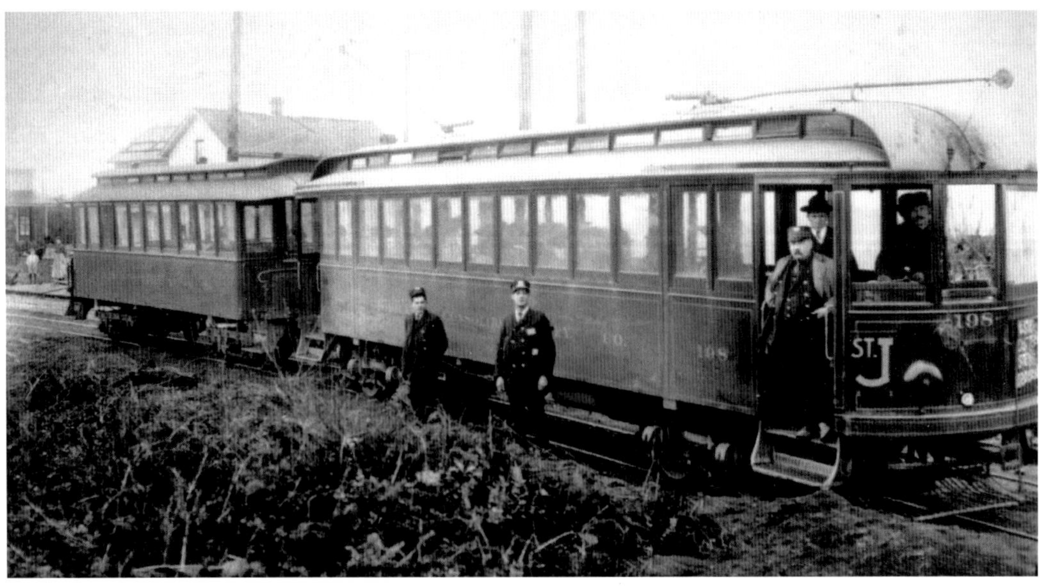

All eyes, including those of the family in the background, are on the cameraman as No. 198 and trailer wait at the Piedmont Transfer terminus. The interurban is now lettered for the Portland Consolidated Railway Company and the open sections on each end of the car have been enclosed. Note the large gong mounted on the dash rather than under the floor.

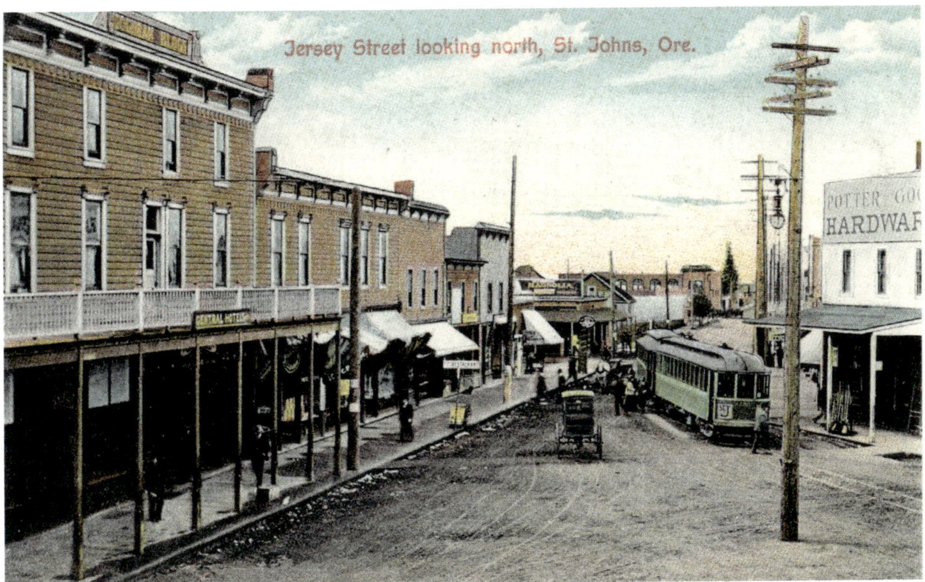

No. 197 and a trailer are seen on N Jersey Street and Philadelphia Avenue during the summer of 1908, when horses and buggies still plied the dirt streets in the center of St. Johns. At right is the Potter and Good Hardware store and the Central Hotel is at far left. Although the colors on this lithographed postcard may not be real, they do portray a representation of the City & Suburban Railway livery, which was olive green with gold detailing.

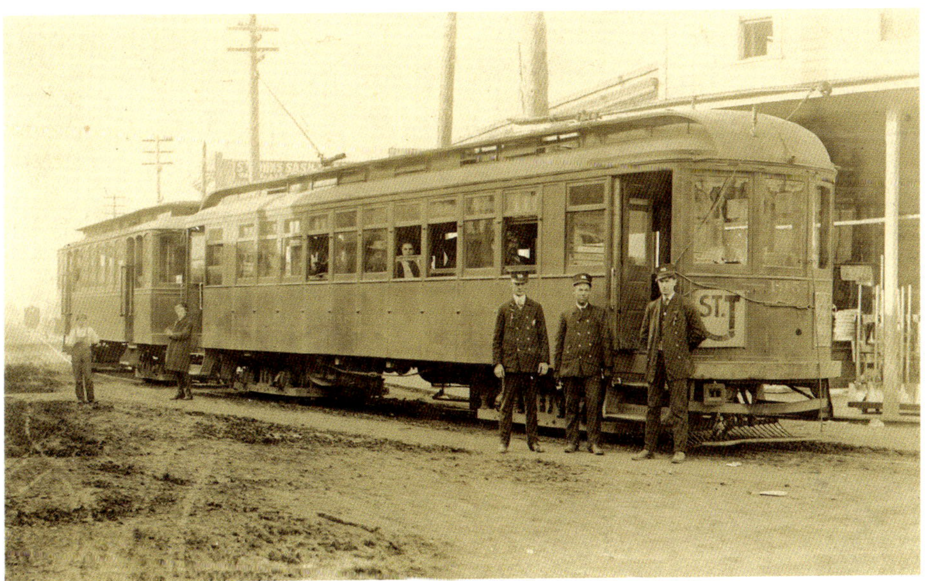

No. 195 is still lettered for the Portland Consolidated Railway and retains its removable side panels in a picture showing it and a new 350-series Fuller trailer at the N Jersey Street and Philadelphia Avenue terminus about 1906. An interurban-style air whistle is mounted on the roof. (*Photograph courtesy Mark Moore*)

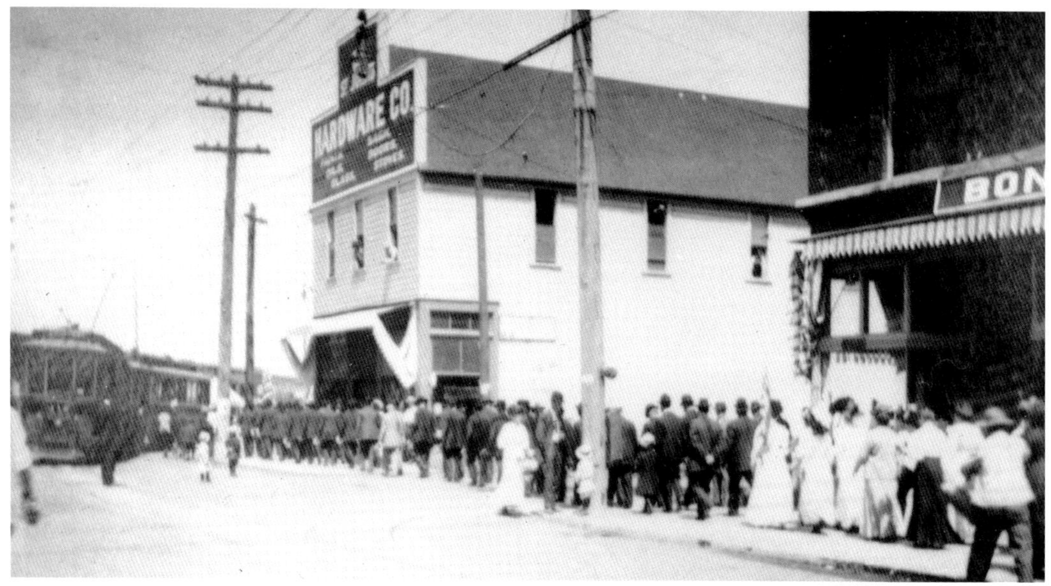

The occasion that has drawn a crowd to N Jersey Street in this 1907 picture is unknown, but it may have been the opening day for the first Portland Rose Festival. Brand new car 415 and its sister have been pressed into duty. The 400–439 series, designed to operate in multiple-unit pairs, were the first group of closed motors ordered by PRL&P following its takeover of the Portland streetcar system.

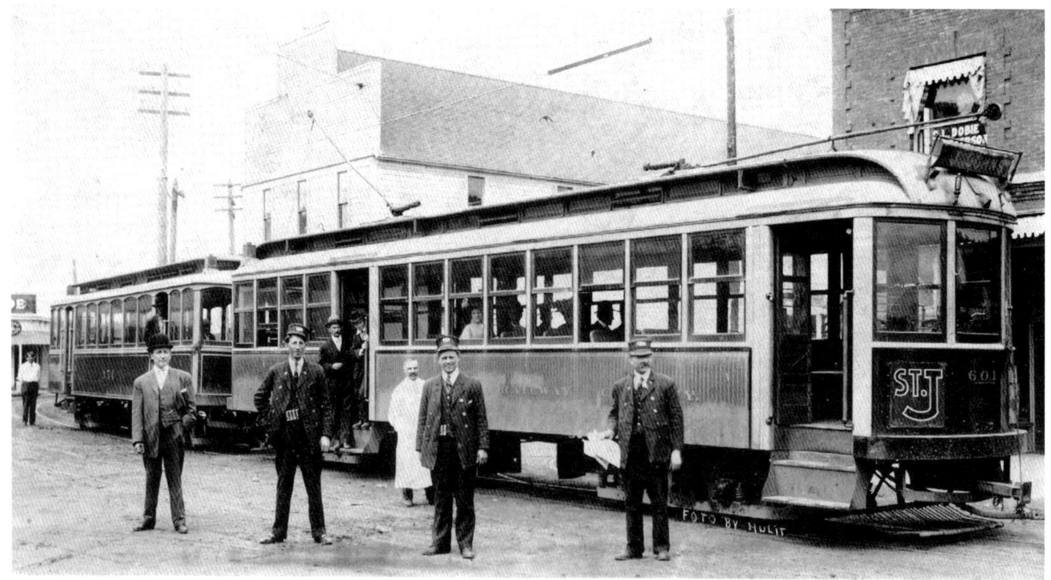

A businessman and a chef are posing with the crew of motor 601 and trailer 354 on N Jersey Street in central St. Johns. The cook may well be from the nearby St. Johns Hotel. The rails curving away beneath No. 601 lead to the storage track used by Portland & Suburban Express box motors. The big combine, known as a "Vancouver" after the line it was designed for, appears to be undergoing refinishing. (*Photograph courtesy Mark Moore*)

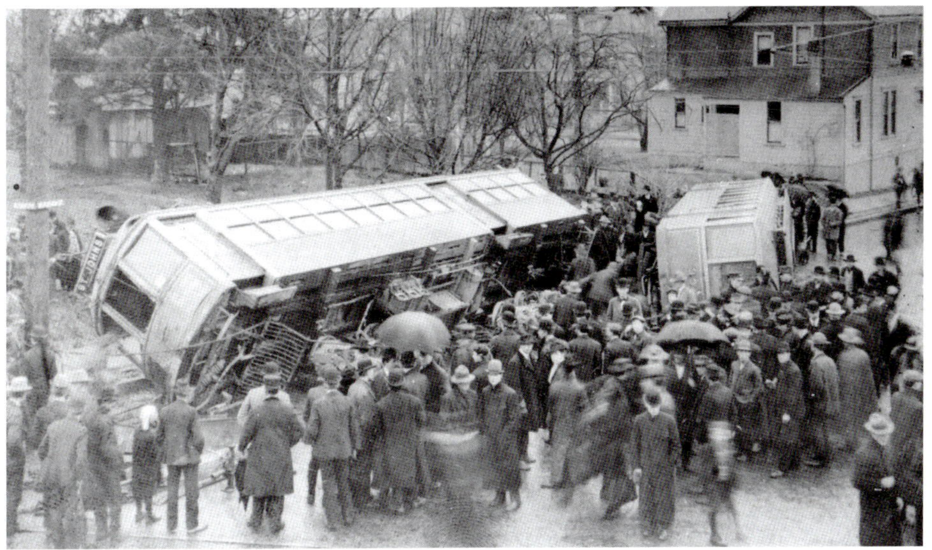

On January 19, 1909, No. 601 suffered an air brake failure and entered the curve on N Williams Avenue at Cherry Street at an estimated 25 miles per hour, derailing and pulling Fuller trailer 353 with it. Newspaper headlines lamented, "Cars Driven at Terrific Speed." Although there were no fatalities, eighteen of the sixty-six passengers were injured. Both cars were repaired and returned to service.

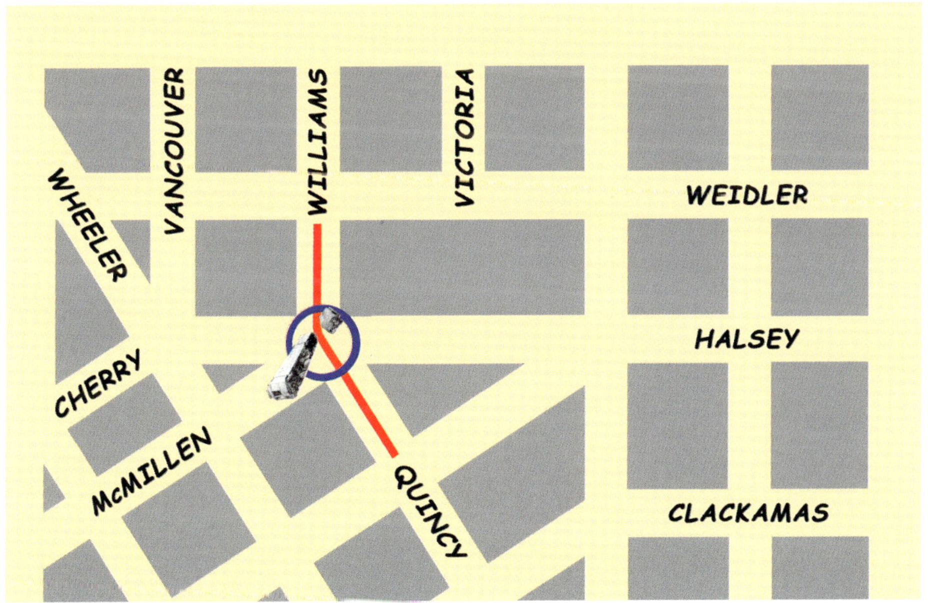

This map shows the location of the wreck of St. Johns Line motor 601 and trailer 353. The curves on the tracks along the diagonal streets of McMillen's Addition were not intended for speed. It is interesting to note that when southbound car 601 ran off the rails it tipped to the left, while its trailer disconnected and leaned the other way.

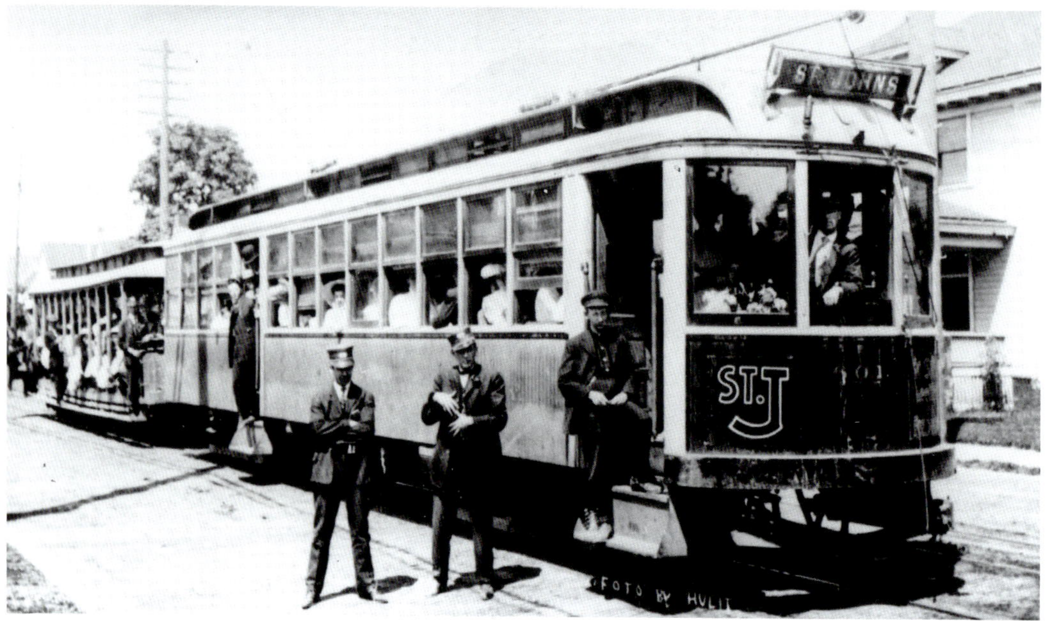

This picture was taken in St. Johns around 1907, before former Portland Consolidated Railway car 601 had been renumbered 192 and the new 274 series open trailer had been enclosed. There are five crewmen in view on what was probably an excursion run. The 600–603 series "Vancouvers" were similar to sisters 191–195 except that they were combines with rear freight compartments. Low demand for freight seems to have encouraged use of these compartments as smoking sections.

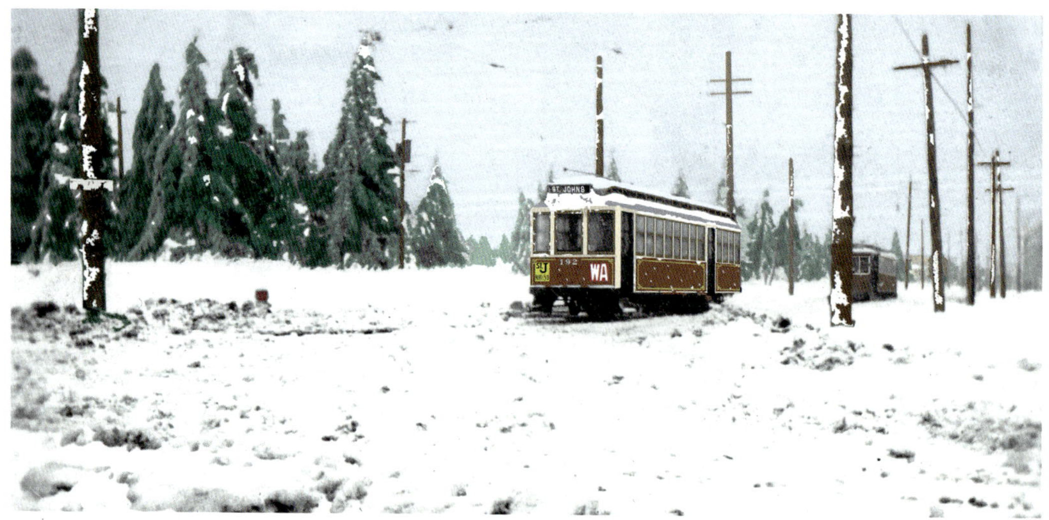

A Williams Avenue streetcar follows as St. Johns Line 192 (ex-601) clears the snow on N Williams Avenue. The picture likely dates from late 1909 or early 1912 when St. Johns and Williams Avenue cars shared these tracks. No. 192 was one of four interurbans built by Portland Railway around 1906 for the Vancouver Line. During the early years, the "Vancouvers," were also used along with the 195 series cars on the St. Johns run. (*Photograph courtesy Don Nelson*)

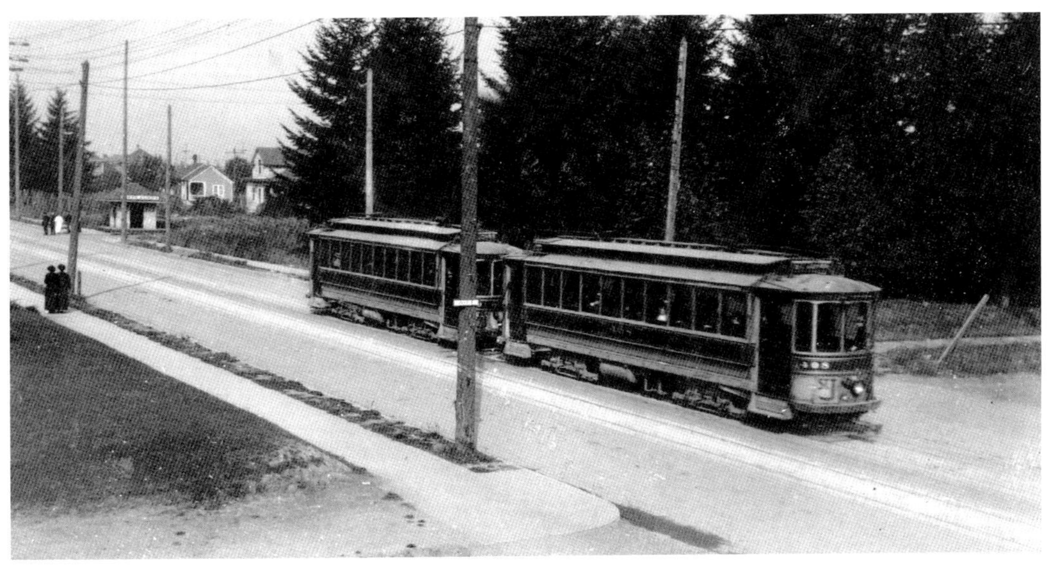

Paired cars 408 and 409 are seen approaching North Albina Station at N Killingsworth Street and Missouri Avenue on October 22, 1909. These cars were more modern-looking than the large interurban-style cars that had inaugurated St. Johns Line service six years before and they were equipped for multiple-unit (MU) operation by a single motorman. (*Photograph courtesy Mark Moore*)

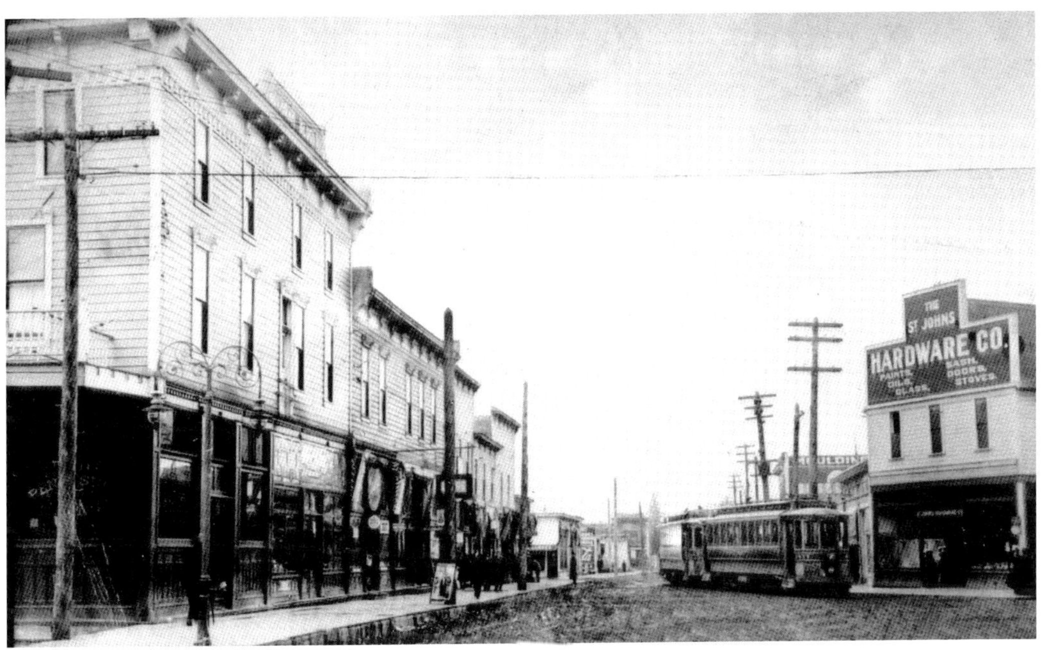

Multiple-unit cars 407 and 411 are seen amid a slightly improved retail district on N Jersey Street in St. Johns in 1909. The street is still unpaved, but the sidewalk in front of the Cochran Building at left has been opened up by removing the Central Hotel balcony and an ornate streetlight has been installed. Note the interurban arc light hanging above the regular headlight.

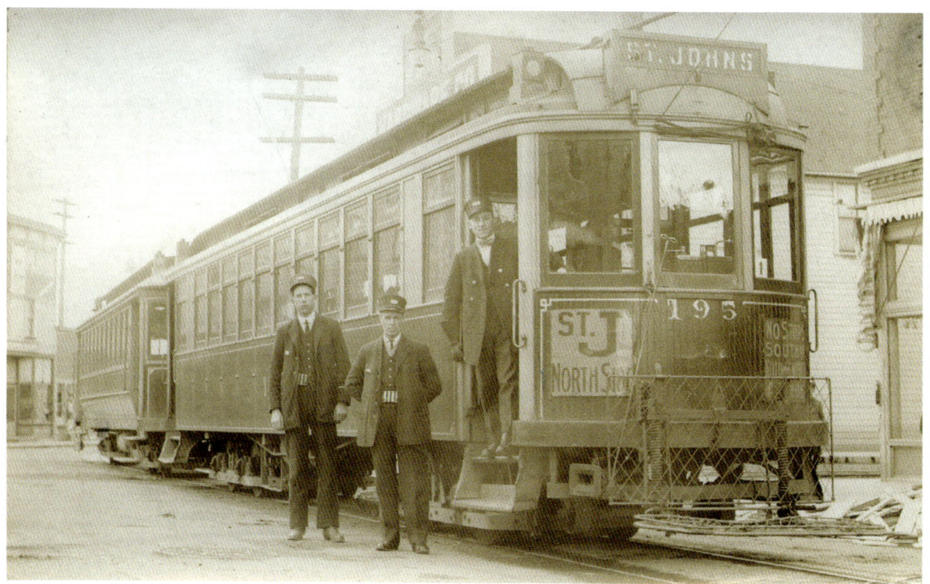

St. Johns motor No. 195 and a 274-class trailer wait in front of the St. Johns Hardware store on N Jersey Avenue about 1913. Motorman Adams and conductors Linkes and Nelsen made up a standard two-car train crew. The dash signs read "St. J North Side" and "No stops south of Killingsworth Avenue." North Side trains entered the St. Johns loop via N Fessenden Street, while South Side trains entered on N Lombard Street.

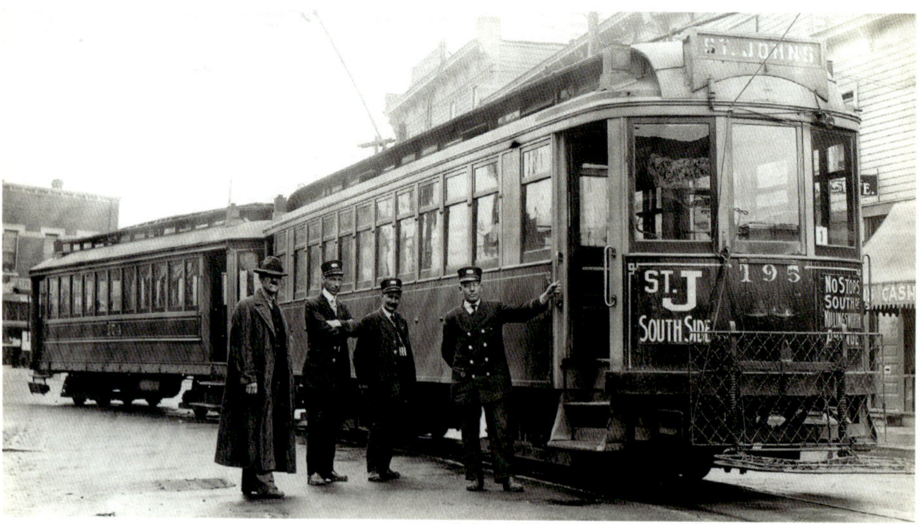

St. Johns Line No. 195 and trailer 274 are working the St. Johns South Side run. Between October 1913 and February 1916, St Johns trains alternated running around the loop from the North Side on N Fessenden Street and the South Side on N Lombard Street. The crew pictured includes motorman Charles Pye and conductors Mollenhour and Lecuyer. Three Lecuyer brothers (Alfred, Phillias, and Raymond) worked out of Piedmont Division. The gentleman in the coat is not identified.

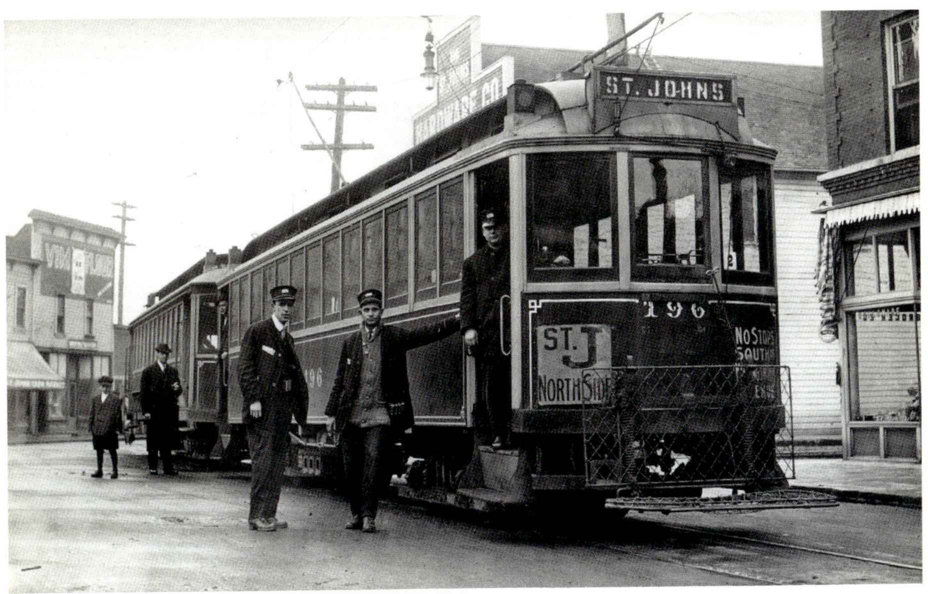

North Side Line motor 196 and trailer are in front of the St. Johns Hardware Company in the St. Johns retail district. In the background, a billboard on the Rostov Bakery advertises Vim Flour, which was produced locally by the Jobes Brothers Flour Mill. The crew on this run includes motorman William Allman and conductor Nelson Shafer (the conductor for the trailer is not identified).

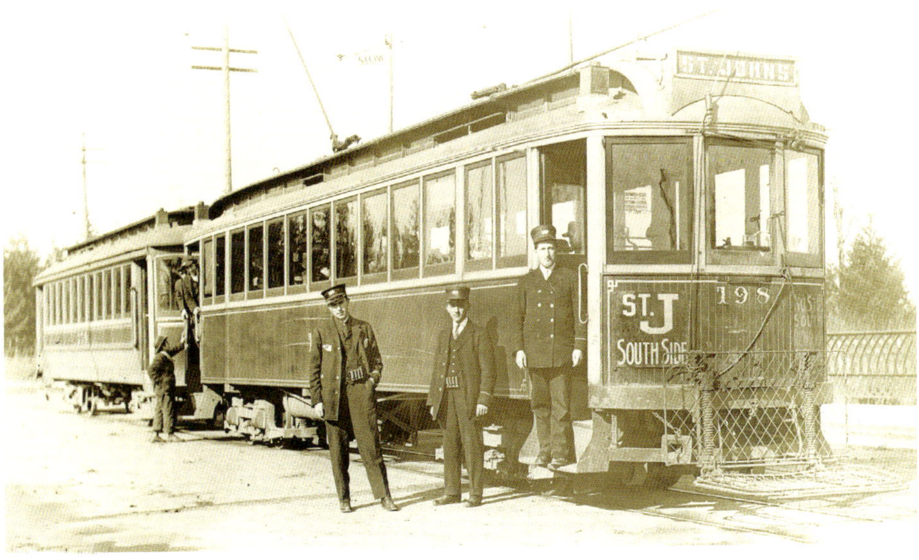

No. 198 and trailer 278 are on the bridge over the railroad cut on N Lombard Street. On May 1, 1918, trains began entering the St. Johns loop via the South Side on N Lombard in order to get wartime workers to the shipyard faster. On October 16, 1919, trains reverted to entering St. Johns via the North Side on N Fessenden and exiting via N Lombard. The crew is listed as Pennington, Ogandyke, and Shafer. (*Photograph courtesy Mark Moore*)

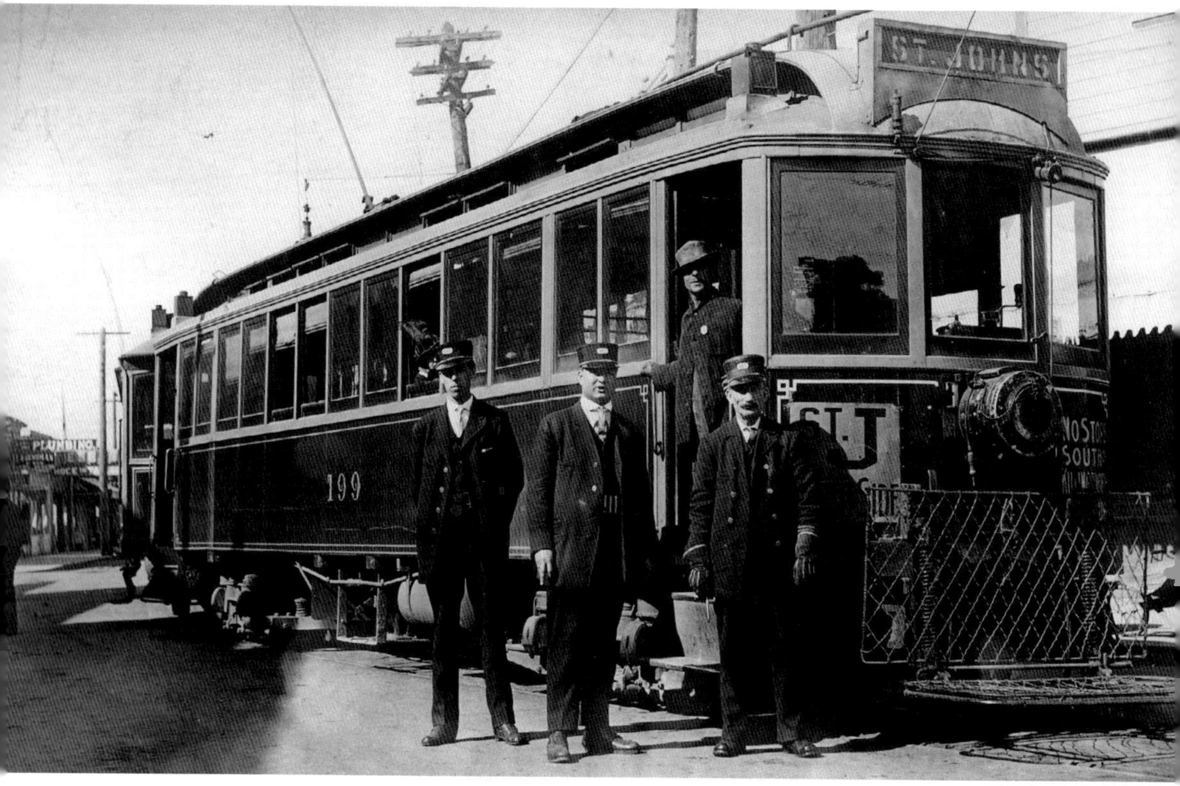

St. Johns North Side Motor 199 and trailer 275 are paused at N Philadelphia Avenue and Jersey Street with a crew consisting of motorman Albert Stein, motor conductor George Foss, and trailer conductor John Neff. As the dash sign proclaims, the two-car train is a limited making "No stops south of Killingsworth Avenue." In the background are the Gilbert Noce Tailor shop and a plumbing store. Note the removable interurban-style, carbon-arc headlight.

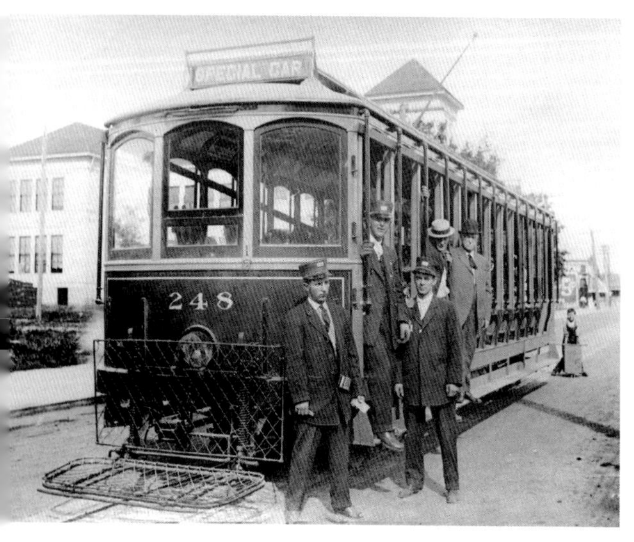

In 1902, Portland Railway built eleven open cars like No. 248. They were popular for warm weather excursions as seen here. In the background is St. Johns Central School, a type of classic two-story frame school that was common in North Portland during the early twentieth century. When these open breezers were hastily enclosed in 1919, the lack of bulkheads created a series of drafty trolleys that earned the moniker "pneumonia cars."

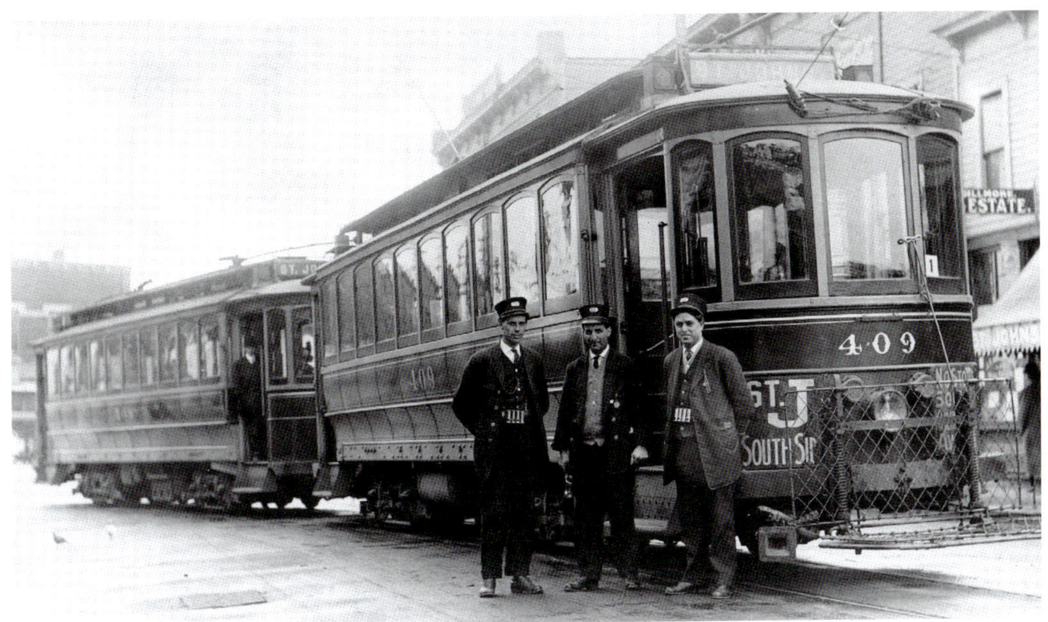

Multiple-unit pair 408 and 409 are seen waiting in front of the King and Gilmore Real Estate Office in a view looking west across N Jersey Street. The Cochran Building is in the center background. The carmen for this St. Johns South Side train are conductor Hulbert Wilkes, motorman Burton or Charles Dean, and conductor Floyd Perry. The picture was taken not long after Nelson Safety Fenders were installed in 1912.

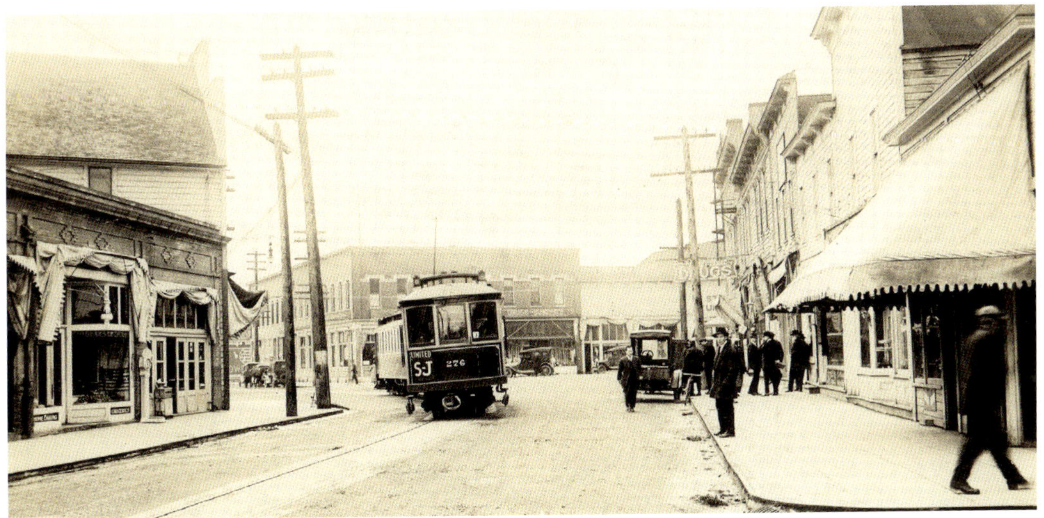

A 195-class motor is pulling trailer No. 276 in a photograph looking south on N Jersey Street at Philadelphia Avenue. The outbound two-car St. Johns Line train leans into the curve as it passes dueling drug stores that face each other on each side of the street. The St. Johns Hardware Company is behind the grocery store at left. Complicated intersections like this still typify St. Johns. (*Photograph courtesy Mark Moore*)

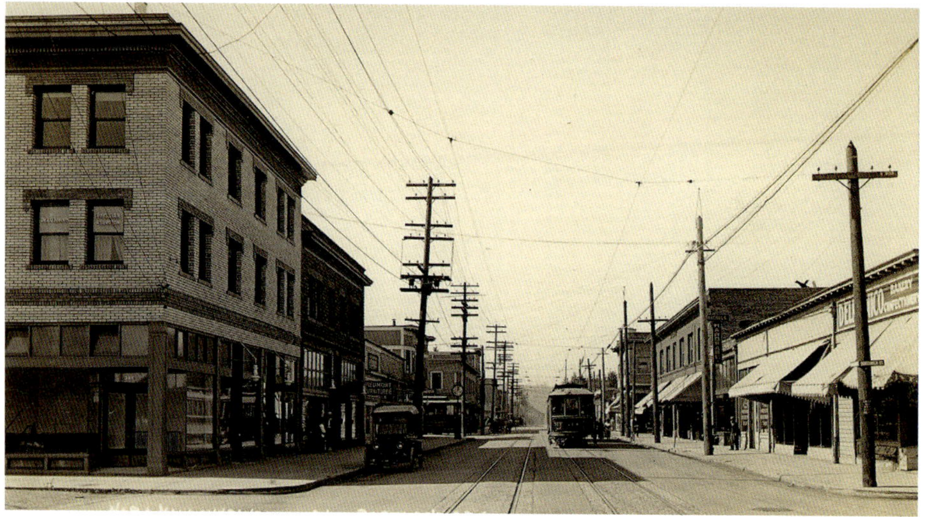

All we can see is trailer 274 on the tail end of a St. Johns train as passengers board on N Killingsworth Street at N Albina Avenue. A Mississippi Avenue Line trolley is waiting behind the street clock at left. Businesses in view along the Piedmont commercial district include a medical building, furniture store, and market at left, and the Delmonico Bakery and Nichols Hardware on the right. (*Photograph courtesy Mark Moore*)

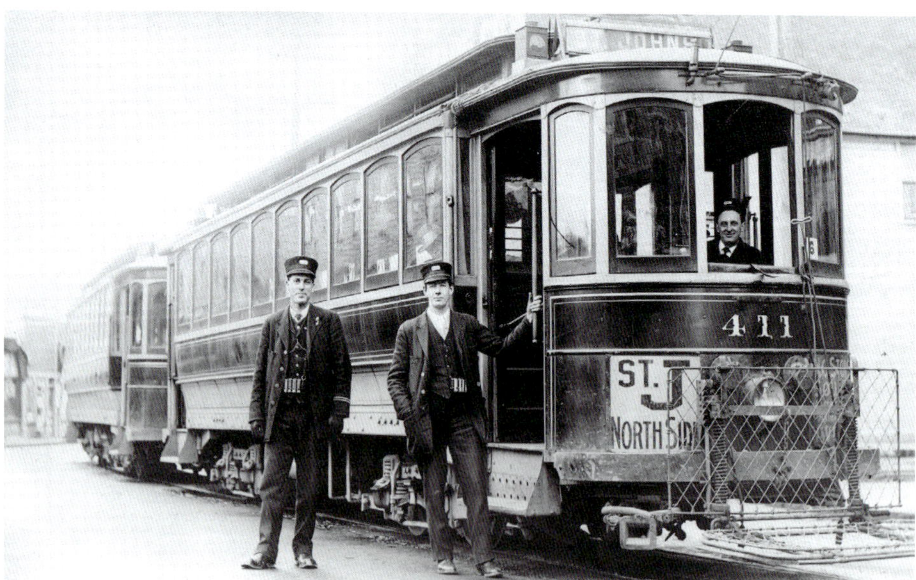

Conductors Anderson and Merton Cline look serious, but motorman Irving Boyce wears a smile in this picture of No. 411 and sister working the St. Johns North Side Line. Cars 400–439 were the only narrow gauge PRL&P streetcars equipped for multiple-unit operation, hence the large round MU connectors seen on each side of the headlight. Although several lines had started using them singly by World War I, St. Johns Line ridership was sufficient to keep them operating in tandem.

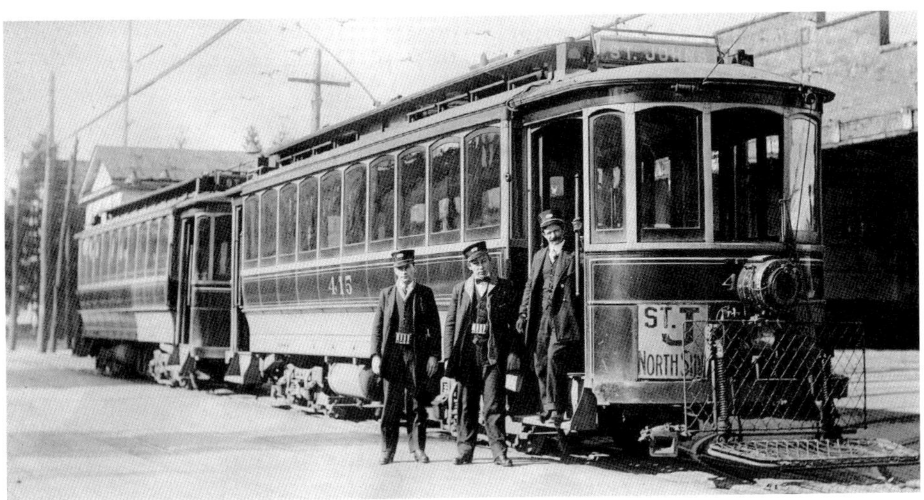

An arc light is hung for evening operation, the rollsign set for St. Johns, and a North Side dash sign placed on the dash as MU pair 414 and 415 pause in front of the Piedmont Carbarn on N Killingsworth Street. Although the late afternoon sun is shining, it must be cold because conductors Lester Chapman and Lloyd Jordan are bundled in extra layers of clothing.

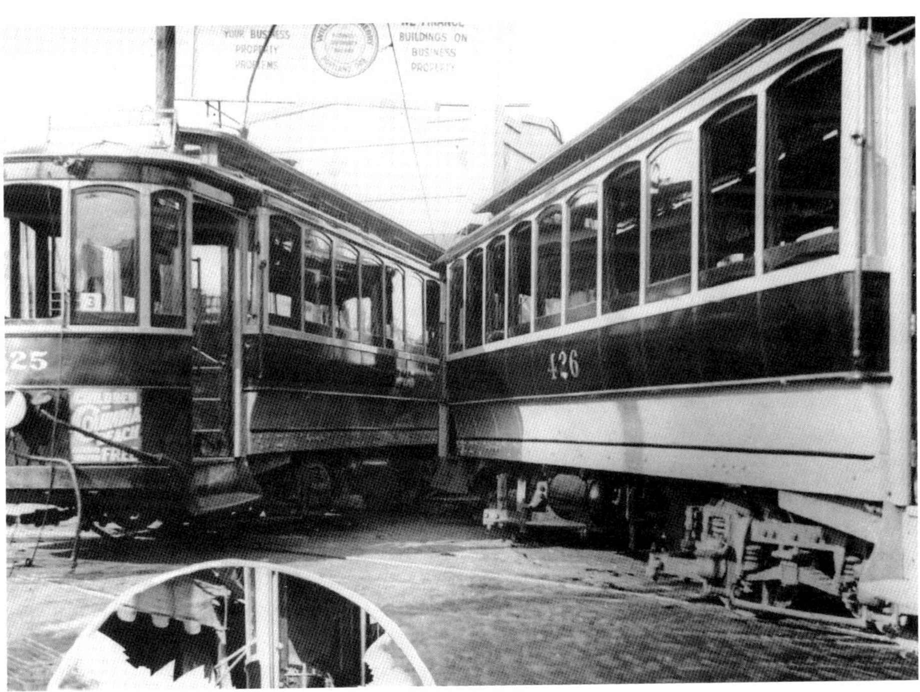

On August 11, 1924, *The Oregonian* reported "Nine women injured, and much damage done when St. Johns trolley train jumps track and crashes into confectionary store at East Broadway and Larrabee street." The store window was broken and traffic at this busy intersection disrupted, but the semi-permanently coupled MU pair do not appear to have been that badly damaged. They were repaired and continued in service until 1946.

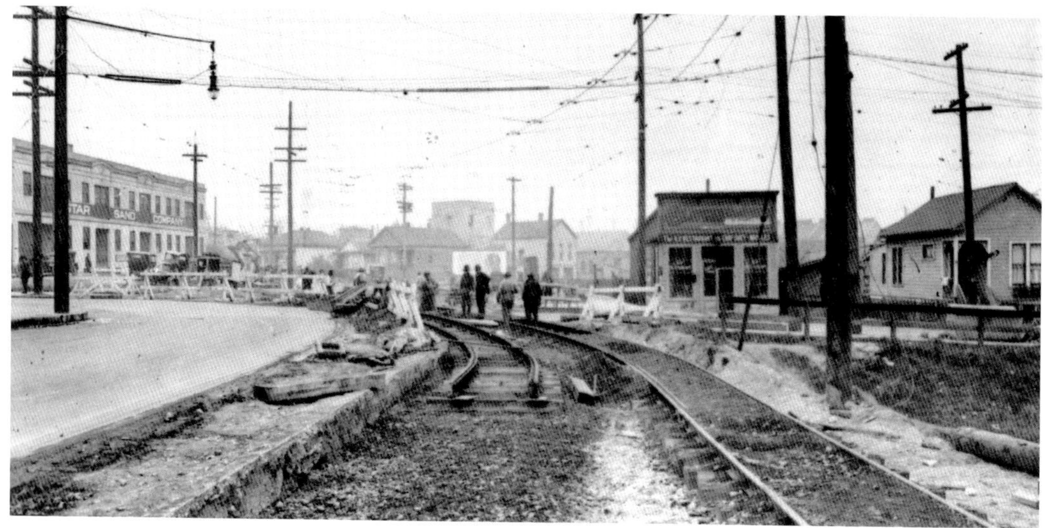

In 1925, work began on the Greeley Cutoff, a double-track private right-of-way alongside N Greeley Avenue that allowed St. Johns streetcars to bypass their former route on N Williams Avenue and Killingsworth Street, and head directly to N Greeley Avenue. Service on the cutoff began in January 1926. This construction scene is on N Interstate Avenue between Russell Street and Albina Avenue with the Gotham Building at left. Compare with pictures on pages 45 and 116.

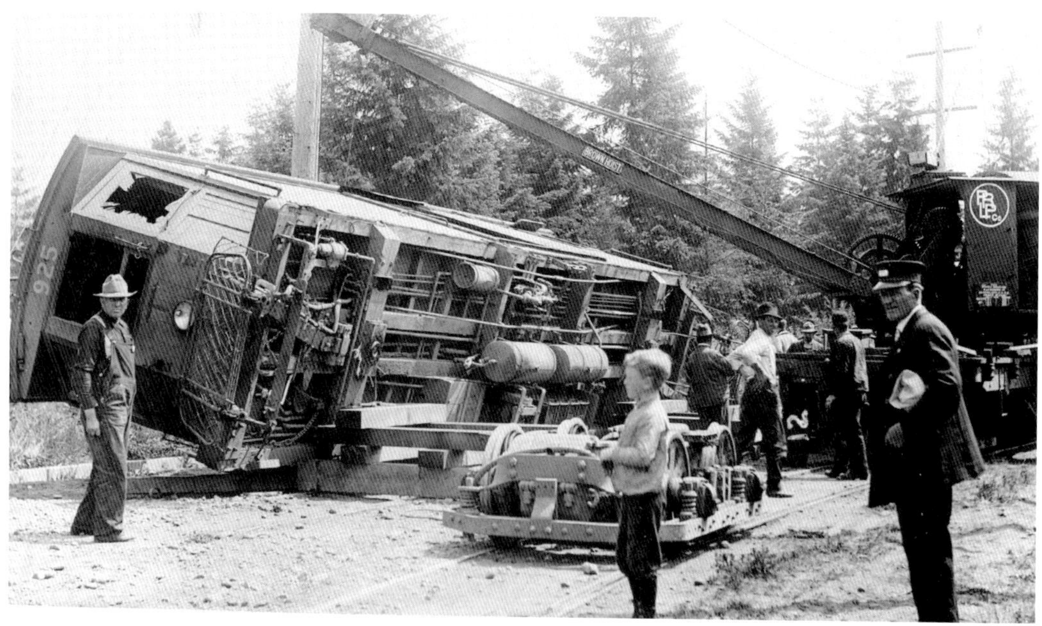

Since its inception, the St. Johns Line hauled freight and it continued to do so into the 1920s. Nothing is known about what caused No. 925 to derail. However, this accident is on double-track private right-of-way, so the location is likely on N Greeley Avenue. Except for broken windows ex-Portland & Suburban Express box motor No. 7 appears intact. "Big Hook" No. 906 has been called in to lift it back onto its trucks. (*Photograph courtesy Mark Moore*)

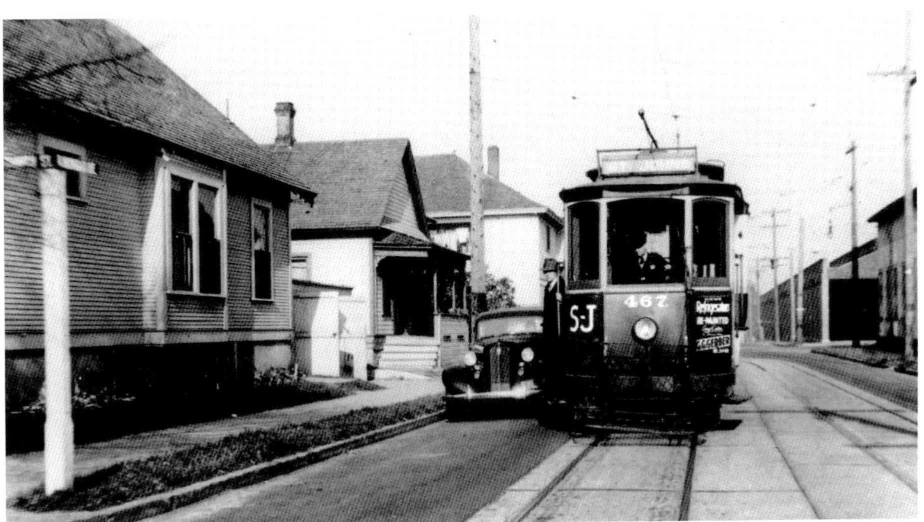

Car 467 is seen here during a 1930s safety demonstration on N Michigan Avenue north of N Jessup Street beside the Piedmont Carbarn. Photographs like this were staged to show the correct method for entrance and exit of passengers on PAYE cars. The dash sign advertisement reads, "Home refrigerators re-painted any color."

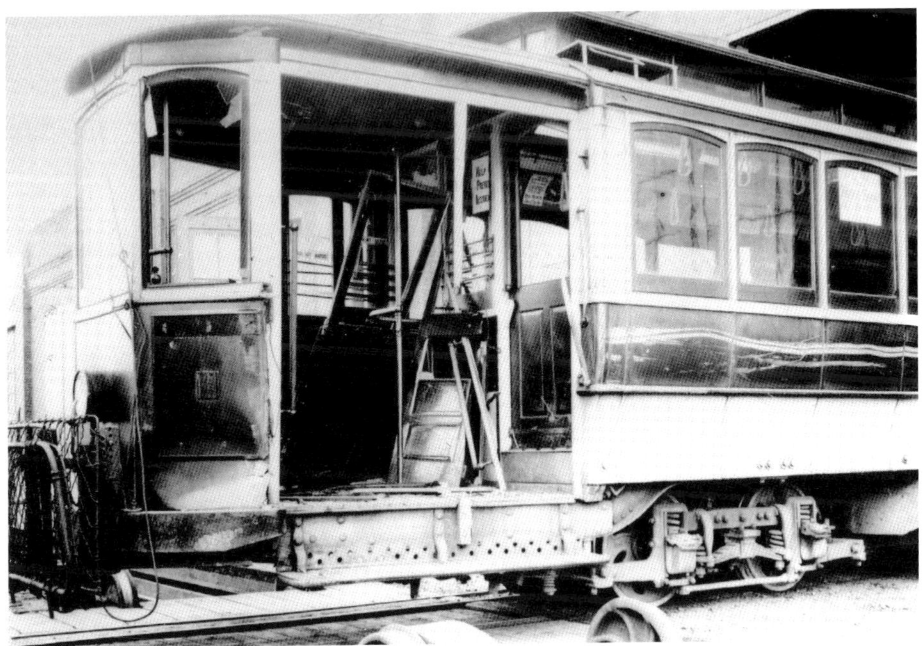

No. 477 is on the transfer table at the Center Street Shops following a mishap with a wood truck on N Interstate Avenue and Tillamook Street on the St. Johns Line on October 21, 1929. The damage was repaired and car 477 returned to service until retirement with the rest of her class in 1948. Note how different the "bay window" vestibules of the 466–485 class PAYEs were from the lower-numbered 400s, whose ends were rounded and included five windows.

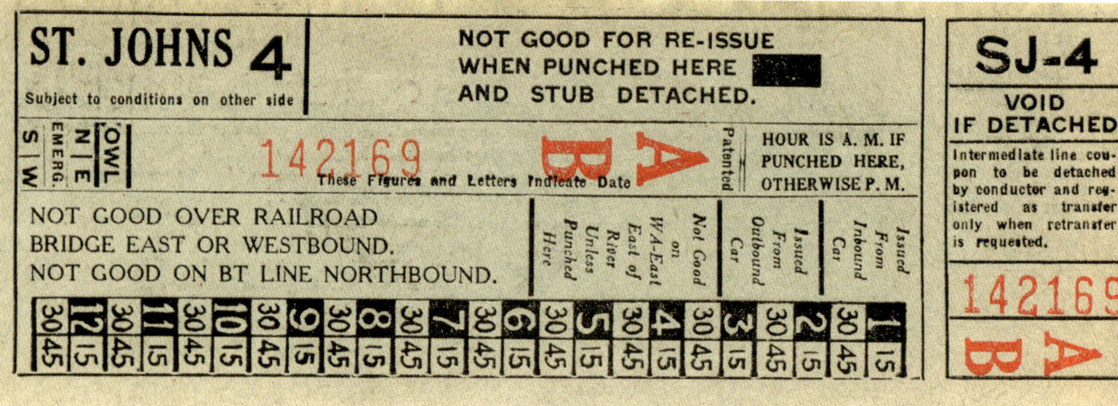

The stub is still attached to this unused St. Johns transfer issued by the Portland Traction Company during the late 1930s, when William H. Lines was first vice president and treasurer. It was "not good for travel over Railroad Bridge east or westbound." The Steel Bridge was often referred to as the Railroad Bridge since it accommodated railroad trains on the bottom deck and streetcars and other vehicles on the top.

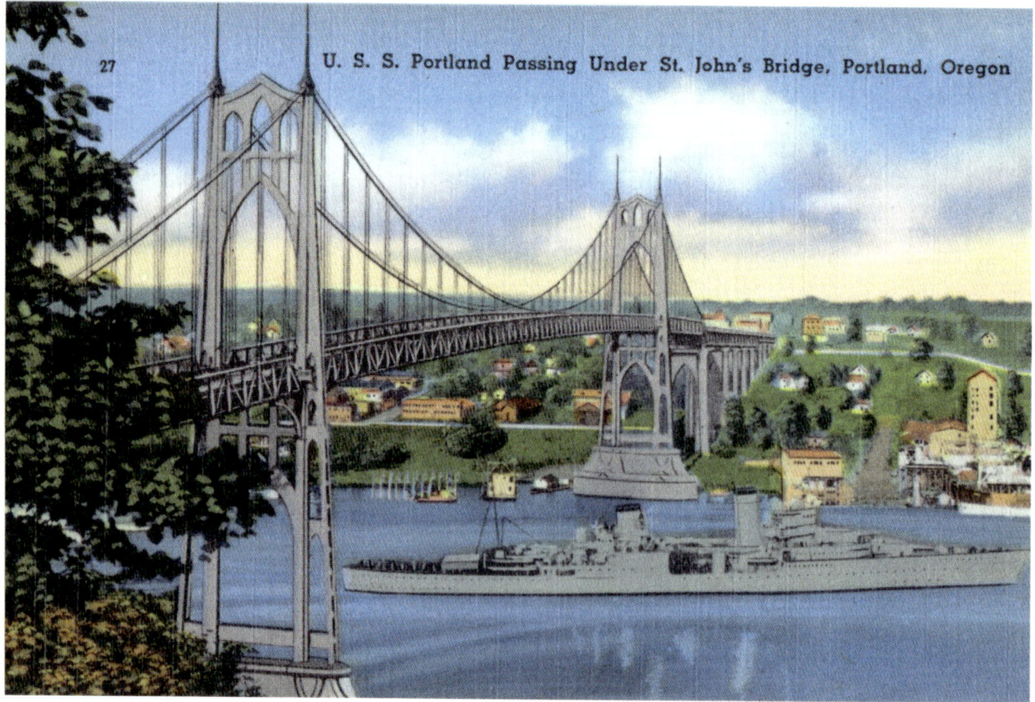

The biggest change in transportation for St. Johns came in June 1931 with the opening of the St. Johns Bridge. This 3,833-foot-long, Gothic-style, suspension bridge is considered the most beautiful in Portland. The ship passing 205 feet beneath the suspension bridge in this postcard is the USS *Portland* (CA-33), which was launched in 1932. The light cruiser accrued sixteen battle stars during World War II.

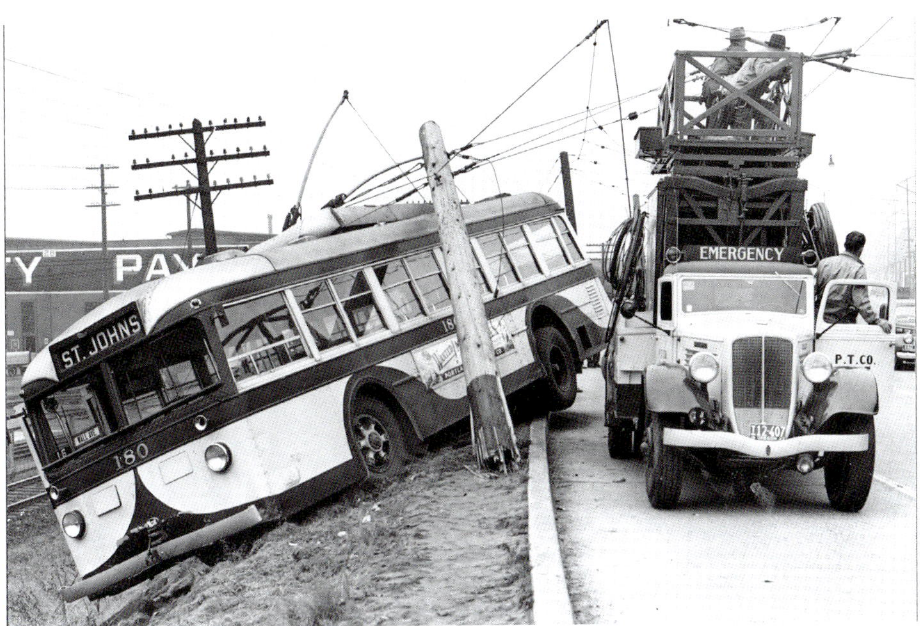

When a Diamond Fuel truck cut in front of St. Johns trolley coach 180, it was forced off the road on N Greeley Avenue just north of Interstate Avenue. The bus jumped the curb and became entangled in wires from a knocked-down pole, which may have prevented it from falling down a 40-foot incline to the railroad tracks below. Five passengers on the loaded bus were injured during the October 16, 1943 accident. (Photograph by *The Oregonian*)

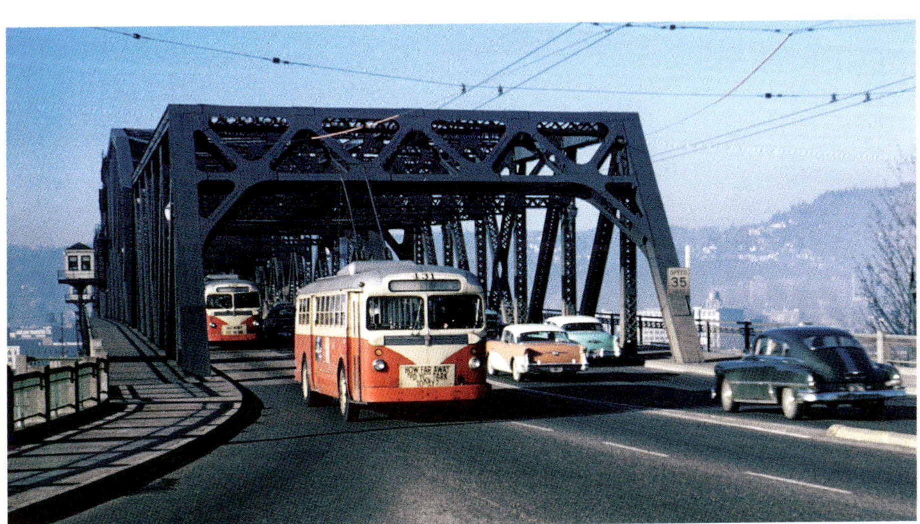

Two Kenworth trolleybuses are outbound on the Broadway Bridge in a slide taken during 1956 or 1957. Bus 431 is on the St. Johns Line with a Rose City Transit advertisement reading "How far away did you park today?" These two were among fifty trolleybuses built by the Seattle company for Portland in 1947–48. Note that the Broadway Bridge was originally black (it was repainted red in 1963). (*Photograph by Al Haij, courtesy Steve Morgan*)

6

Stub Lines

Lines that begin at the outer end of another line, rather than running from a downtown terminus, are called stub lines. North Portland was home to four such lines, each of which was unique in its own way. The oldest crossed the Willamette River for a time, but did not run into the central retail district, the second was a stub on a stub, the third was operated by a private company, and the fourth by a governmental agency. The first of these lines began and ended as a stub operating from NE Union Avenue (now Martin Luther King, Jr., Boulevard) and Russell Street to N Shaver Street and what is now N Concord Avenue in the Overlook Addition. It was originally the Portland Railway Company's short-lived Albina Line, which had been intended to extend to St. Johns. Within months of opening in August 1903, the route had been reimagined by successor Portland Consolidated Railway Company as the Russell–Shaver Line. More distant termini were added twice.

In 1907, PRL&P extended the Russell–Shaver Line across the river to NW 16th Avenue and West Burnside Street. The west side connection was dropped in April 1908. However, a second experiment saw Russell–Shaver combined with the East Side Line in October 1909, which gave it a southern terminus on SE Grand Avenue and Hawthorne Boulevard in the East Portland commercial district. Interestingly, an alternate northern terminal on N Maryland Avenue and N Prescott Street was in operation from January 27, 1913, until January 1, 1916.

The Russell–Shaver stub was cut back to NE Union and Russell again on January 1, 1915. This would remain the Russell–Shaver route until the line was discontinued on April 17, 1937. Although only a handful of trolleys were needed for Russell–Shaver service a wide variety appeared over the years, including C&S Standards, old Pullmans, 466-class PAYEs, and Birney Safety cars.

Next we come to the two Kenton lines. On September 14, 1909, stub line service was inaugurated between N Killingsworth Street and Albina Avenue in the Piedmont District and N Kilpatrick and Derby streets (now Denver Avenue) in the company town of Kenton. On October 13, 1912, this Kenton line merged with the Mississippi Avenue Line. Regular Mississippi Avenue streetcars began using the Broadway Bridge when it opened in April

1913, but Mississippi Avenue–Kenton trolleys continued crossing via the Steel Bridge for a few months. After both lines began using the Broadway Bridge in 1914, Kenton faded away as a separate line.

The second Kenton Line was a stub on a stub. In 1909, Swift & Company built the company town of Kenton to house employees of its large meat packing plant 2 miles away on the south bank of the Columbia River. On March 22, 1909, the Kenton Traction Company was incorporated to operate a streetcar line from a terminus in Kenton to the Union Stockyards. Old City & Suburban Standards were leased for the Kenton–Stockyards Line, which operated from October 18, 1909 until December 1928.

The Municipal Terminal Line was the last new streetcar line in Portland when it opened on November 6, 1920. The 1.5-mile stub was built by the Commission of Public Docks to provide access to new Terminal Number 4, which was located in a remote area north of St. Johns. On April 8, 1922, a short extension was added along N Terminal Road to Pier No. 1. On October 31, 1929, the city replaced streetcars on this stub with a bus. Equipment on this line consisted of a single 100-class car.

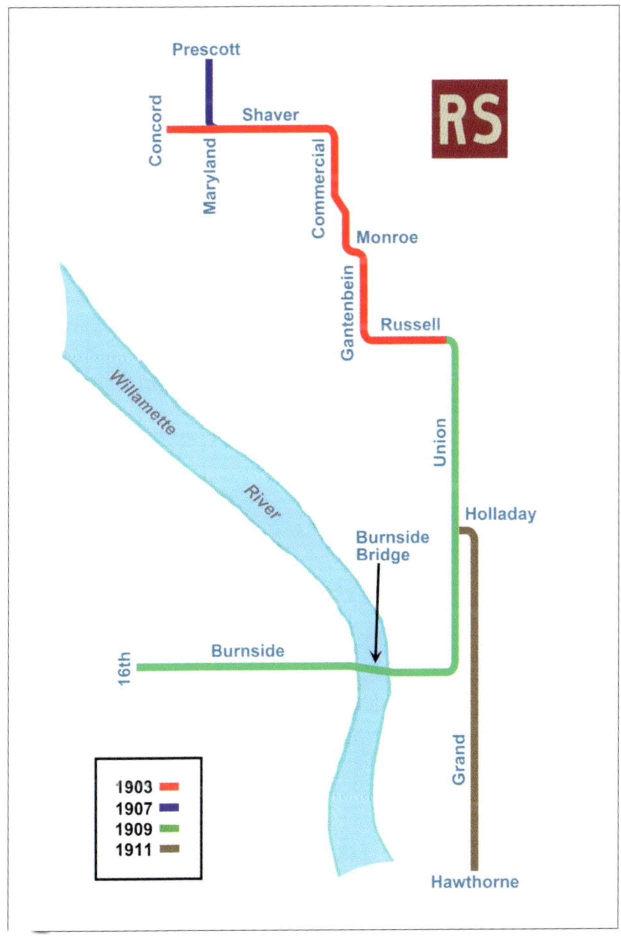

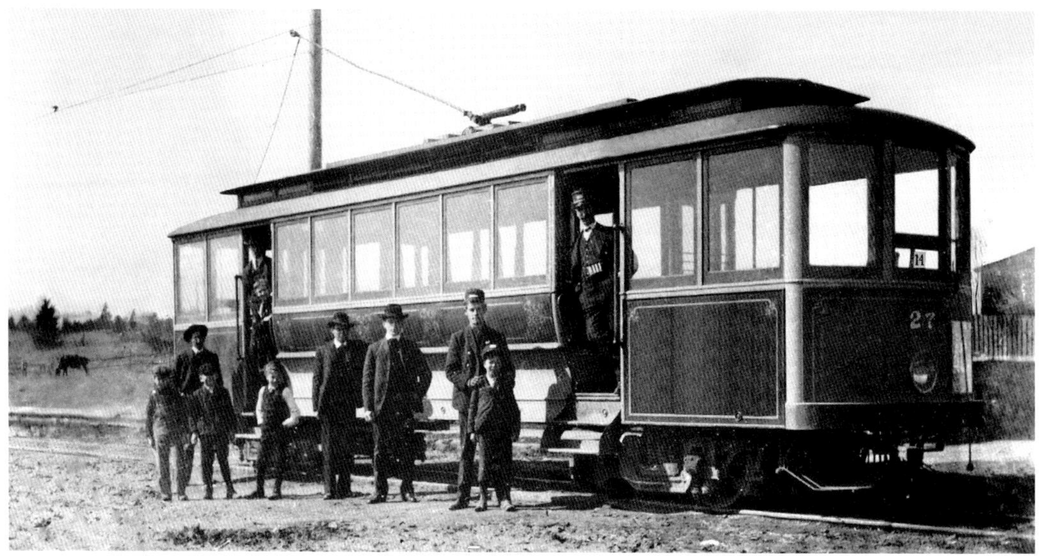

Cows graze behind No. 27 as construction is getting started in the Overlook neighborhood in a view thought to be at the terminus on N Shaver Street and Concord Avenue. The picture dates from around 1904 because the first-series Fuller car is lettered for the Portland Consolidated Railway yet the dash sign still reads "Albina" rather than Russell–Shaver.

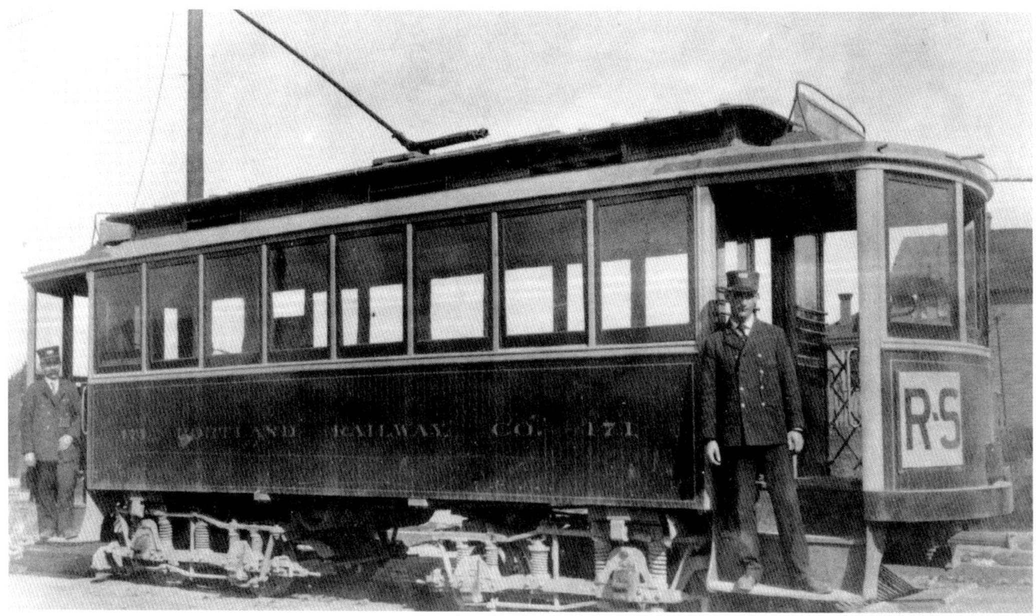

This photograph of car 171 at the Overlook terminus of the Russell–Shaver Line was taken around 1905 during the short tenure of the third Portland Railway Company. The once-proud trolley was one of the open-platformed white-and-gold painted Pullmans ordered by the City & Suburban Railway in 1891. However, by this time, little 171 had been relegated to stub-line duty. The motorman, also a veteran, is Frank P Love.

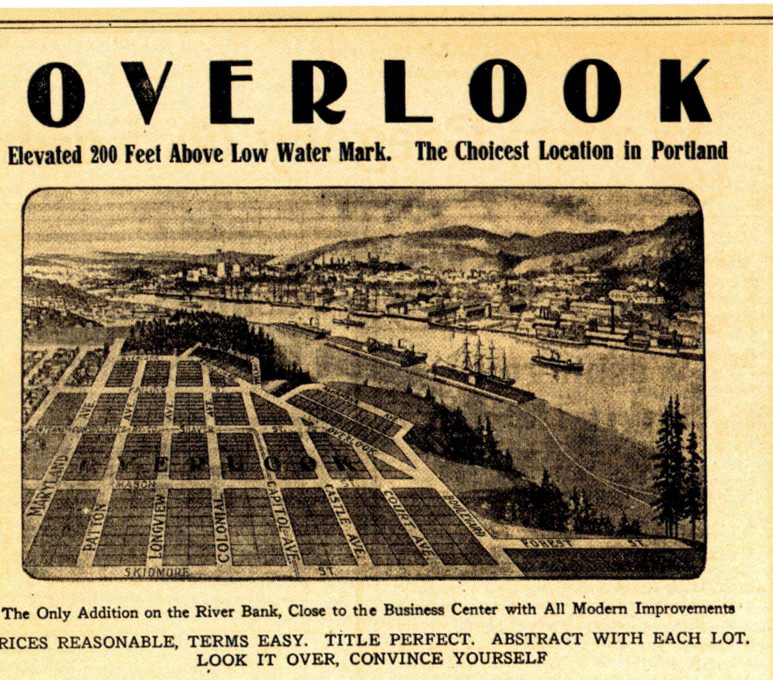

The Russell-Shaver Line helped promote the sale of lots in the new Overlook Addition. As explained in this advertisement "R-S Cars Take You to the Center of the Addition." After years of delay, the Overlook neighborhood was platted for development in 1905. The addition's name comes from its location on a bluff overlooking Swan Island and the Willamette River.

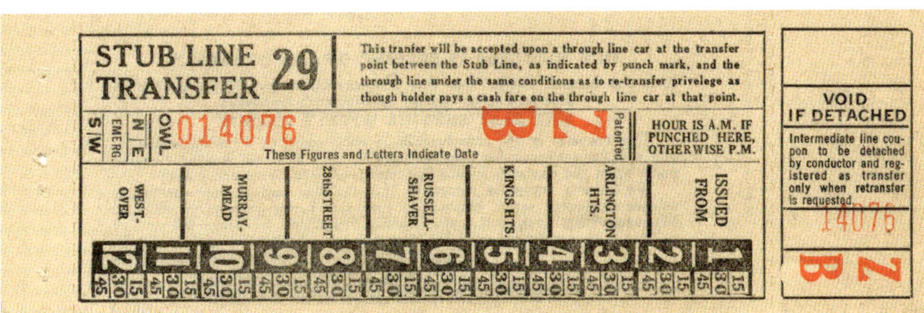

By the early 1930s, Russell–Shaver was the only stub line remaining in North Portland as can be seen in this stub-line transfer issued by the Pacific Northwest Public Service Company. At one time, Portland could boast of fourteen stub lines. By the time this transfer ticket was issued, there were just six.

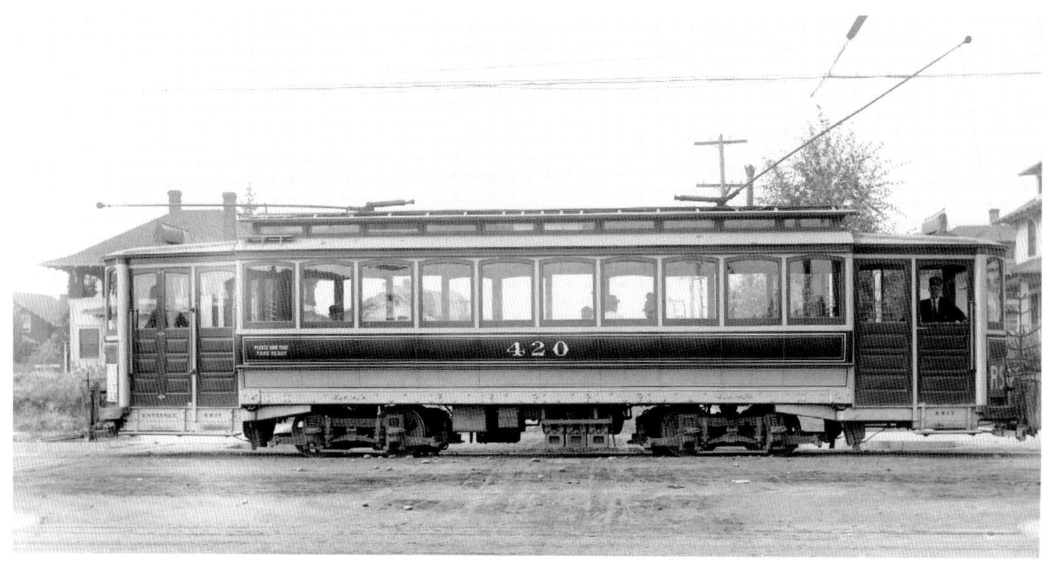

No. 420, seen here at the Russell–Shaver Line terminus in Overlook, was a one-of-a-kind streetcar. Originally one of the 400–439 class ordered from the American Car Company in 1907, she was rebuilt in 1909 with large PAYE vestibules. The remodel was not successful, however, since the excessive overhang created by extending the platforms produced a harsh ride. This was not a problem with the later PAYE cars because their trucks were farther apart.

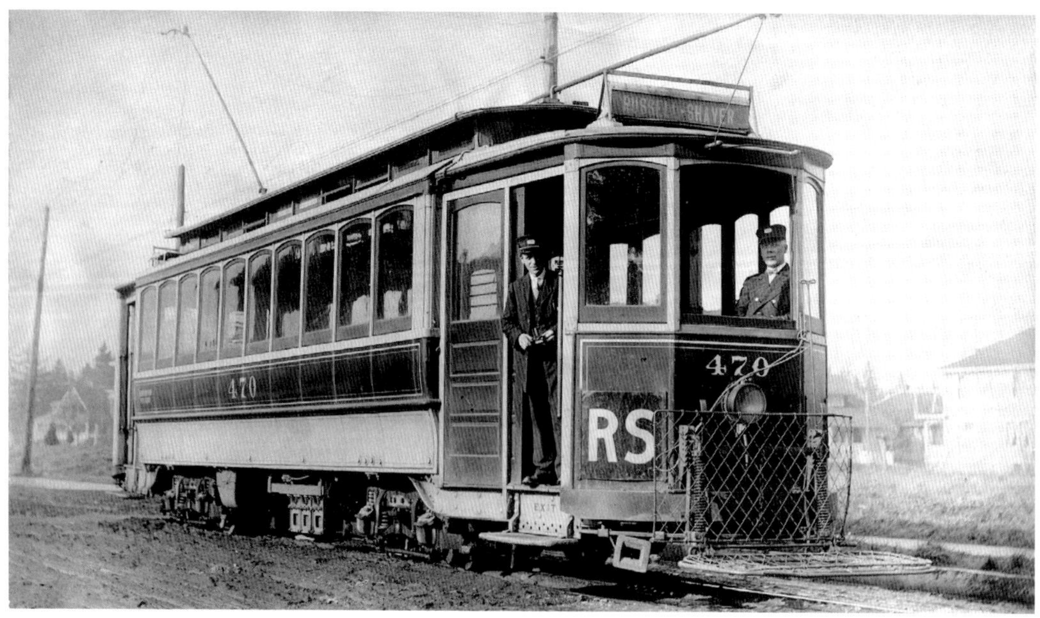

Conductor William Older and motorman Elmer Stark wait with their trolley at the western Russell–Shaver Line terminus in a picture dating from the mid-1910s, when the neighborhood had begun to fill in. PAYE car 470 would be converted to one-man operation during the early 1920s. and given two additional GE-58 motors.

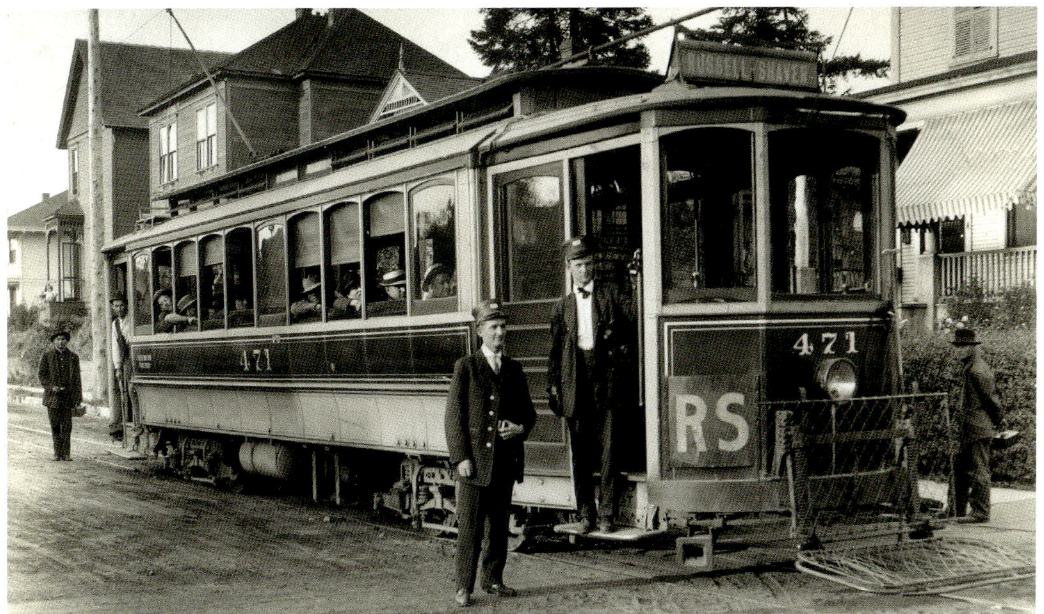

Motorman Earl Crosson and conductor Paul Emanuelson are about to depart with crowded Russell-Shaver car 471 from what must be the terminus on N Russell Street and NE Union Avenue since few Victorian houses like those in the background were built in Overlook. Note the workmen with lunch boxes standing near each end of the trolley.

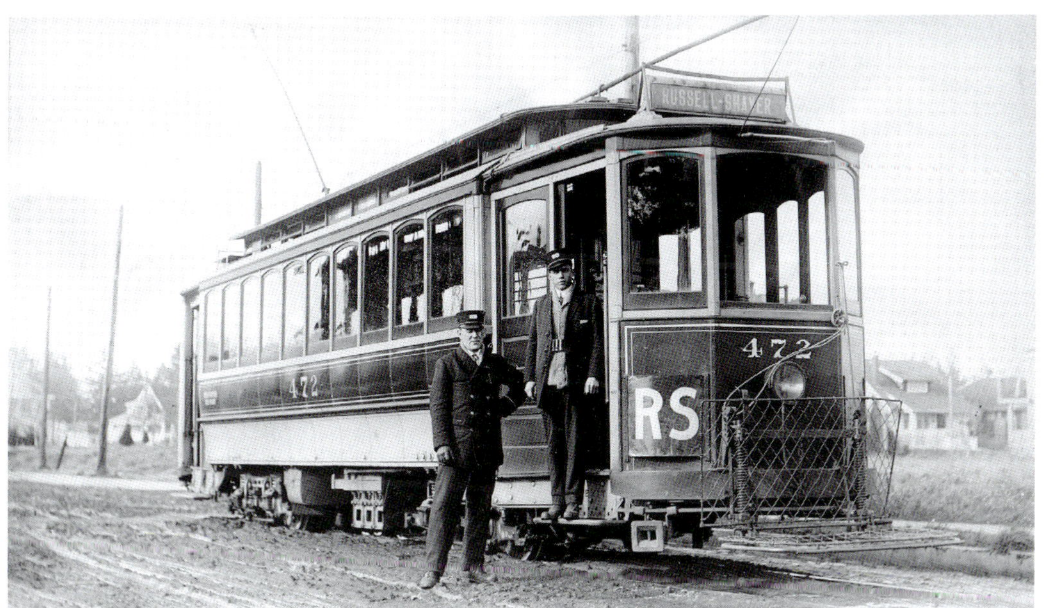

No. 472 is pictured at the Russell–Shaver terminus in the Overlook neighborhood on unpaved N Shaver Street near Capitol (now Concord) Avenue with motorman John Crowe and conductor J. R. McGinnis. Both carmen lived nearby and rode streetcars to work at the Piedmont Carbarn.

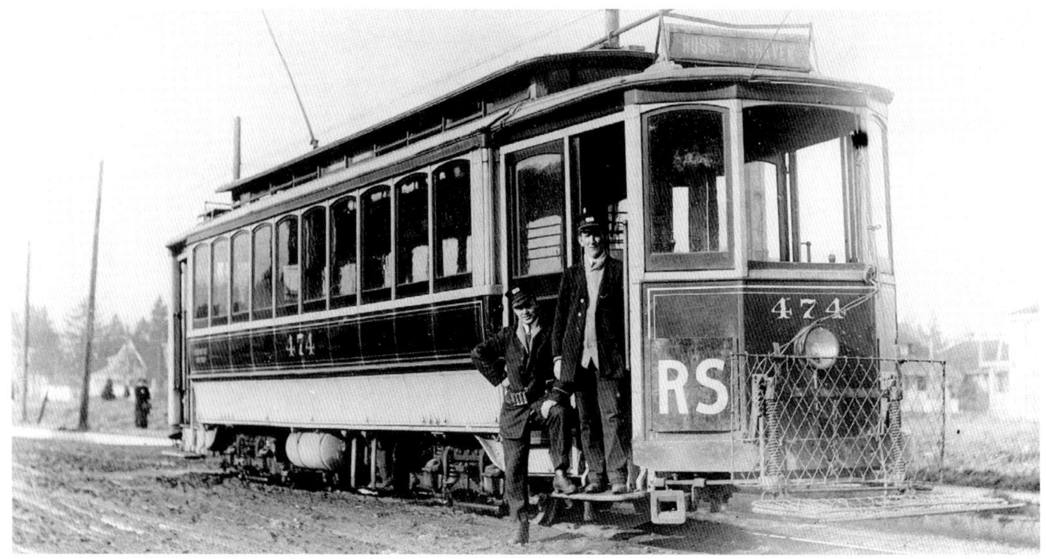

A woman waits in the background while conductor Arne Hellerud and motorman Willard Corwin pose with No. 474 at the Overlook end of the Russell-Shaver route, *c.* 1916. The front window is open, as was typical during a layover, yet it must be a chilly day since the crew are bundled in sweaters.

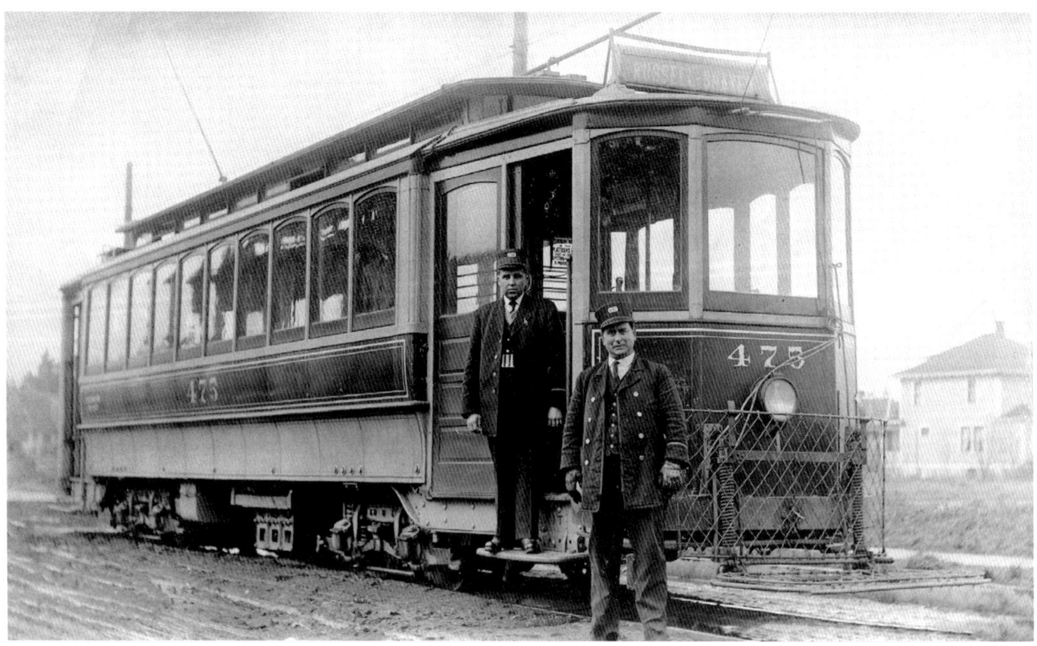

Motorman James Grogan looks pleased as he stands next to conductor Frederick Gosnell in front of Russell–Shaver Line car 475 at the Overlook terminus. As can be seen, many PRL&P streetcars lacked retrievers during the 1910s, so the trolley rope was merely lashed to the front of the car. All twenty PAYE cars in this 1908 vintage American Car Company series lasted until 1947–48.

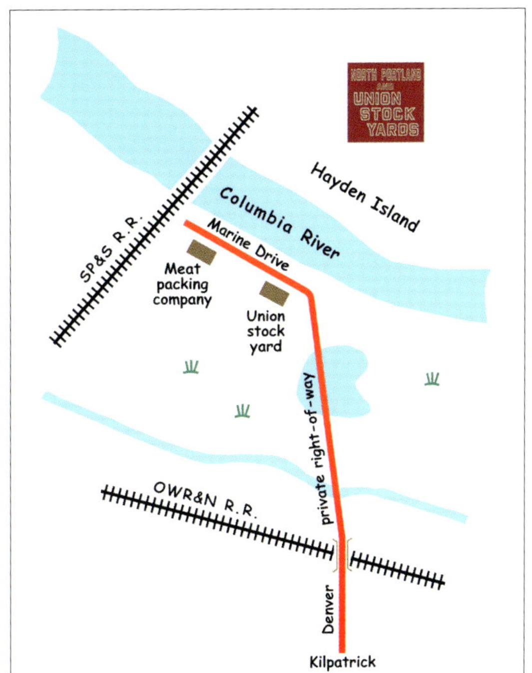

Below: No. 110 could be working either the Kenton stub line or the Union Stock Yards Line in this postcard dating from 1910. The streetcar is waiting on N Derby (now Denver Avenue) and Kilpatrick Street with the Bank of Kenton in the right background. In Kenton, the Swift Meat Company provided executive row houses, family homes, and apartments for its 250 employees.

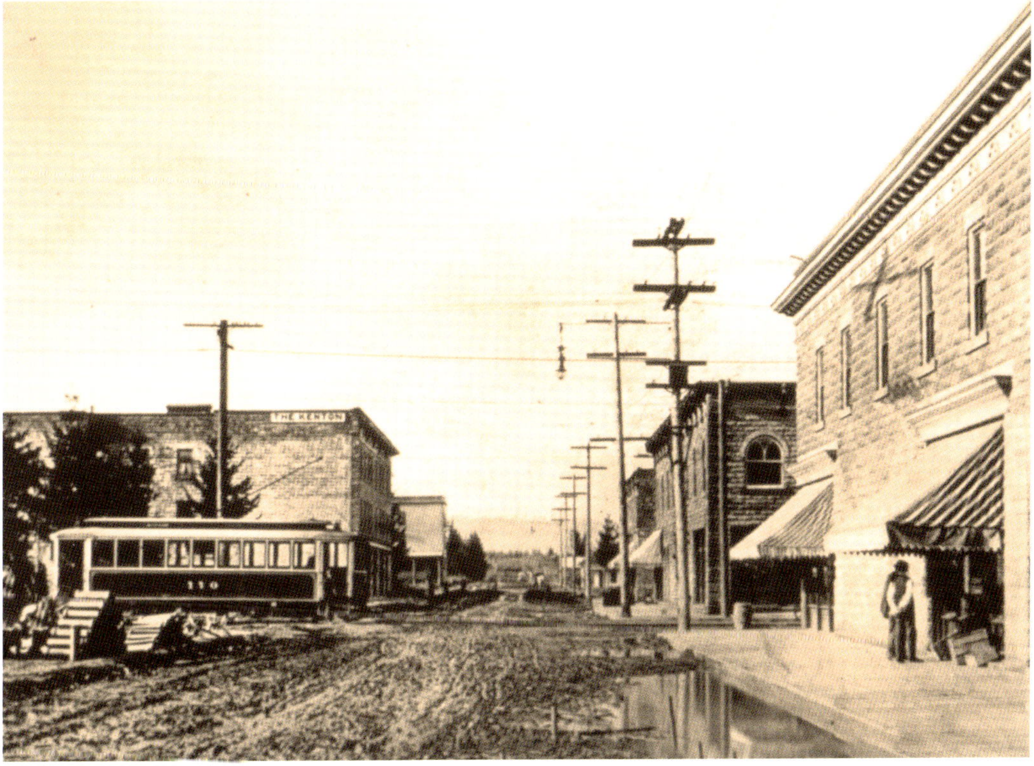

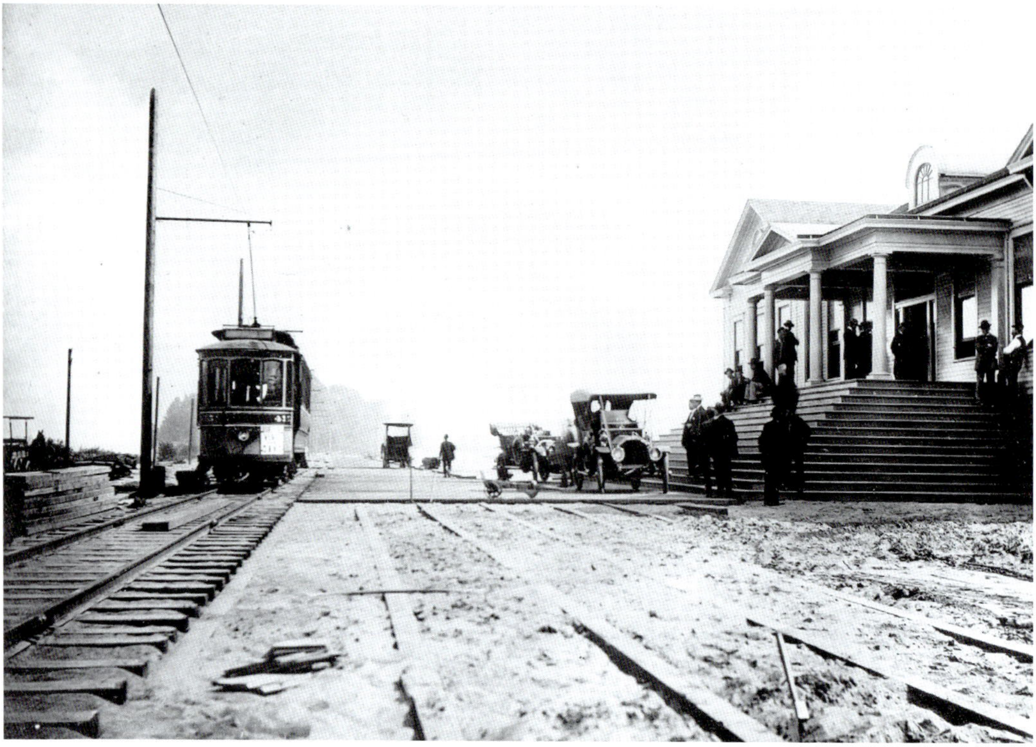

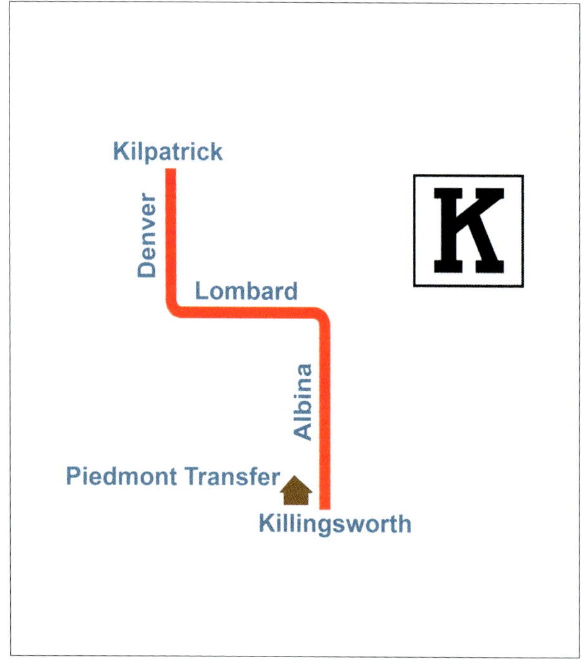

Above: The Kenton Traction Company borrowed car 417 for opening day at the Portland Union Stock Yards on September 15, 1909. Trolleys ran over a new bridge across Columbia Slough to reach what the newspapers called "Packingtown." No. 417 is seen on newly laid track in front of the Stock Exchange building on what is now N Marine Drive. (*Photograph courtesy Oregon Historical Society 28232*)

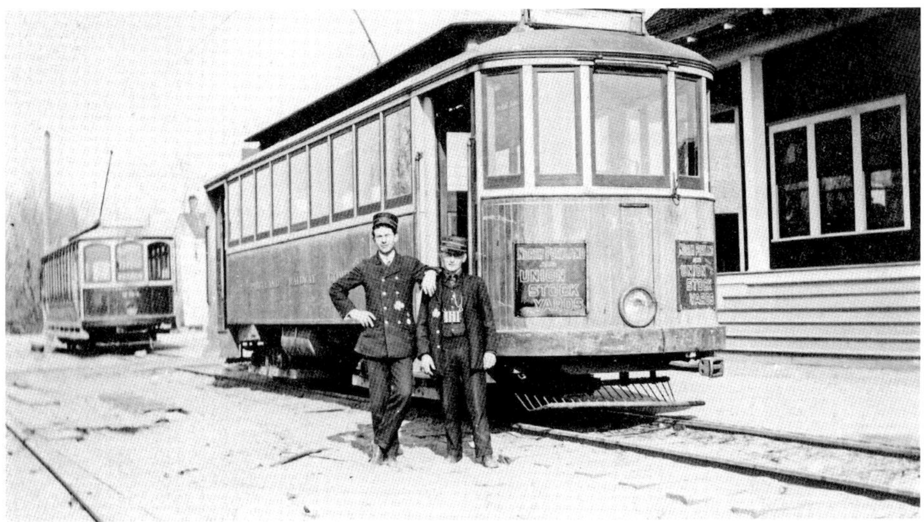

The crew posing with No. 137 in front of the Red Steer Café at the Union Stock Yards are wearing shamrocks in this 1909 St. Patrick's Day scene. This trolley and open car 251 in the background were leased from PRL&P by the Kenton Traction Company. No. 137, still lettered for Portland Railway Company, was a C&S Standard recently rebuilt with drop platform and five window ends. In 1910, 251 would also be rebuilt, to an enclosed car. (*Photograph courtesy Mark Moore*)

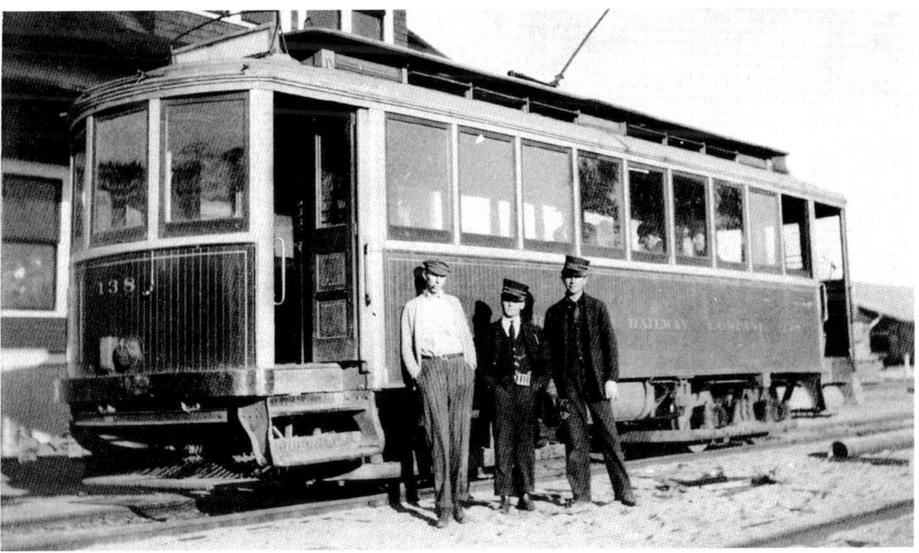

Veteran No. 138 still wears the Portland Railway Company name in this *c.* 1909 scene on the Kenton Traction Company's North Portland and Union Stock Yards Line. City & Suburban Railway Standards like this were available for lease because they were slower and could only accommodate fifty-two passengers (with standees), about thirty-five fewer than newer trolleys. Note the different-style uniform hats for Kenton crews. (*Photograph courtesy Mark Moore*)

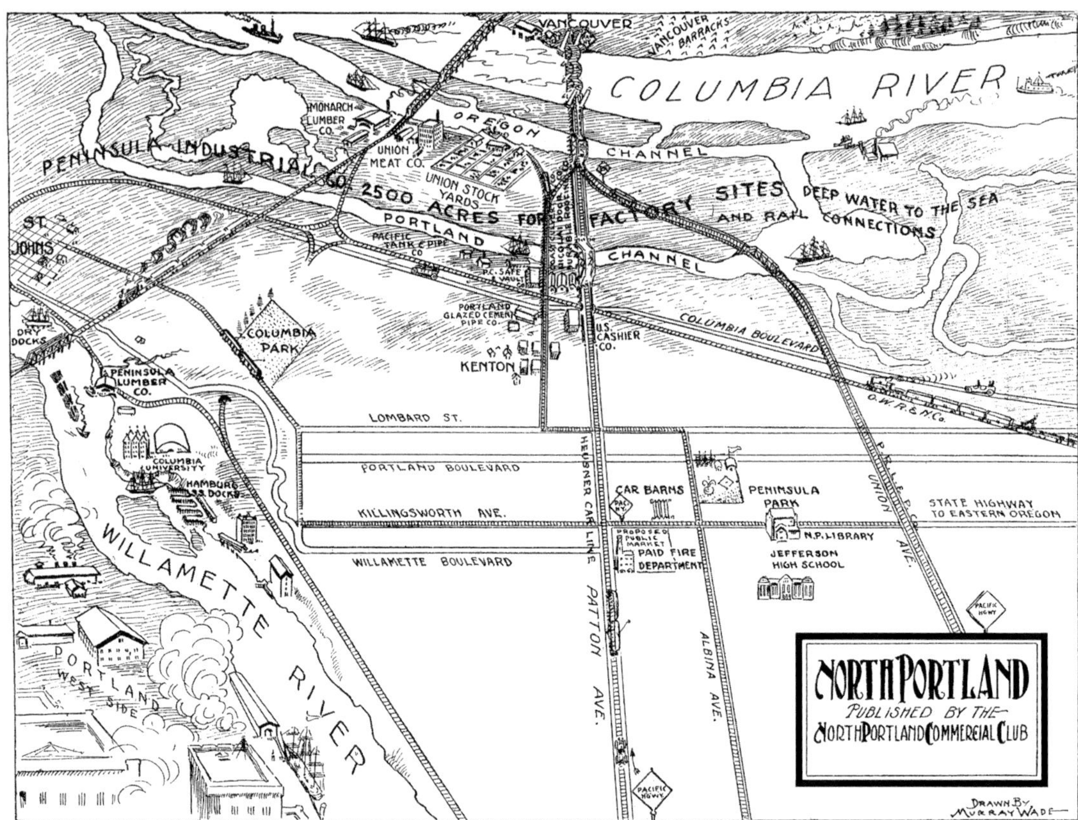

This map of North Portland published by the Commercial Club in 1909 includes landmarks like Kenton, the Union Stock Yards, Columbia University, Columbia Park, Jefferson High School, and the Piedmont Carbarns. It also promotes things that would not be realized for years, such as the Interstate Bridge, which opened in 1917, and the "Heusner Car Line" on Patton (later Interstate) Avenue. That streetcar line was never built, although a similar Interstate trolleybus service began operating on May 5, 1940.

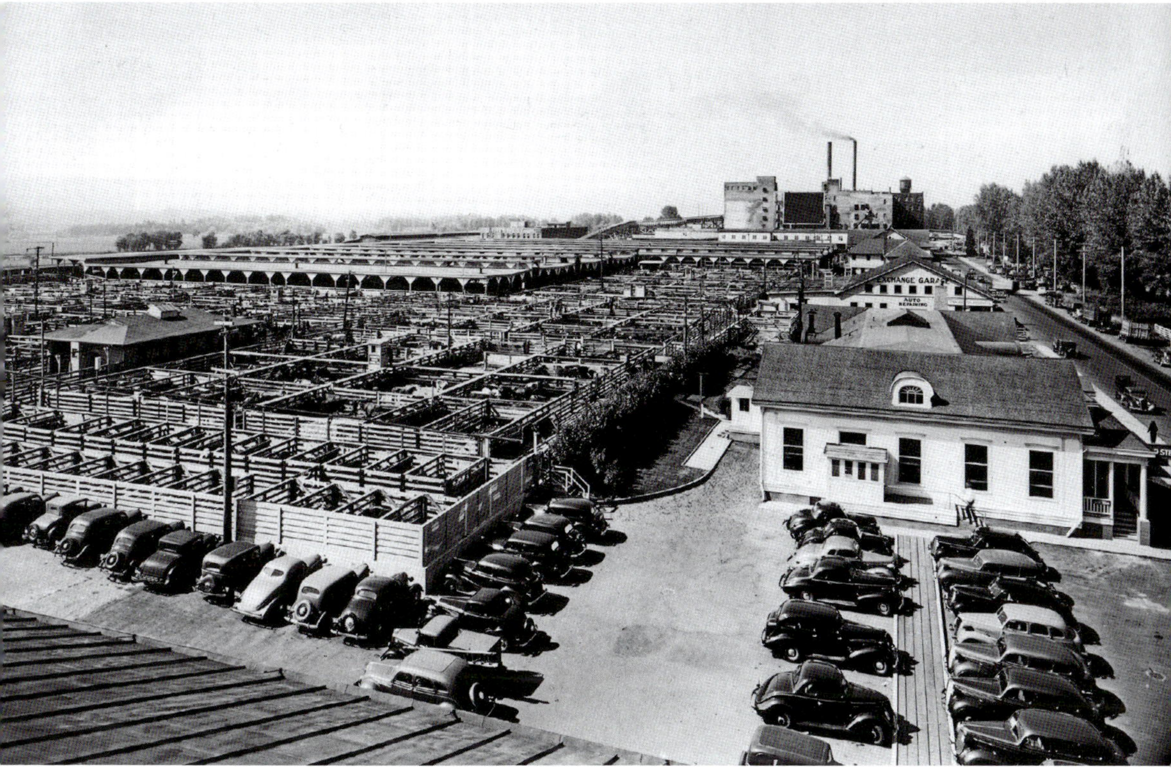

Above: The Union Stock Yards and Swift meat processing plant along N Marine Drive are seen in a photograph taken in 1937. Chicago-based Swift & Company built the facility in 1909 following its 1906 purchase of the Union Meat Company. By 1911, it had become the largest livestock exchange business on the Pacific Coast. (*Photograph courtesy Norm Gholston*)

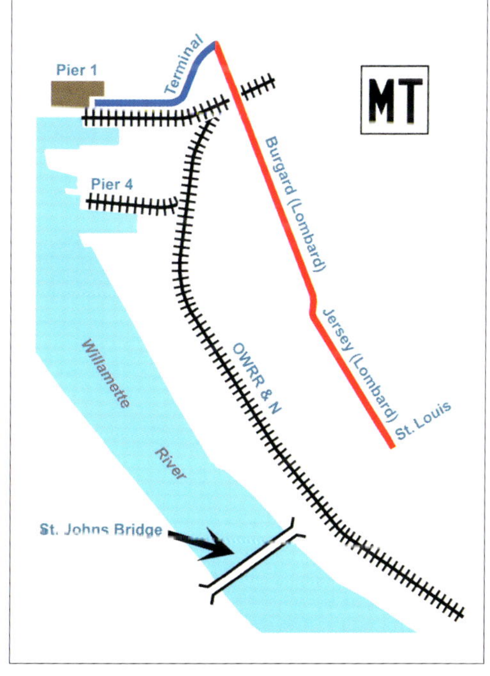

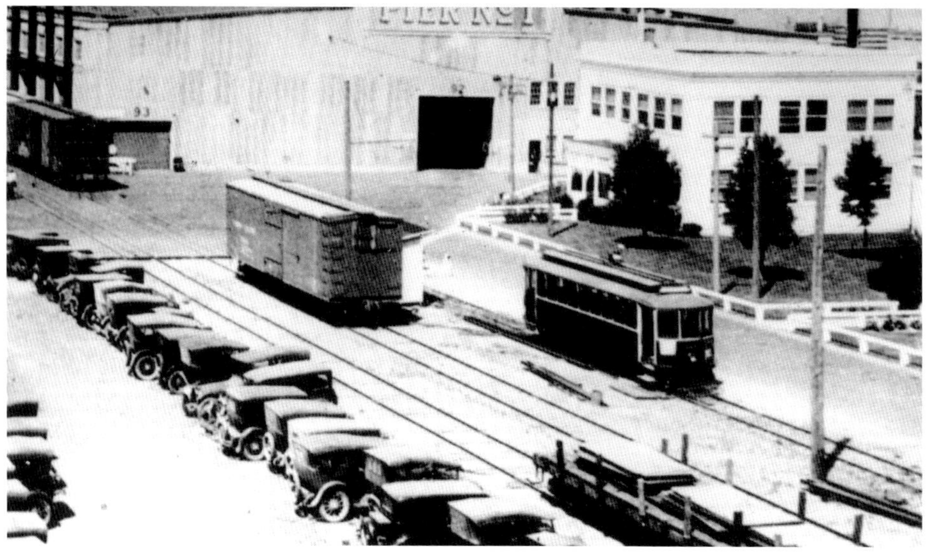

Old City & Suburban Standard No. 107 is in front of Pier No. 1 in the only photograph the author has seen of a trolley on the Municipal Terminal Line. By the time this picture was taken in 1926, it would appear that quite a few were able to drive private automobiles to this once-remote work location.

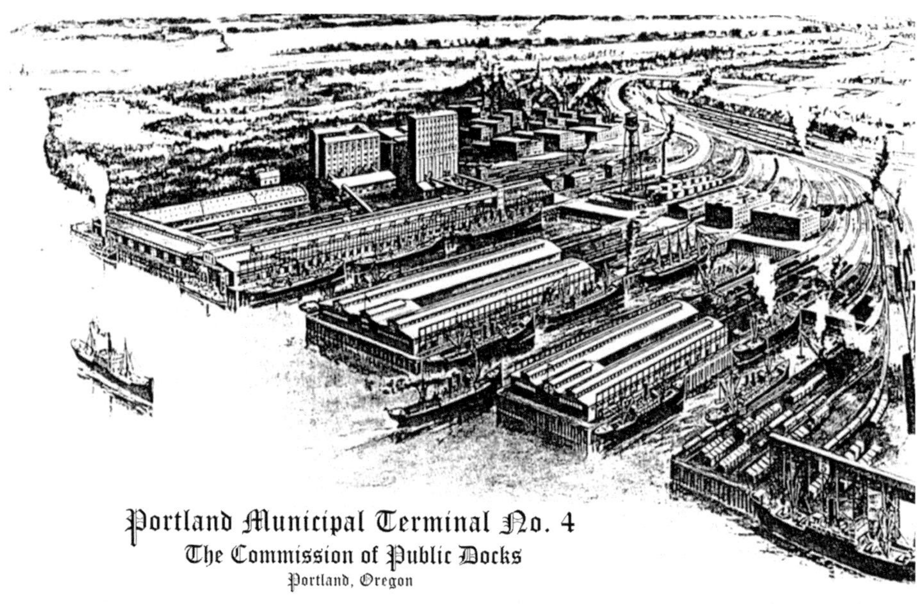

This artist's rendering of the plan for Municipal Terminal No. 4 is from the 1921 Annual Report of the Commission of Public Docks. The commission was an independent agency created by voters in 1910 in order to break the monopoly held by railroads and shipping companies and acquire land for public docks. It built Portland's fourth terminal in 1920. (*Photograph courtesy Port of Portland Archive*)

7

The Piedmont Carbarn

North Portland was home to three carhouses over the years. The first two, both of which were built around 1890, were located at opposite ends of the St. Johns Motor Line and served mainly as engine sheds for steam dummy locomotives. On the other hand, the Piedmont Carbarn, on N Killingsworth Street between N Michigan and N Mississippi avenues, was built to house electric streetcars. When it opened in 1905, it was described as the largest and most completely equipped carhouse in the northwest. This long-lasting facility would be the operating division headquarters for eleven streetcar lines serving north and northeast Portland, including Alberta, Broadway, Irvington, Kenton–Stockyards, Mississippi Avenue, Municipal Terminal, Russell–Shaver, St. Johns, Vancouver, Williams Avenue, and Woodlawn. In later years, trolley coaches for North Portland lines also operated out of Piedmont Division.

Construction of the Piedmont Carbarn got underway in 1904 while the new Portland Consolidated Railway Company was in the process of merging the City & Suburban and Portland Railway companies. The new carhouse combined the functions of the City & Suburban's St. Johns Carbarn on N Commercial Avenue and Stanton Street in Albina and the Portland Railway's Woodlawn Carbarn on NE Dekum and Madrona streets.

The original barn was of wooden-frame construction with corrugated iron walls. It featured four bays and a headquarters building. The headquarters in the southwestern corner of the block was less utilitarian in appearance, with drop wood siding and a bay window for the superintendent's office. At first, bay A included an electric substation consisting of control switchboards, a motor-generator set, and hundreds of glass storage batteries. These Edison batteries had been placed there after the recently electrified St. Johns Line was found to be underpowered.

The substation was removed in 1907 and the space remodeled for use as employee club rooms. This was an important addition since 300 men were assigned to Piedmont Division. Around the same time bays C and D were extended for the full length of the block, brick firewalls were built between each bay, and the original north-facing wall, with its elegant arches, was replaced to make room for a new water tower and an oil storage room.

During 1910–11, an additional block-long brick carbarn was built on the block located to the north of the first barn. It had been planned as a two-bay barn, but only single bay E was built. Instead, the vacant land to the east, along N Mississippi Avenue between N Simpson and Jessup streets, became a five-track storage yard. A long, curving, test track was also installed there.

After the Piedmont Division closed in 1958, the property was sold to the Albertson's grocery chain. Today, the supermarket is long gone and most of the former carbarn site is taken up by a parking lot and a fire station.

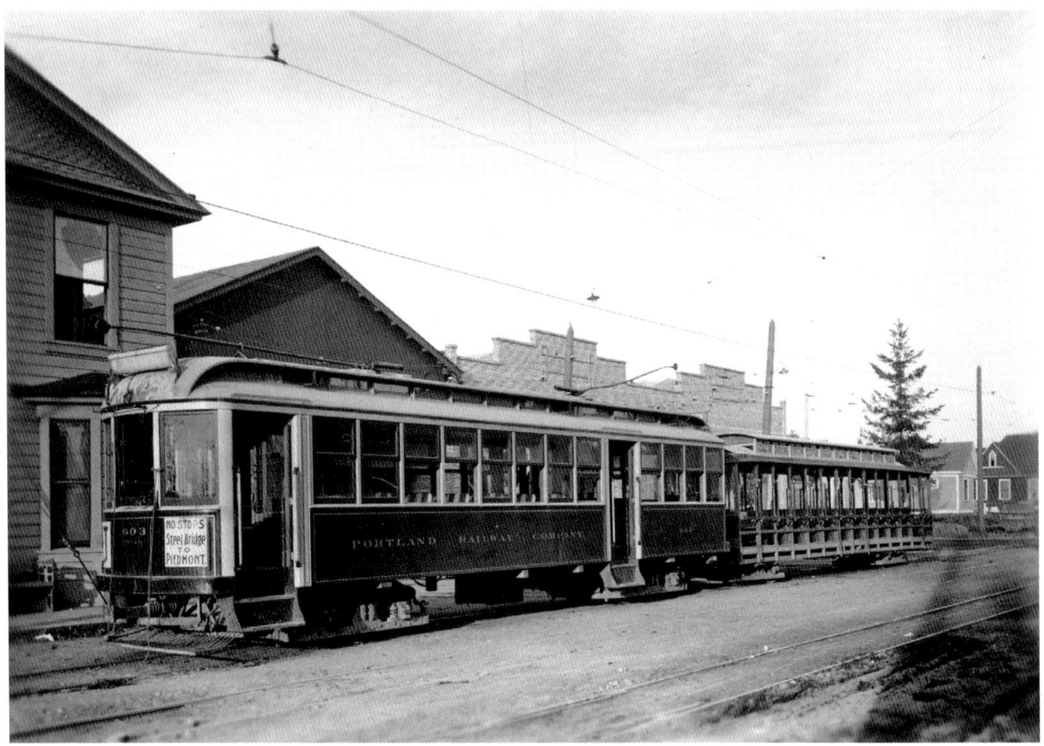

Portland Railway Company St. Johns car 603 is seen around 1905 in front of the new Piedmont Carbarn on N Killingsworth Street. No. 603, soon to be renumbered 194, is pulling an open trailer. Trailers 89 and 90 were built in 1893 from spliced horsecars. By 1913, they were stored out-of-use at Piedmont. (*Photograph courtesy Mark Moore*)

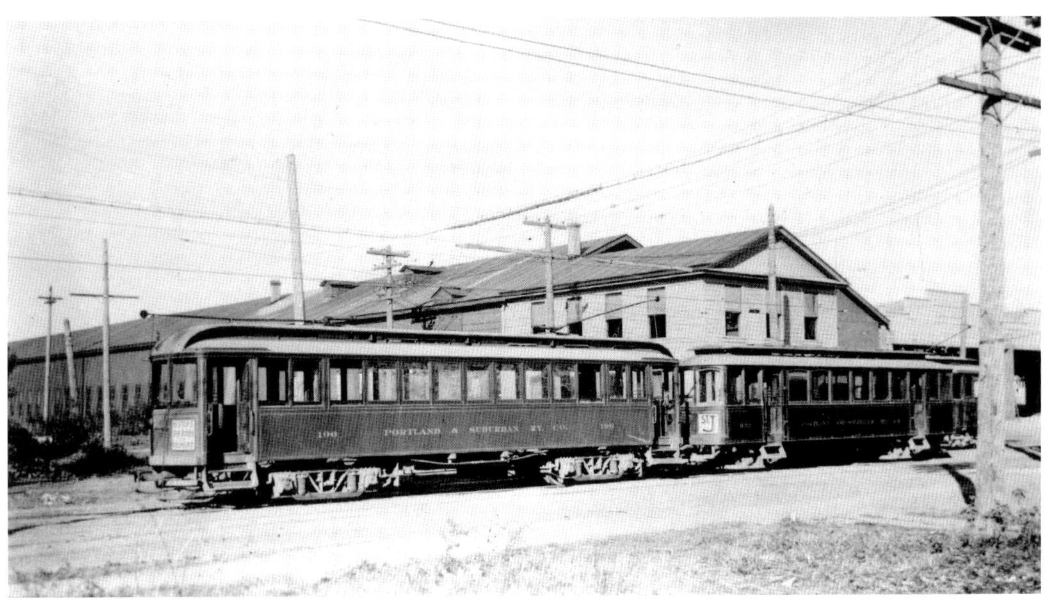

St. Johns motor 196 and Fuller trailer 351 bear different company names in this *c.* 1906 picture at the Piedmont Carbarn. No. 196 was one of the cars lettered for the Portland & Suburban Railway Company in 1904 before it was discovered that a freight company was already using that name. The corrected name can be seen on trailer No. 351, which is lettered for the Portland Consolidated Railway Company.

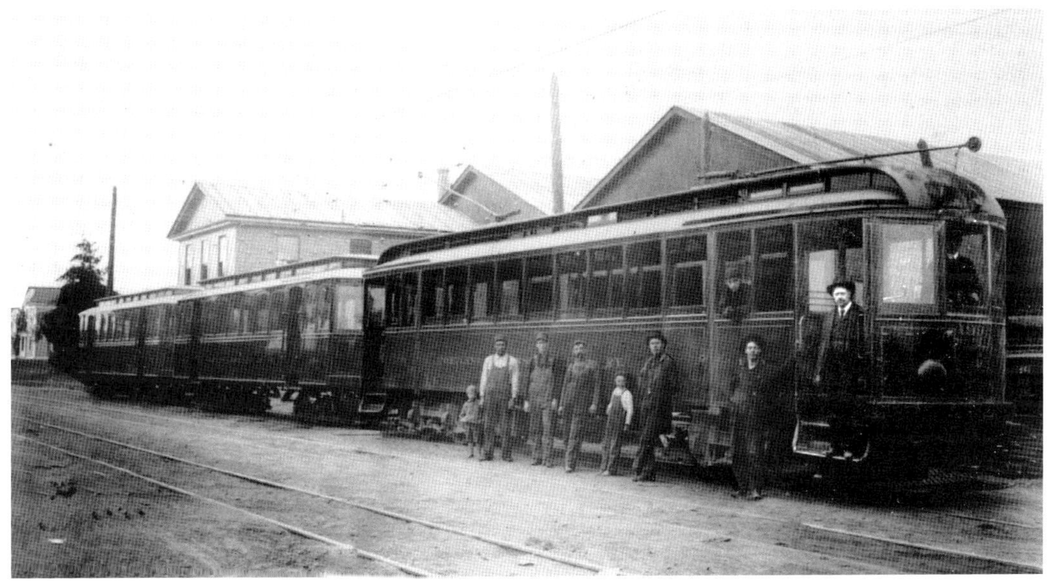

Members of the Piedmont Carbarn shop crew are posing with motor 199 and two Fuller trailers in a rare picture of a St. Johns train with three cars. This is an early view because the Telephone Exchange building has not yet been built next door and No. 199 is still lettered for the Portland Consolidated Railway Company. Portland Railway built five Fuller trailers like these in 1906.

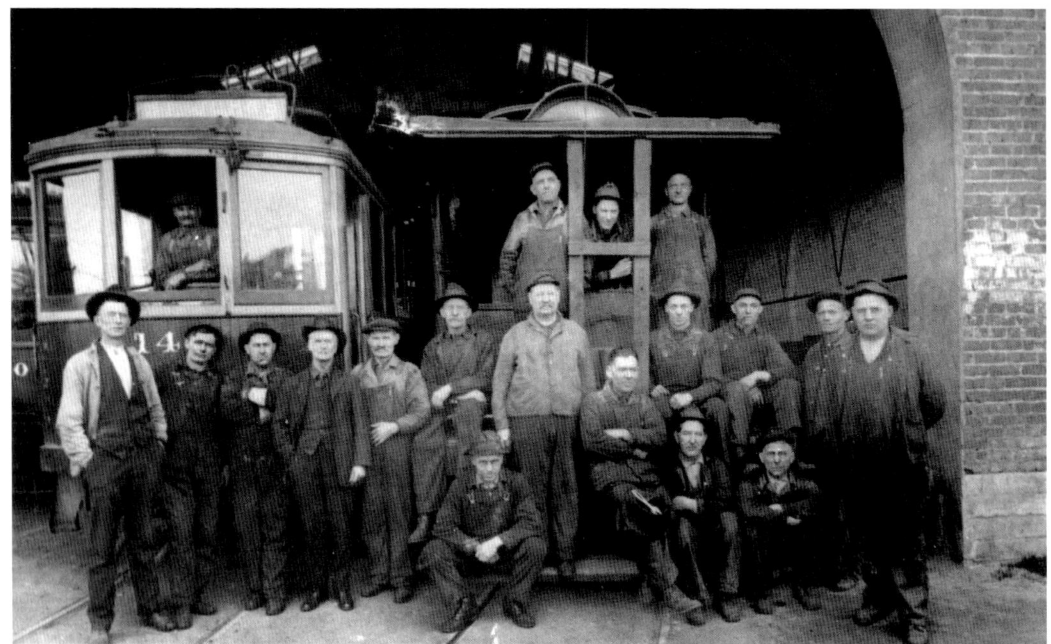

These shop employees are posing beneath an arched entrance on the N Jessup Street end of the original Piedmont Carbarn with a car described at the time as one of the three oldest streetcars still in use in the U.S. Much modified No. 921 at right, which had become a "hog" used to move cars around the yard, started life in 1891 as a passenger motor for the Barnes Heights & Cornell Mountain Railway in Northwest Portland.

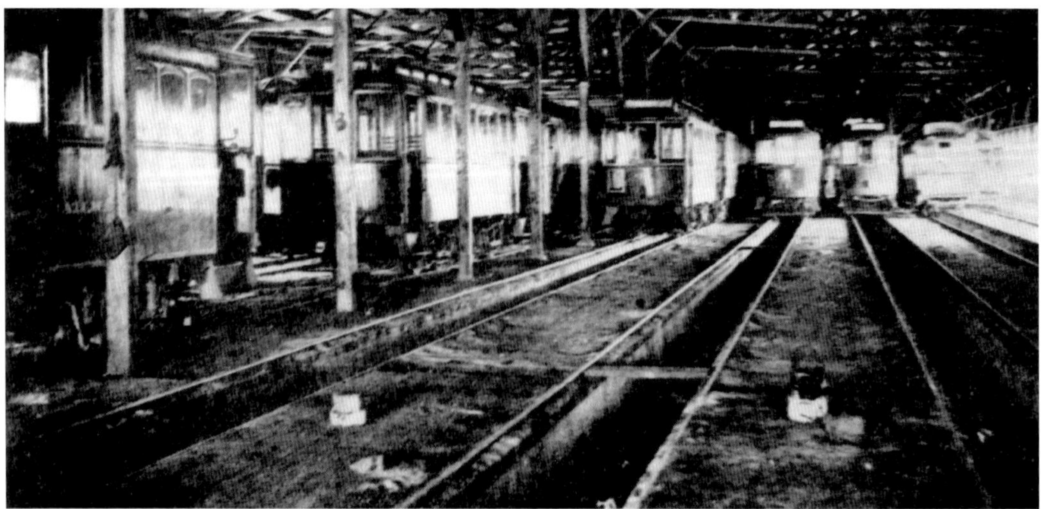

This scene at "the largest and most completely equipped carbarns in the Northwest" was published by *The Peninsula* magazine in 1909. Eight City & Suburban Standards can be seen inside the original barn. In 1910, the addition of brick fire walls and concrete work pits made the structure much safer.

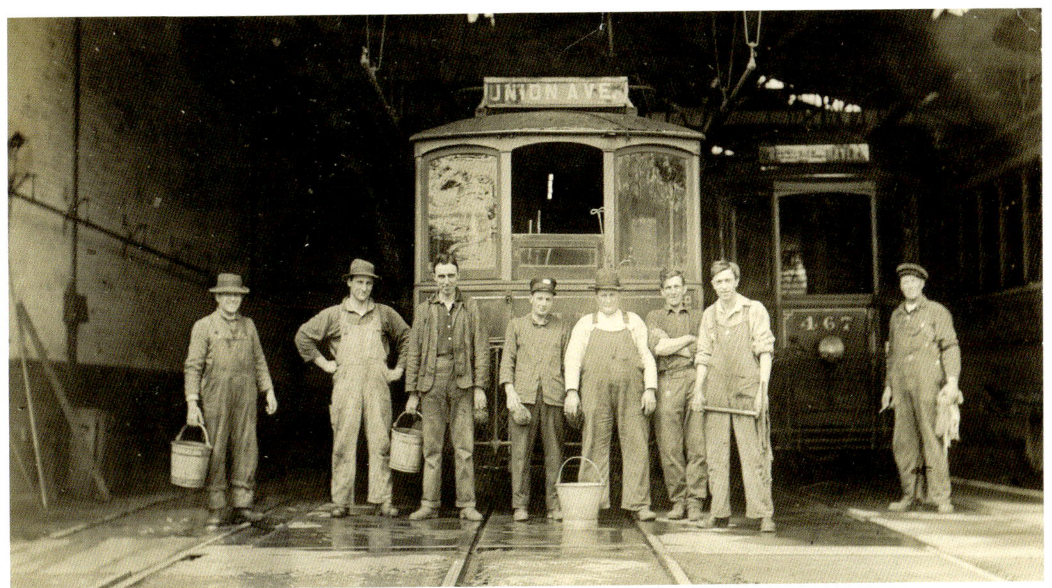

These proud-looking Piedmont Carbarn employees have just washed No. 311, the first second-series Fuller car, in a picture taken about 1909. Car 311 is signed for Union Avenue, an Alberta Line tripper service. PAYE No. 467 in the right background is signed for the Russell Shaver Line. (*Photograph courtesy Mark Moore*)

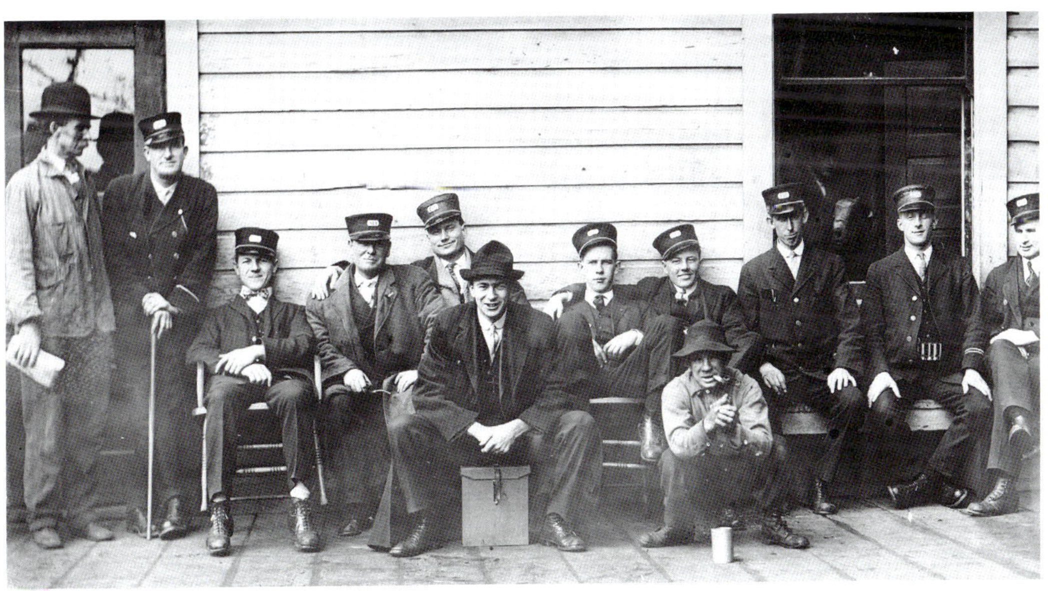

A dozen cheerful employees are gathered outside the clubhouse at Piedmont Carbarn in a scene that resembles a Normal Rockwell painting. They are identified as "Looley, Hubbard, Conrad, Countryman, Roach, Enhi, Ryan, Douglas, Slocomb, Leonard, Anderson, and Campion." Note the man at left wearing a work jacket over a shirt and tie, the motorman next to him leaning on a cane, and the crouched shop man smoking a stogie.

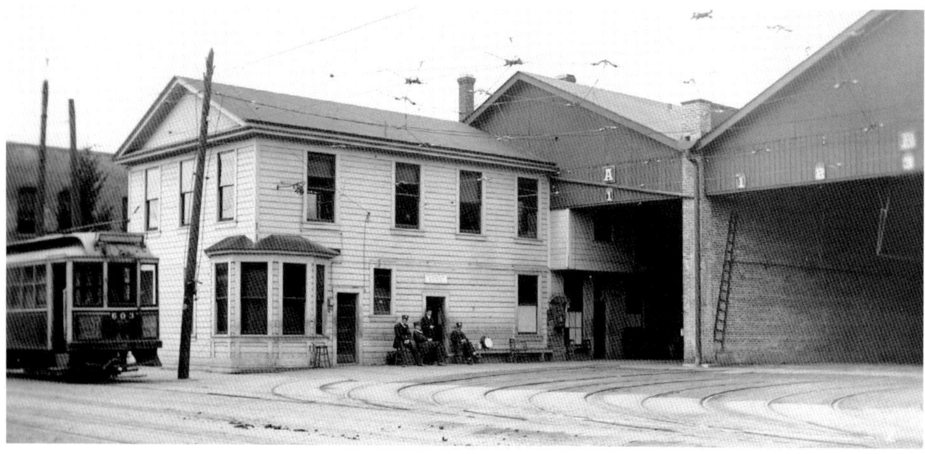

Carmen are relaxing next to the clubhouse entrance at the Piedmont Carbarn. The sign above the doorway reads, "No one except employees of this company allowed on these premises." The Telephone Exchange building is behind streetcar 603 at the corner of N Killingsworth Street and Michigan Avenue. (*Photograph courtesy Oregon Historical Society 128-15*)

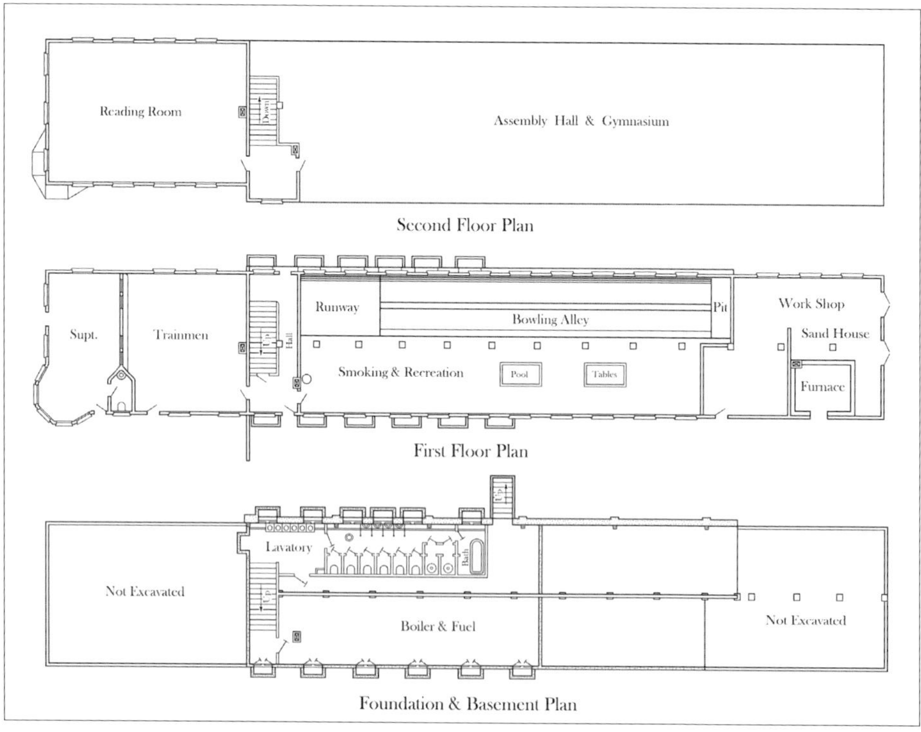

A powerhouse occupied most of this space before it was replaced in 1908 by the splendid facility illustrated in this *Street Railway Journal* floor plan for the office and clubhouse at Piedmont Carbarn. It was equipped with a reading room, gym, bowling alley, and recreation room, as well as an office for the superintendent.

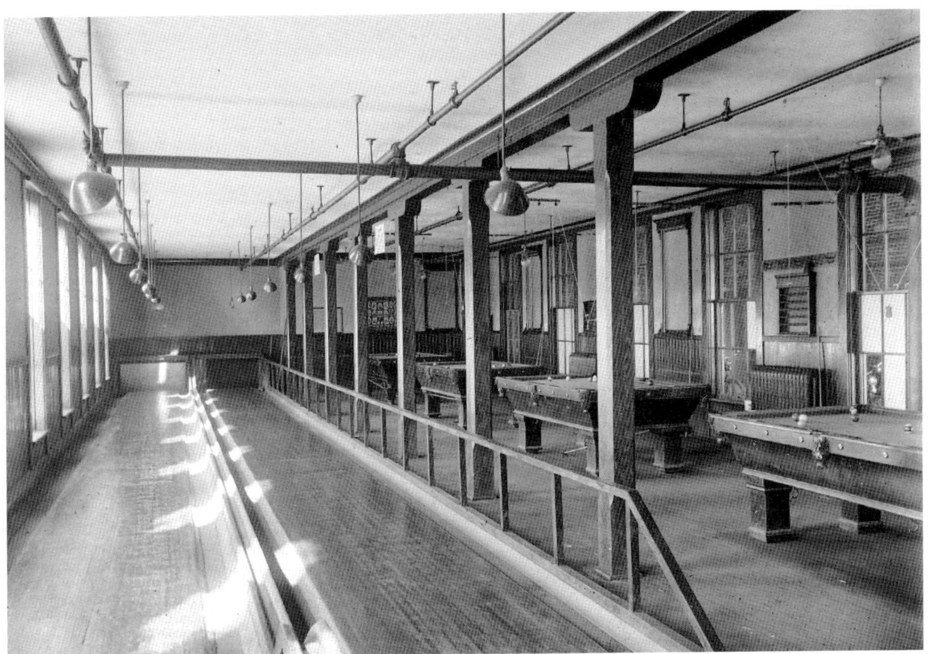

The first floor of the clubhouse at Piedmont Carbarn featured a smoking and recreation room with a bowling alley and pool tables. Unlike the second story, the walls on this floor were plastered. (*Photograph courtesy Mark Gilmore*)

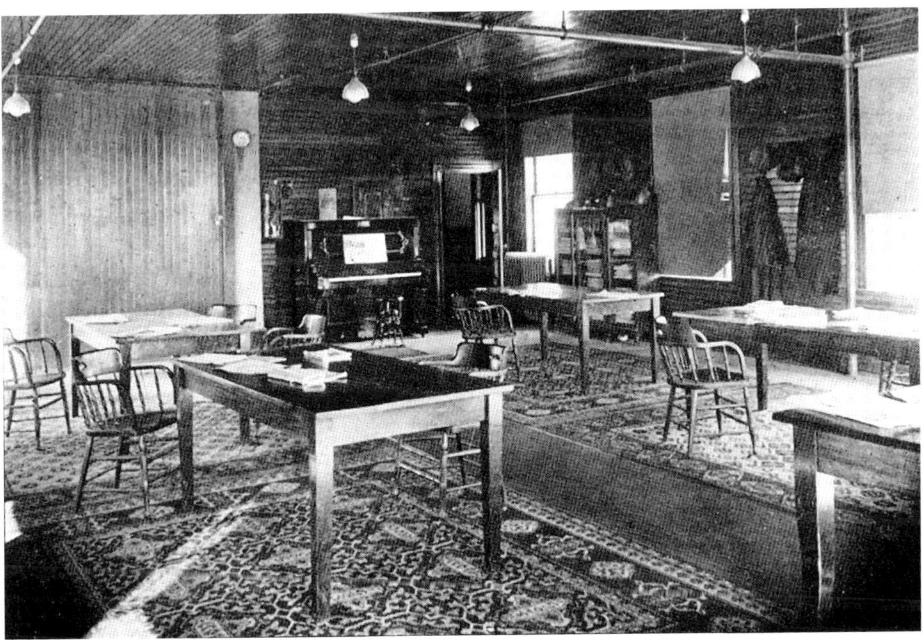

The second-floor assembly room at the Piedmont Carbarn clubhouse is furnished with rugs, tables, reading material, and a piano in this 1910 illustration from *Portland Carman* magazine.

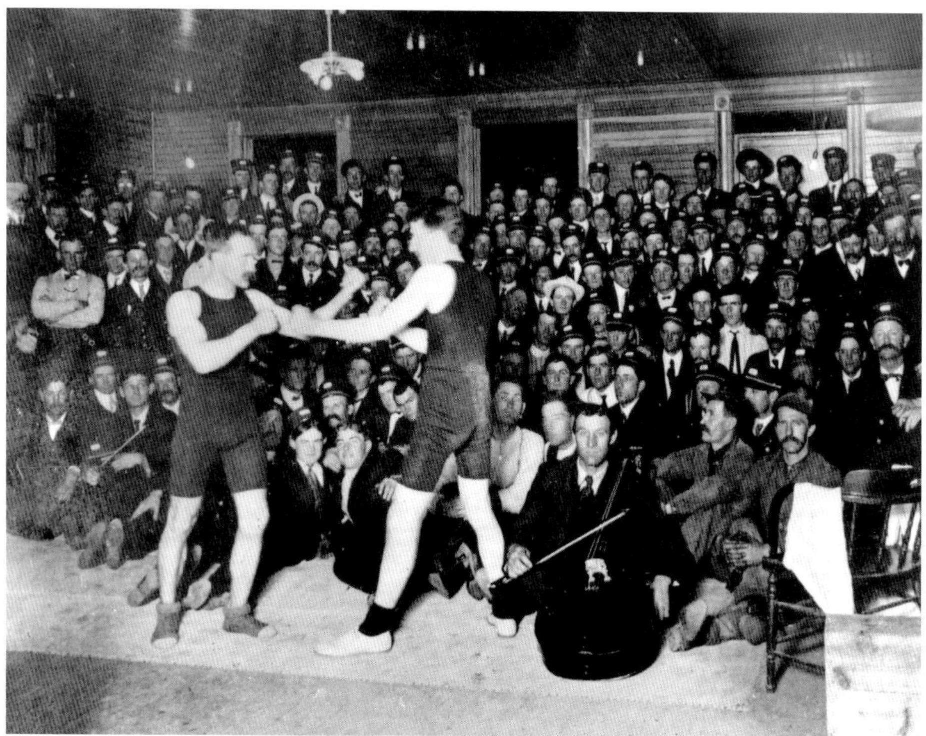

The assembly room at Piedmont Carbarn could be cleared for sporting events like this boxing match. We are not sure what the musician with the cello was doing, but he appears to be oblivious to any danger that might have resulted from the lack of ropes.

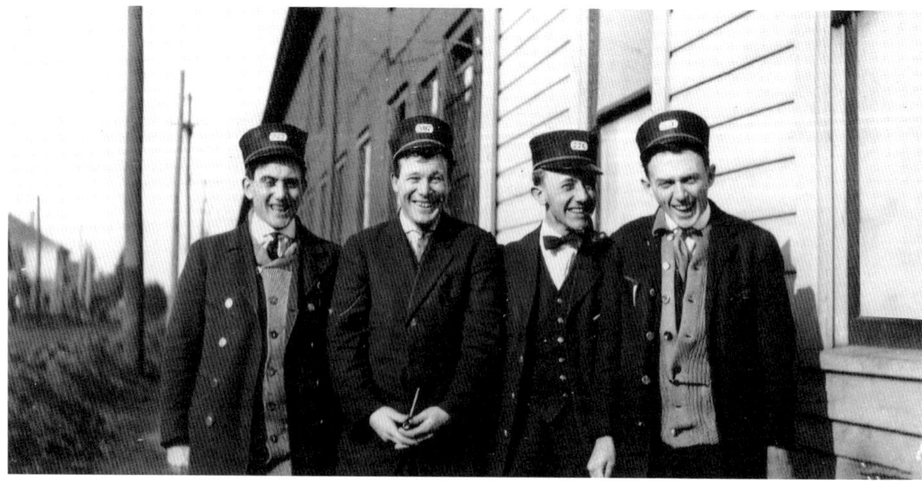

The life of a carman was not all work as can be seen in this picture of Roma Sly, Raymond Lindsay, William Ojendyk, and John Kindred "horsing around" in between shifts. This 1910s view was taken on N Michigan Avenue alongside the Piedmont Carbarn. The car house in the background was sheathed in corrugated metal.

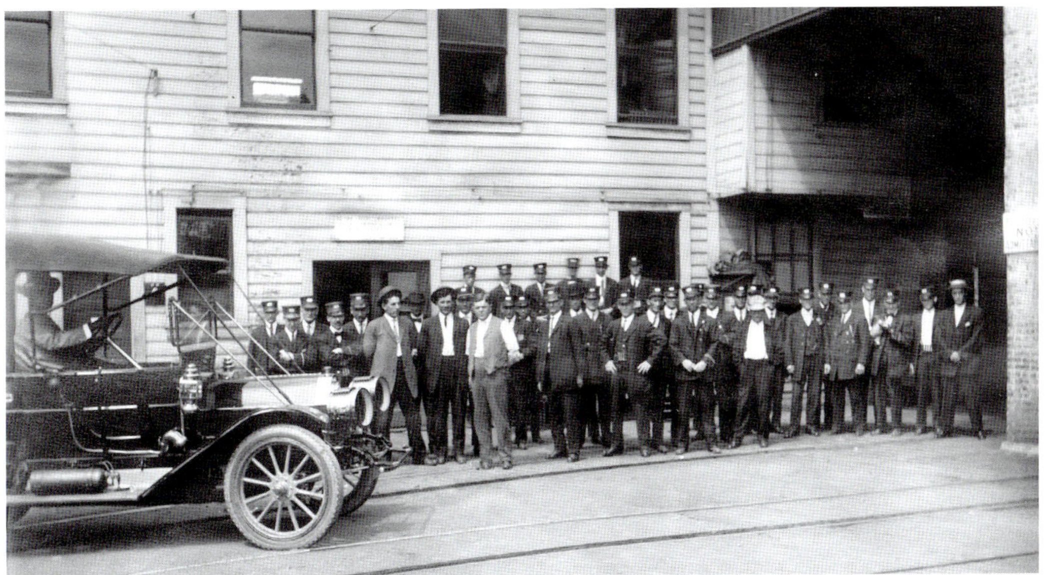

Most of the men pictured in front of bay A-1 at the Piedmont Carbarn would have ridden a streetcar to this unidentified occasion, but when the top man arrived, he came by private automobile. Five office personnel and thirty-three carmen can be seen in this *c.* 1912 view.

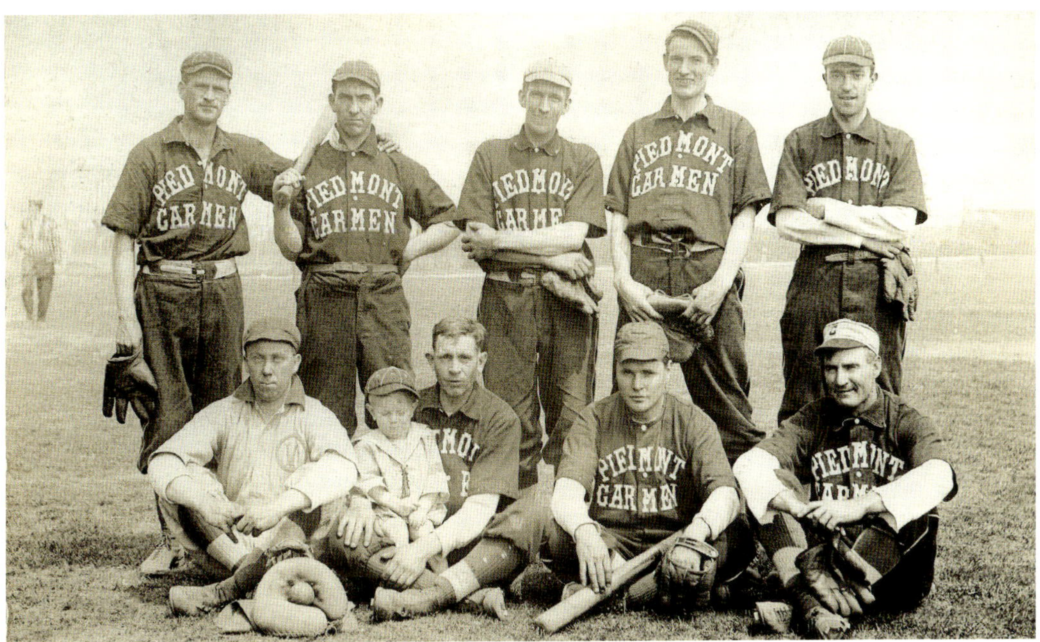

Although street railway men often worked ten hours a day, seven days a week, prior to the formation of Street Railway Employees Local 757 in 1917, they still found time to participate in baseball teams. The Piedmont Carmen are seen here around 1914 on the baseball diamond at Overlook Park on N Interstate Avenue near N Fremont Street.

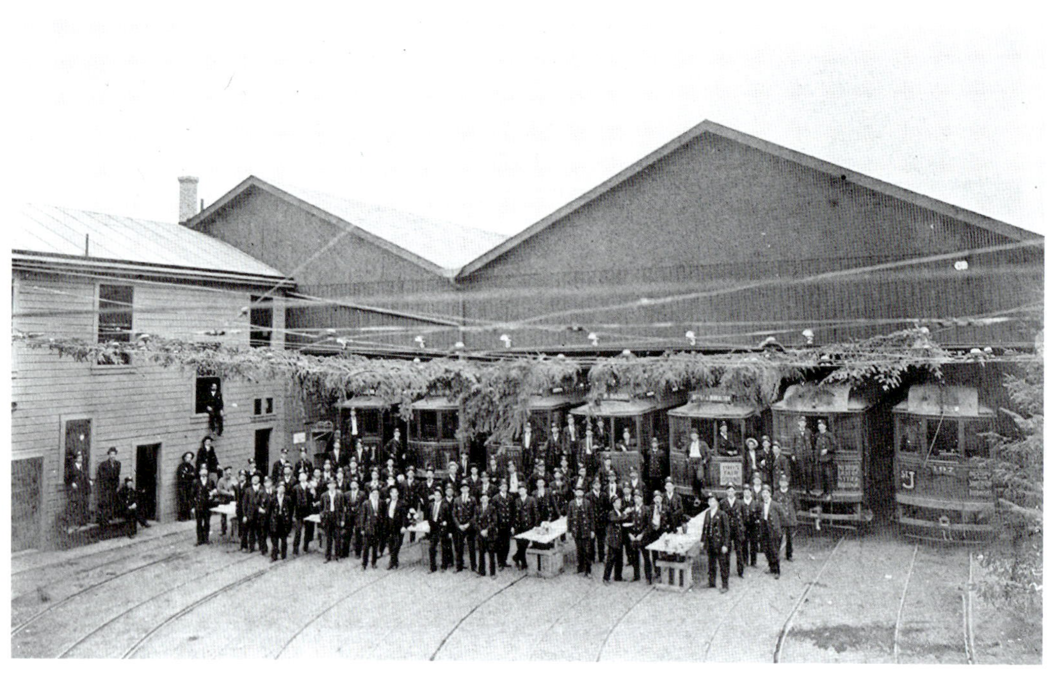

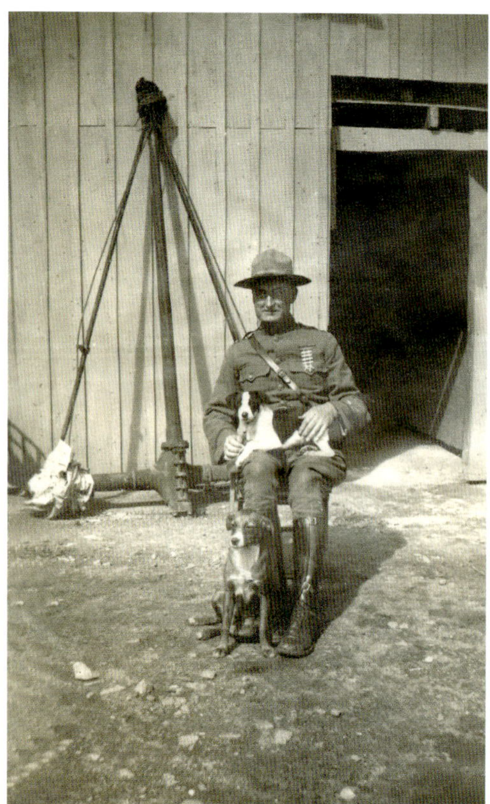

Above: More than eighty employees (one even sitting on a window ledge) can be seen in this Christmas celebration at the Piedmont Carbarn. The overhead has been decorated with fir boughs and tables of goodies are on the apron. Two St. Johns interurbans and five City & Suburban standards are neatly arranged in bays A and B. The third car from the right may be a visitor from the Savier Carbarn since it is signed for the "1905 Fair Ground."

Left: Some of the carmen who answered the call to arms during World War I kept in touch with their workmates. This postcard from First Lieutenant A. A. Schwarz mailed on September 15, 1918, was addressed to Piedmont Superintendent R. A. Bird. His two canine friends are not identified in a scene simply labeled "somewhere in France." The truck axle, leaning against the barn in the background, suggests Schwarz may have lent his expertise to a mechanized division.

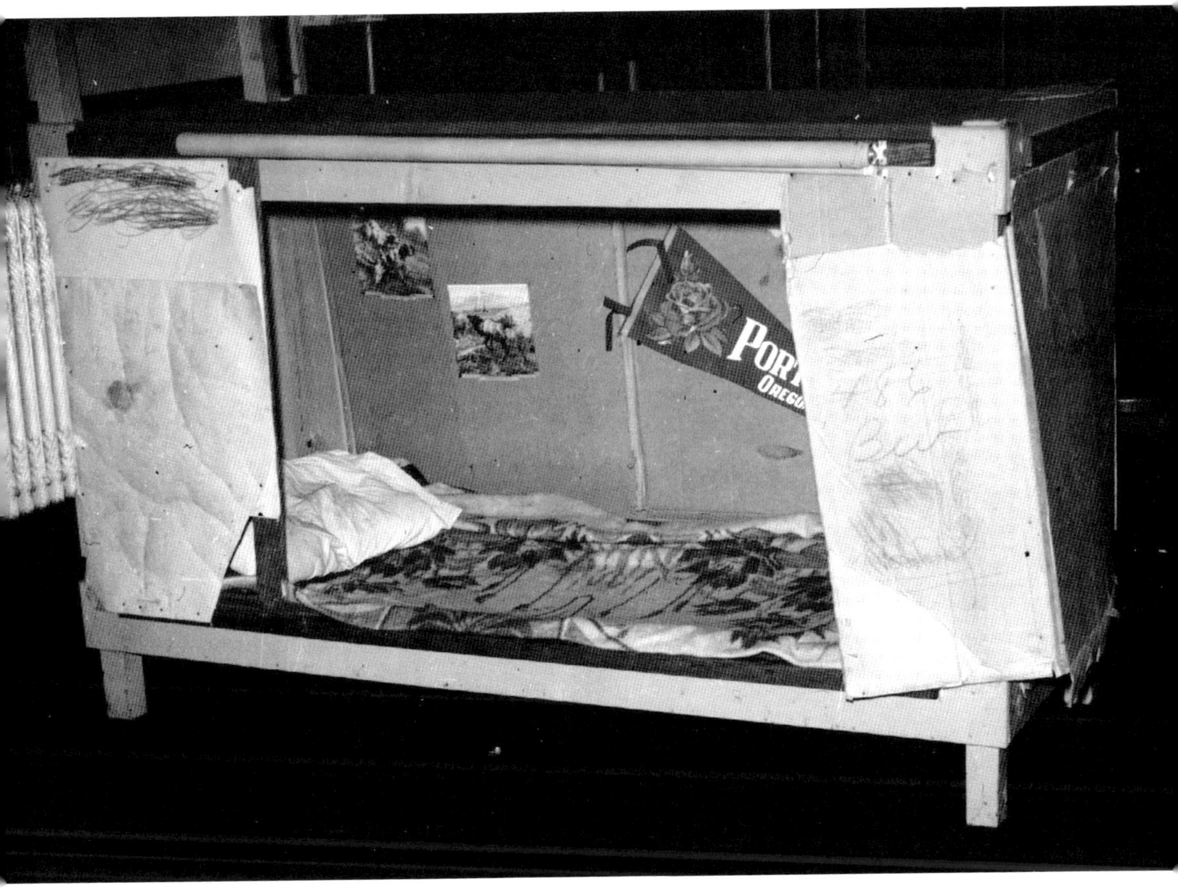

Shift changes at shipyards and war plants during World War II resulted in long hours for Portland Traction Company operators. "Doghouses" like the one seen here at Piedmont Carbarn were used by carmen needing to sleep between split shifts. Cardboard doors covered with notes provide limited privacy on a doghouse decorated with pictures of pets and a Portland pennant.

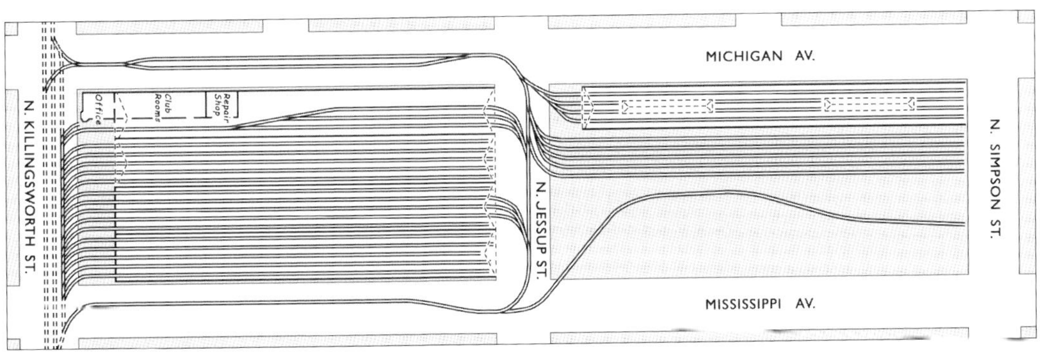

Piedmont Carbarn Track Plan.

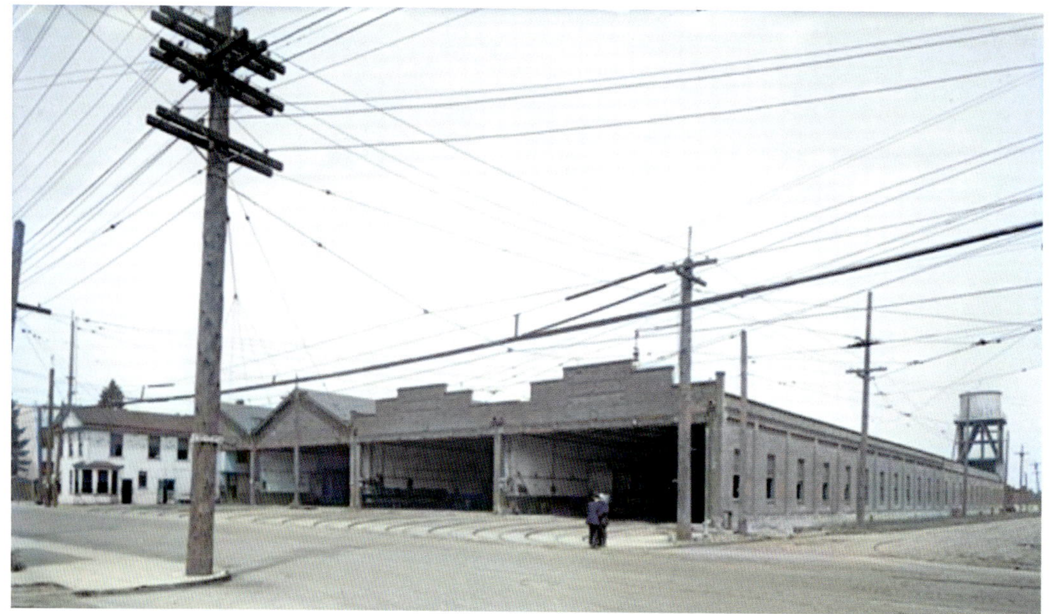

It must be rush hour because two carmen are conferring in front of empty bays A, B, C, and D in this undated picture taken at the Piedmont Carbarn on the corner of N Killingworth Street and N Mississippi Avenue. The headquarters and clubhouse building stands out at far left, as does the prominent water tower at right, which was added in 1910.

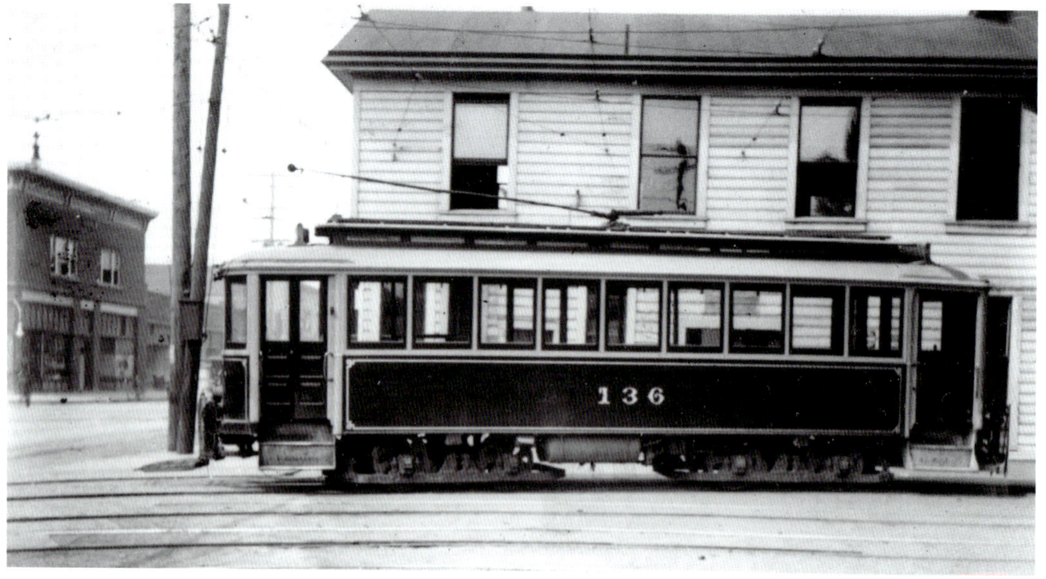

The oldest streetcars kept at the Piedmont Carbarn were the 100–146 series Standards built by the City & Suburban Railway at the Savier Street Shops in Northwest Portland in 1892. These forty-seven cars were the largest group operated by the C&S. During the PRL&P years they were still in regular use as trippers or for fill-in duty. With the exception of one, they lasted well into the 1930s.

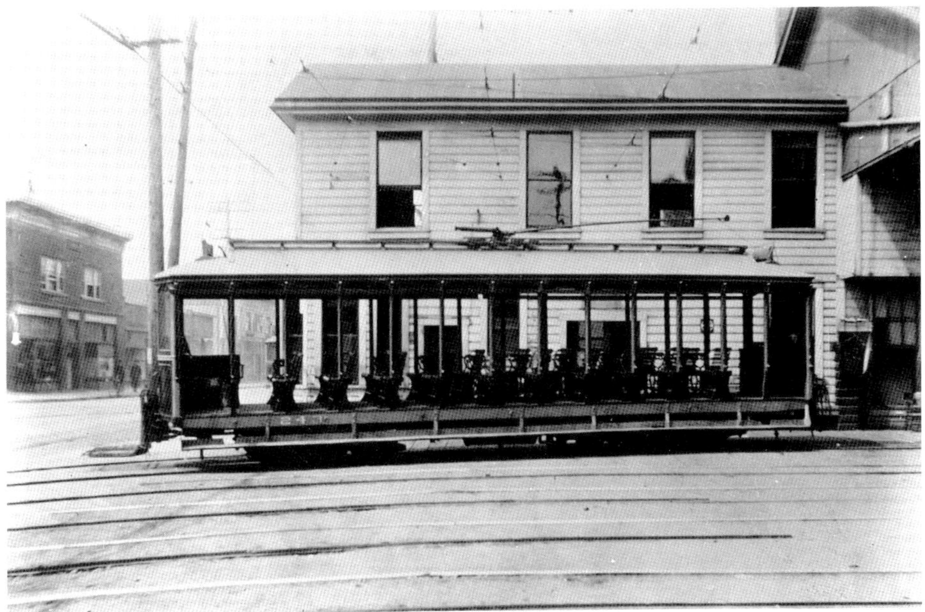

No. 243 is still an open car in this scene on the ladder tracks in front of Piedmont Carbarn bay A. However, it would soon be remodeled as one of the eleven drafty trolleys that would be nicknamed "pneumonia" cars. Open 241–251 series cars were sporadically enclosed between 1910 and 1919.

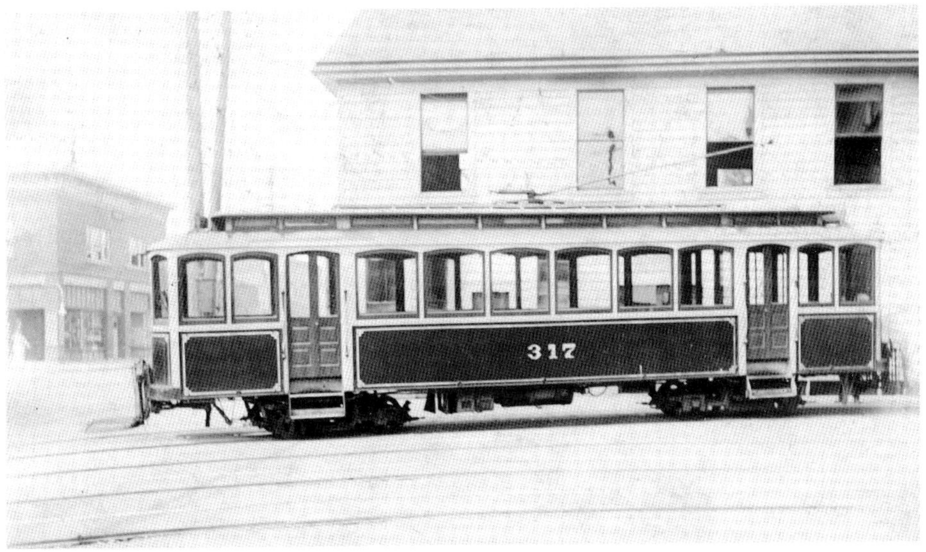

No. 317, shown in front of the headquarters building at the Piedmont Carbarn, was a second-series Fuller car built by the Portland Railway Company at their Washington Street Shops in 1903. This picture was taken ten years later after Nelson Safety Fenders had been installed. This trolley was originally No. 117. Series 311–340 were remodeled for one-man operation in 1922 and continued in service until 1933.

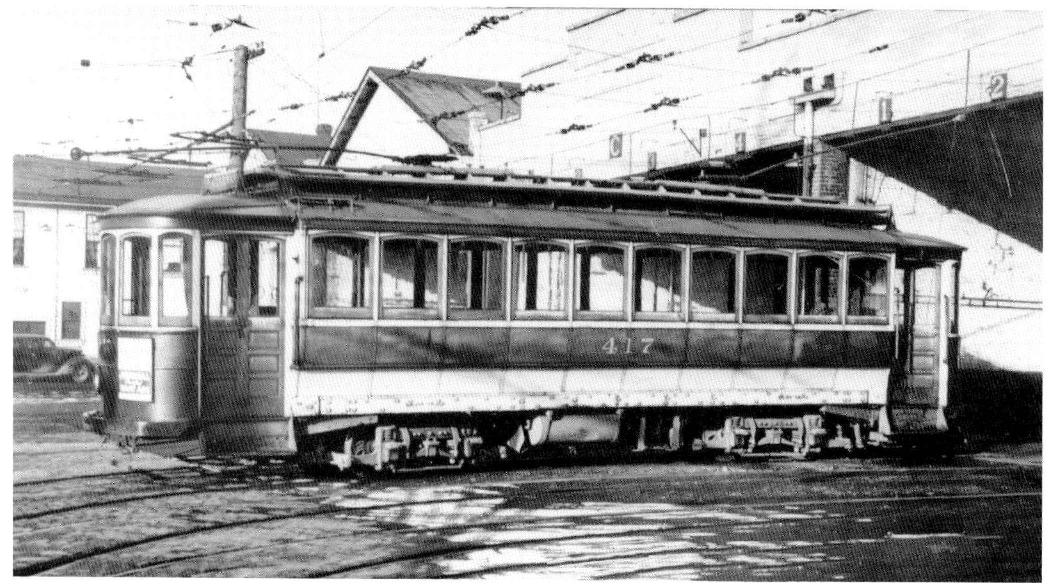

Veteran No. 417 basks in the sun in front of Piedmont Carbarn D on a cold winter day in the 1940s. By this time, multiple-unit cars in the 400-439 class were being operated singly on the Alberta Line, instead of being assigned to the St. Johns run. Most of the cars in this series continued in use until 1947–48.

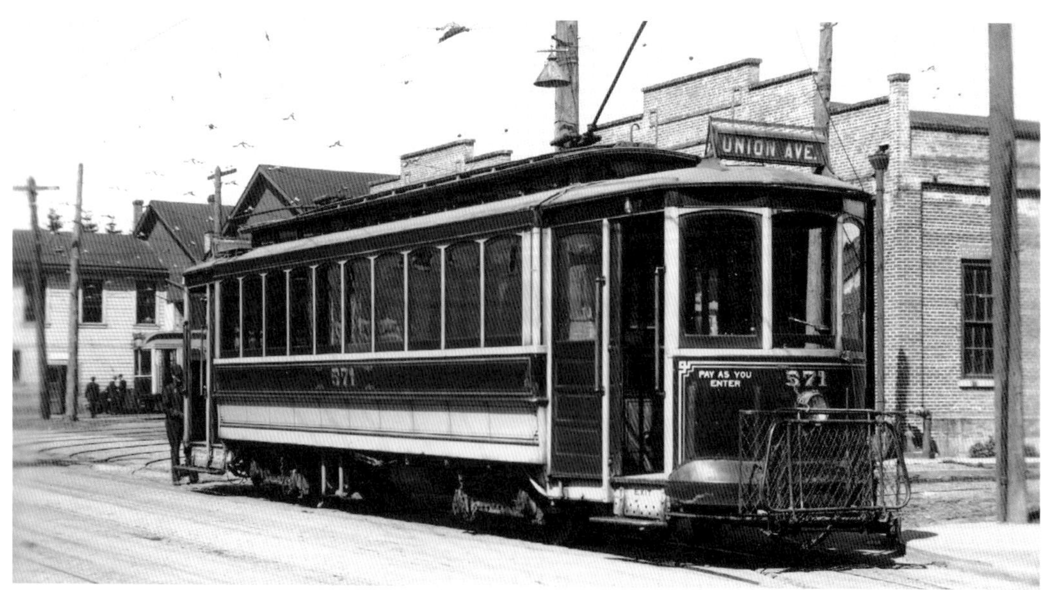

Prior to the arrival of the streamlined Broadway cars, No. 571 was one of the newest trolleys based out of the Piedmont Carbarn. She was built in 1910 by the American Car Company and retired in 1940. Seen here as a Union Avenue rush hour tripper, Car 571 was one of the 144 PAYEs that comprised PRL&P's largest group. (*Photograph courtesy Oregon Historical Society 129-62*)

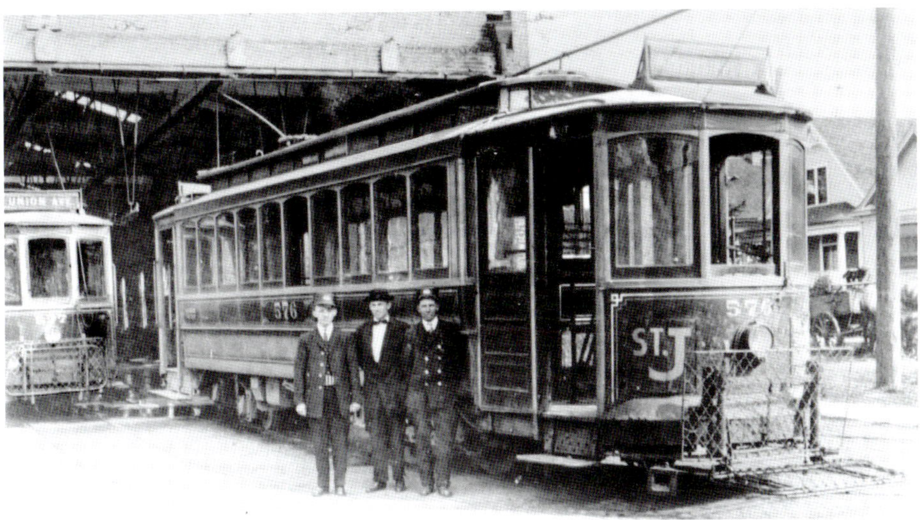

Cars 577 and 576 in front of Piedmont Carbarn Bay D are both trippers; 576 wears a Mississippi Avenue rollsign, which signifies it as a tripper on the St. Johns Line, while car 577 sports a Union Avenue sign used for short-turn cars on the Alberta Line. Today, two PAYEs like this survive—No. 611 in a spaghetti restaurant in Newport Beach, California, and standard gauge sister No. 1351 as a novelty shop in Lincoln City, Oregon.

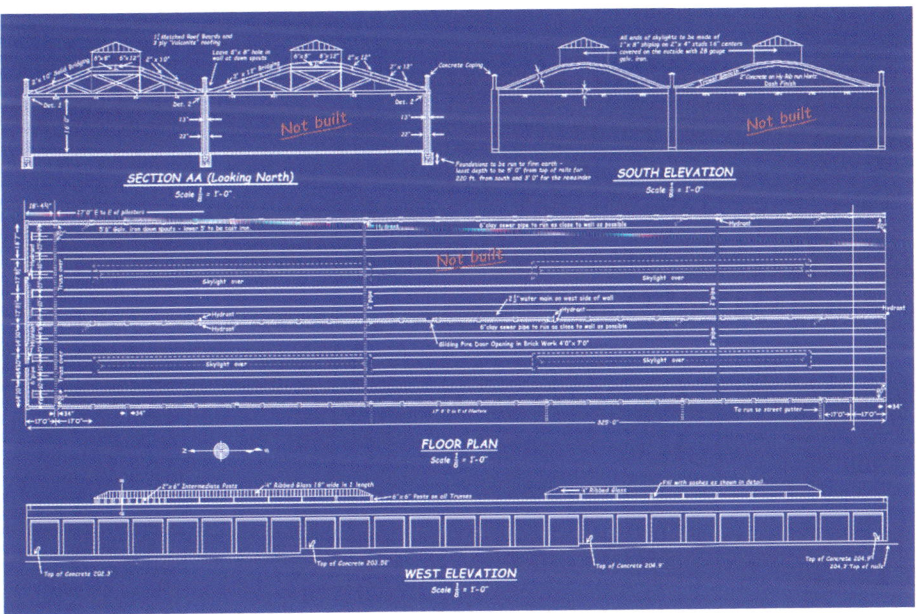

This blueprint is evidence that the second Piedmont Carbarn was intended to have two bays, E and F. However, when construction was completed in 1910, the lot reserved for bay F had been put to use as a storage yard and test track instead. With completion of the second carbarn Piedmont Division occupied two long blocks. (*Photograph courtesy Oregon Electric Railway Historical Society Archive*)

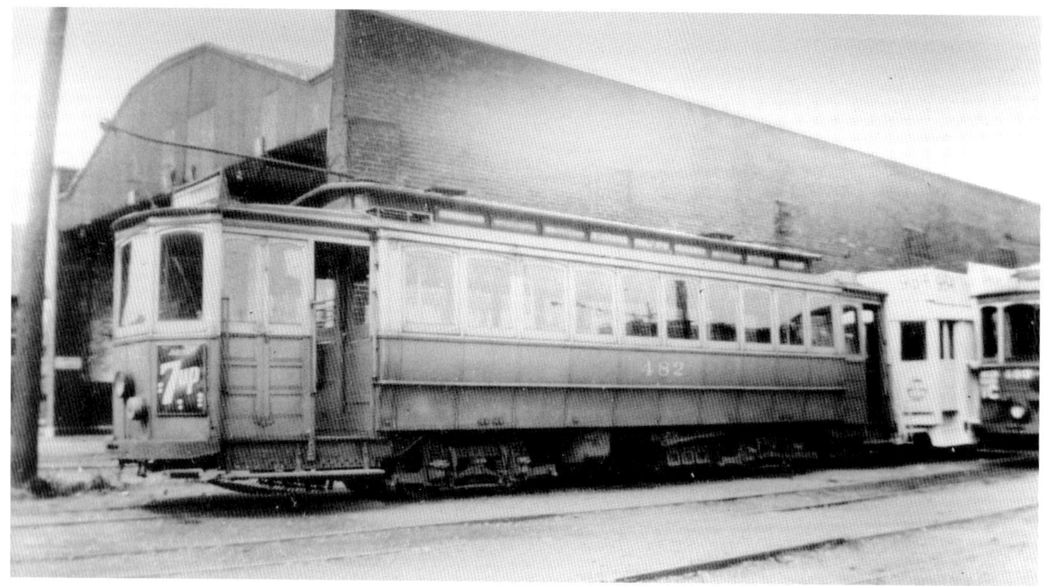

No. 482, one of the first PAYEs ordered by PRL&P in 1908, was housed at Piedmont during its last years. It is seen here wearing 1930s green and cream livery in the storage yard next to bay E. Behind it is old City & Suburban standard 123, which was painted white and survived as an advertising car. Although the last of its class to be officially retired in 1938, it was stored inactive after its motors were removed in 1927.

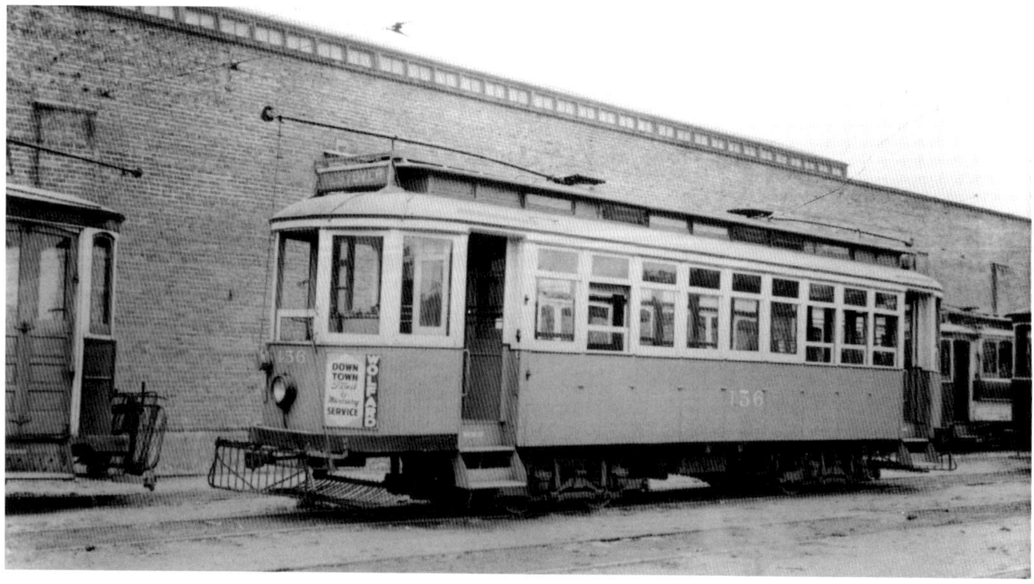

Another foreign visitor to the Piedmont Carbarn was "Toronto" No. 456, which operated out of the Piedmont Carbarn after the Savier Street Carbarn closed in 1937. It is seen here alongside bay E, wearing green and cream colors and sporting a Westover rollsign. The Westover stub was discontinued in 1941.

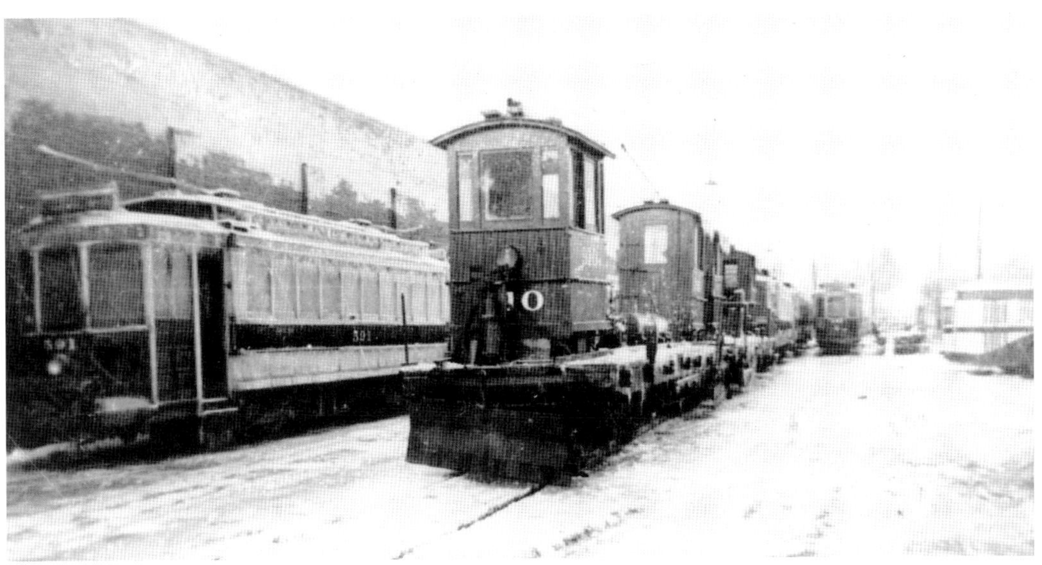

Work equipment was also stored at Piedmont as can be seen in this 1940s snow scene. Two-cab construction flat No. 910 heads a row of work cars in the Piedmont Yard. Construction flat 910 was built in 1911 by adding cabs and motors to a 1904 vintage Portland Railway Company flatcar. The 39-foot-long vehicle was retired in 1946. (*Charles Hayden photograph*)

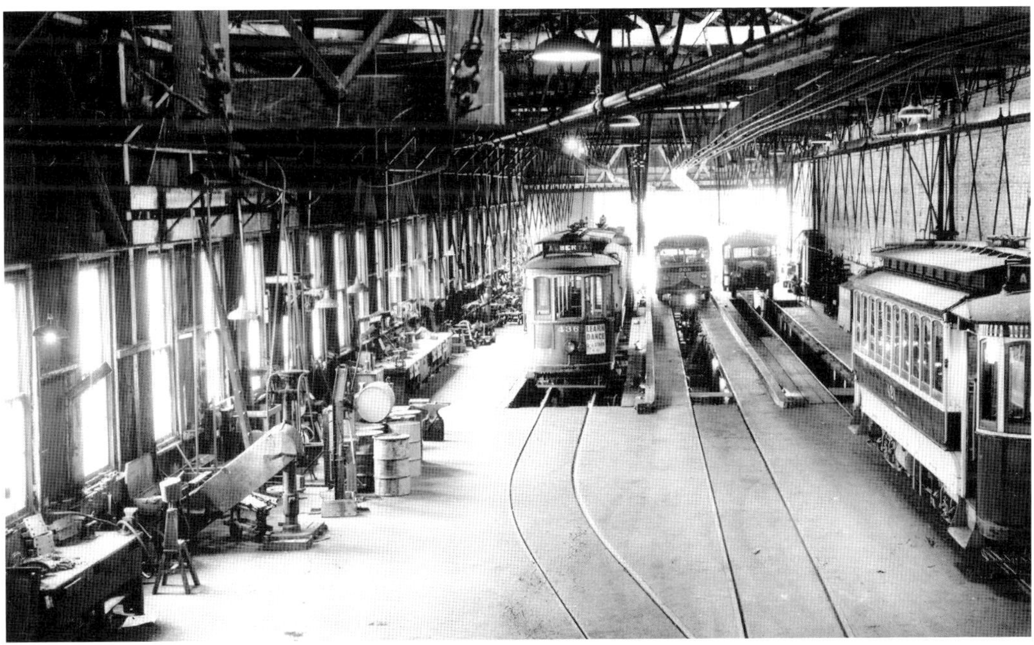

The roof of an 800-series Broadway car peeks from behind Alberta Line No. 436 in this World War II scene inside Piedmont Carbarn bay A. In the right background are bus 206 and a Reo shipyard bus. The track at left curves in from the side to make room for the clubhouse and headquarters building. Work benches, tools, oil drums, and acetylene tanks line the outside wall.

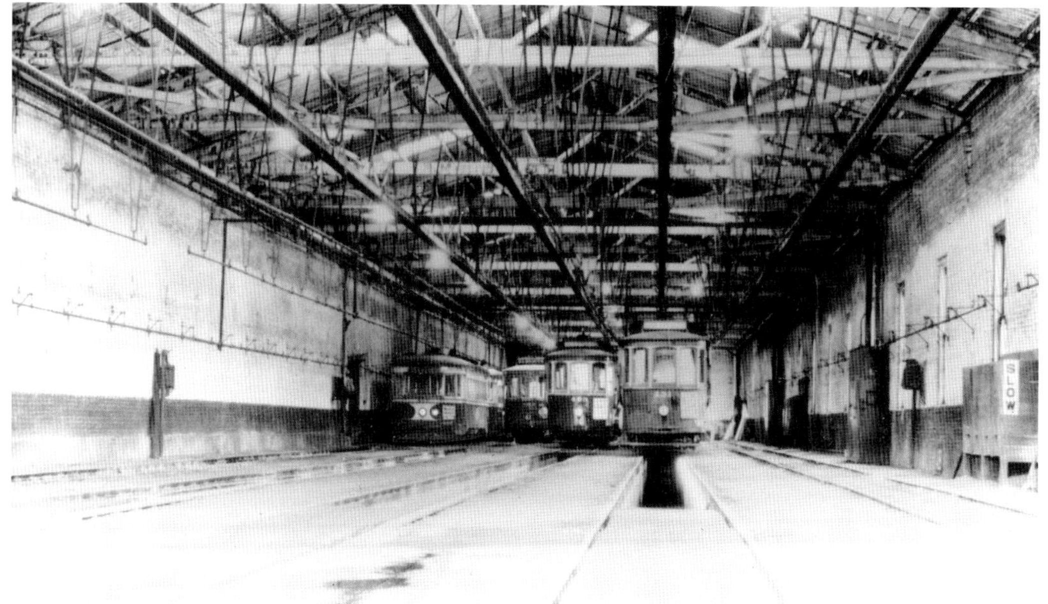

The trolleys seen at the back of Piedmont Carbarn bay D are all signed for service on the Alberta Line in Northeast Portland, which is not surprising since all but one line serving North Portland had been discontinued for a decade when this picture was taken around 1946. Broadway car 800 is on the left, next to multiple-unit cars 404, 403, and 431.

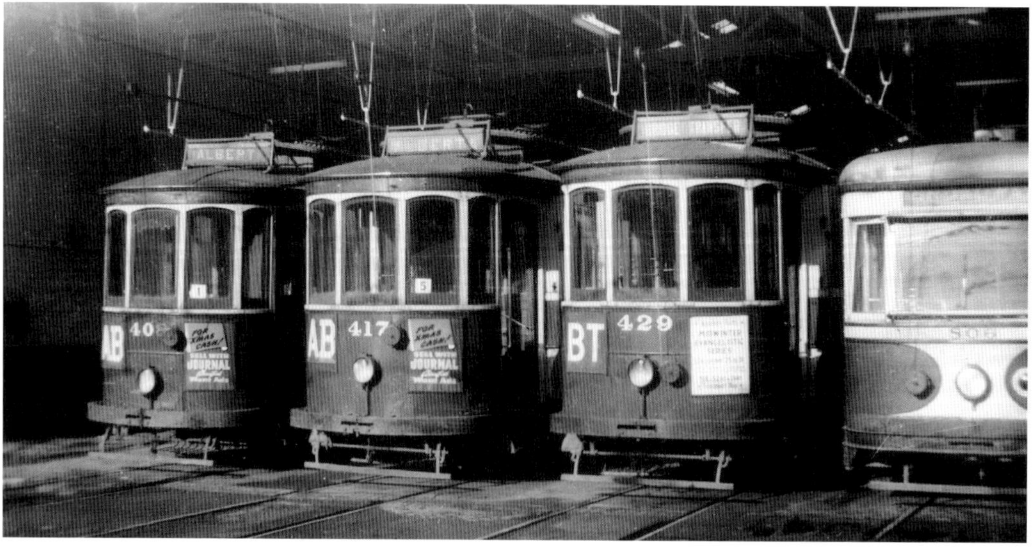

The bell will soon be tolling for cars 408, 417, 429, and 806, seen in the Piedmont Carbarn in 1948. The lines each car is signed for have already ceased operation or are about to. The Bridge Transfer Line closed in 1947, and the Alberta and Broadway lines went in 1948. Lines serving the Portland Peninsula, including Mississippi Avenue, St. Johns, Williams Avenue, and Russell–Shaver had been discontinued much earlier, during 1936 and 1940.

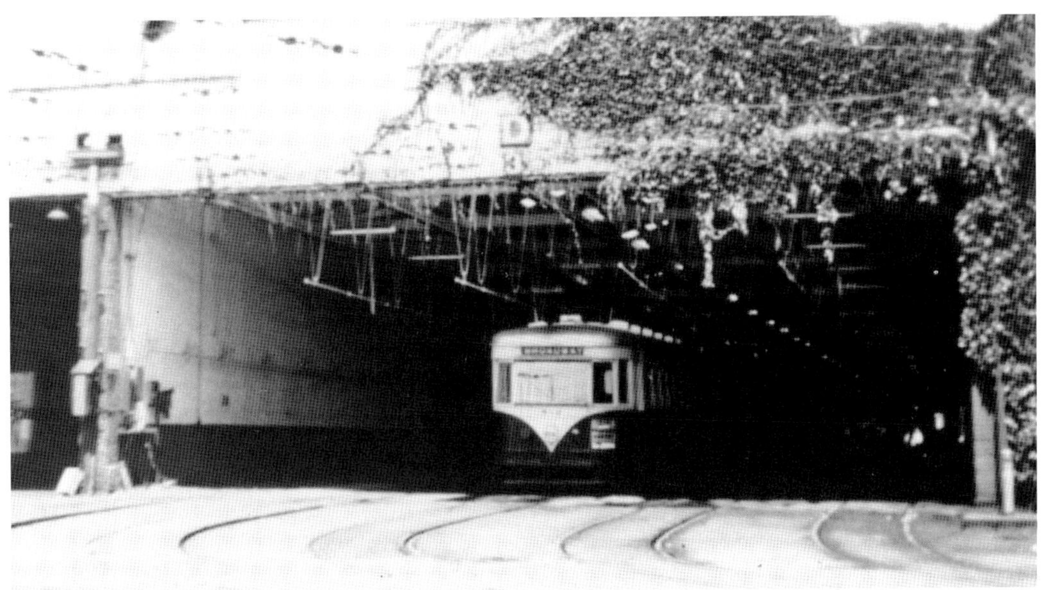

Broadway car No. 812 is a forlorn-looking single occupant inside ivy-covered bay D at the Piedmont Carbarn. In addition to their namesake line, the Broadways saw service on the Alberta, Mississippi Avenue, 23rd Avenue, and Willamette Heights lines. Cars 801–812 and 814 were retired in 1950, and 800 and 813 followed in 1954 and 1958 after having been converted for operation on the standard-gauge lines.

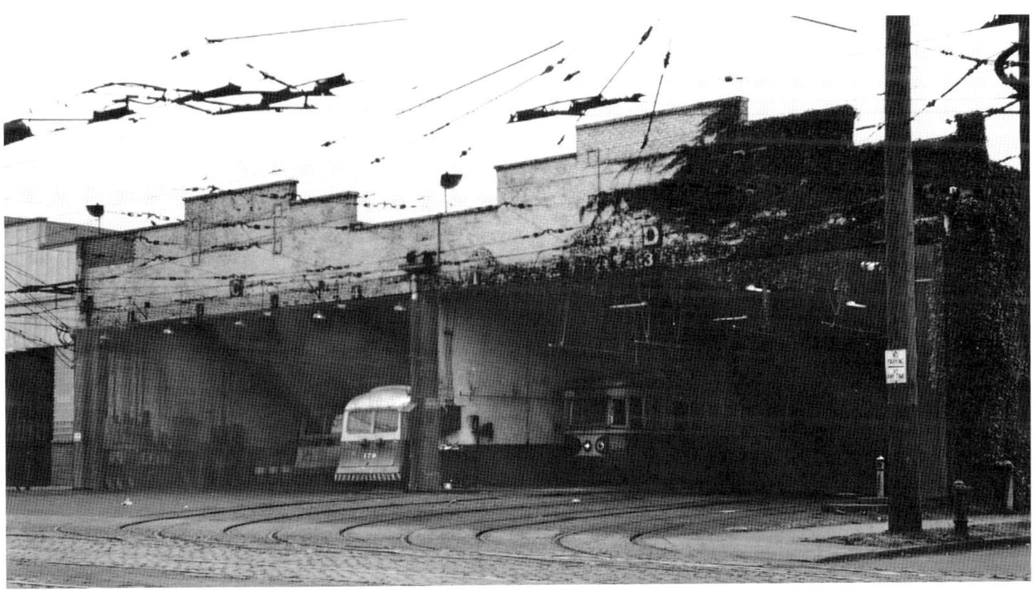

Broadway car 807 sits beneath a plethora of wires next to trolley coaches 170 and 179 at the Piedmont Carbarn. The Williams Avenue, St. Johns, Interstate Avenue, and Mississippi Avenue trolley coach lines operated out of Piedmont. The first began operation in February 1937, and the last ceased running on October 23, 1958. This marked the end of all trolleybus service in Portland.

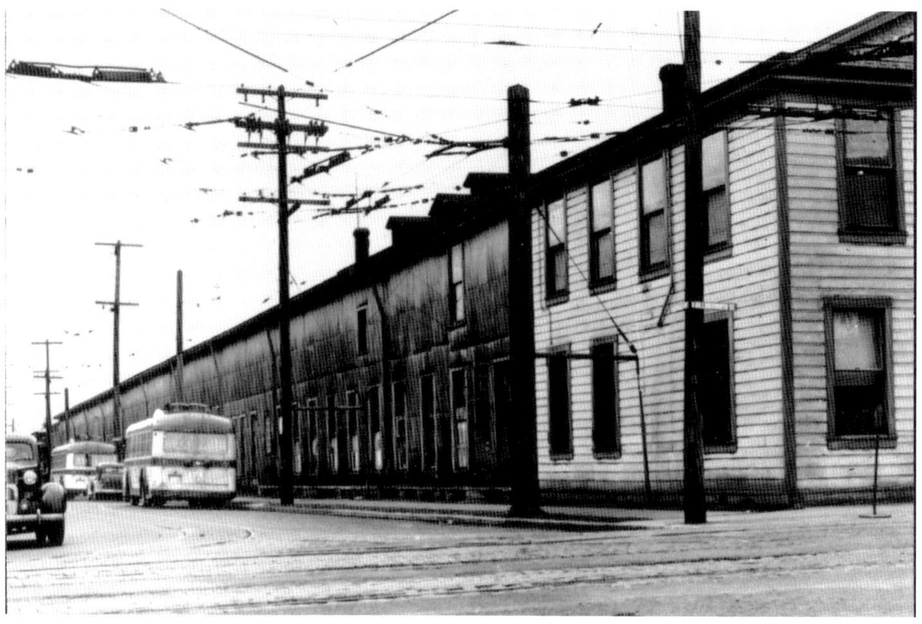

The two trolleybuses in this view looking northward alongside the Piedmont Carbarn on N Michigan Avenue from Killingsworth Street are wearing the red, cream, and silver color scheme adopted by Portland Traction Company in 1939. Mack built 120 trolley coaches like this for Portland in 1936 and another twenty in 1937. Numbers 126–198 featured Westinghouse motors, while numbers 301–370 were equipped with General Electric motors.

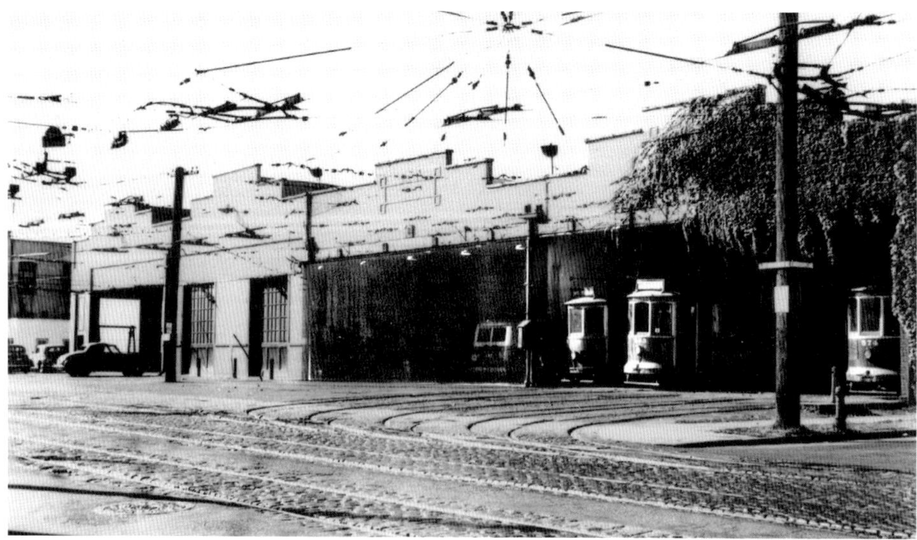

Streetcars 530, 563, and 564 await their fate in bay D at the Piedmont Carbarn on September 6, 1949, while trolleybus 137 sits in adjacent bay C. Note by this time the office and clubhouse have been razed and bays A and B remodeled for other use. (*Photograph courtesy Warren Wing*)

8

Trolleys Return to North Portland

Trolleybuses served North Portland until October 23, 1958, but their streetcar brethren had disappeared long before. Streetcars had ceased running out the Portland Peninsula in 1940, and by 1948, the last Piedmont Division trolley lines had been discontinued. For more than fifty years afterward, the familiar sounds of the conductor's bell, the squeal of flanged metal wheels, and the growl of electric motors were gone from North Portland.

Things changed on May 1, 2004, when the Tri-County Metropolitan Transportation District of Oregon, known less formally as TriMet, opened the Interstate MAX (metropolitan area express) Yellow Line as its fourth light rail line. TriMet adopted the use of color to identify separate routes in 2000.

The Interstate MAX Line was originally intended to be part of a "South/North Line" that would have connected Clackamas Town Center mall and Vancouver, Washington, via downtown. However, after failing to gain needed support from voters in Clark County, Washington, TriMet was persuaded to build the line as a MAX extension to North Portland only. Construction got underway in 2001.

At first, the Yellow Line ran from the Expo Center in North Portland to the Library and Galleria stations in downtown Portland. On August 30, 2009, a new southern terminal was created when tracks were added to the Downtown Transit Mall, taking light rail to the Portland State University campus. The Interstate MAX Yellow Line now operates from the PSU South Station on SW 6th Avenue and Jackson Street in Portland to the Portland Expo Center on N Marine Drive. The 5.8-mile, double-tracked light rail line crosses the Willamette River via the Steel Bridge. The line serves ten stations along the Interstate MAX corridor and seven stations in downtown Portland.

The first LRVs used on the Yellow Line were Type 1 cars 101–126, built by Bombardier between 1983 and 1986. Those were followed by four groups manufactured by Siemens. Type 2 SD660 models 201–252 arrived in 1996–2000 and Type 3 SD660 cars 301–327 came in 2003–05. Type 4 S70 series 401–422 were built in 2008–09. The newest additions to the fleet are S700 cars 521–538, which made their debut in 2015. An order for twenty-six more S700 light rail vehicles was placed in 2019, and these are expected during 2022–23.

In addition to MAX, two contemporary streetcar lines curved through a small portion of North Portland as they crossed the Willamette River on the Steel and Broadway bridges, although they did not run out the Portland Peninsula. From November 29, 1991, until July 6, 2014, TriMet operated the Portland Vintage Trolley heritage streetcar service, which ran on a portion of the MAX light rail tracks between the Lloyd Center Mall in NE Portland and the Downtown Transit Mall using four reproduction "Council Crest" streetcars manufactured in Iowa. Then, in September 2012, the Portland Streetcar opened the Central Loop (later the CL Line), which operates across the Broadway Bridge and into the Lloyd District before turning south into the Central Eastside.

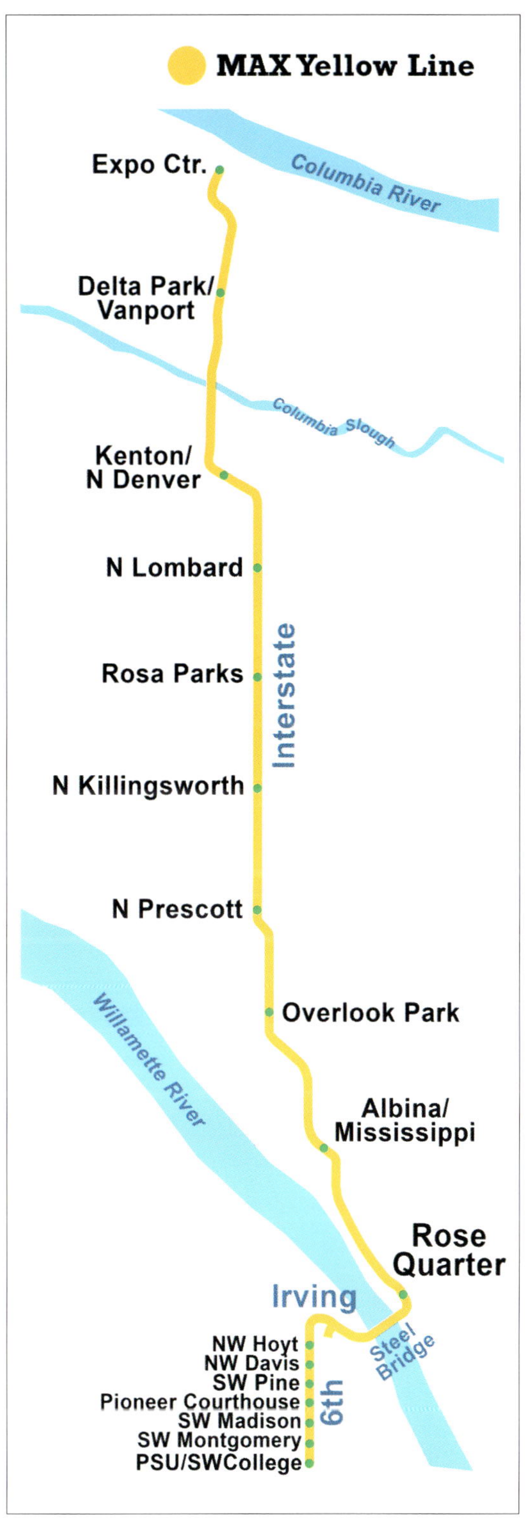
MAX Yellow Line
Expo Ctr.
Columbia River
Delta Park/
Vanport
Columbia Slough
Kenton/
N Denver
N Lombard
Interstate
Rosa Parks
N Killingsworth
N Prescott
Willamette River
Overlook Park
Albina/
Mississippi
Rose
Quarter
Irving
Steel
Bridge
NW Hoyt
NW Davis
SW Pine
Pioneer Courthouse
SW Madison
SW Montgomery
PSU/SWCollege
6th

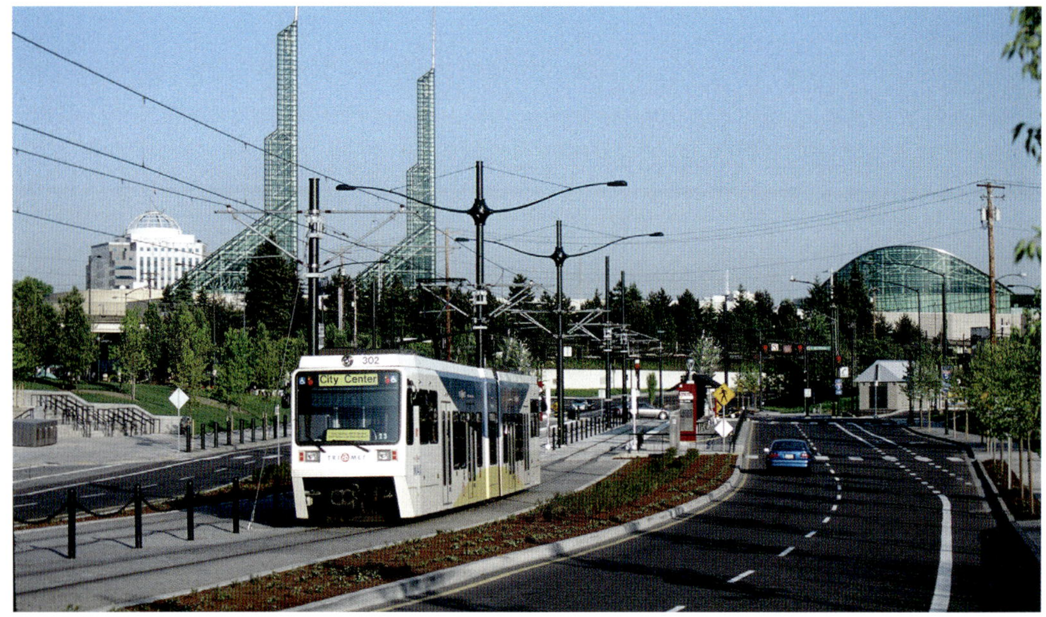

No. 302 is pulling into the Interstate/Rose Quarter station during simulated Yellow Line service on April 26, 2004. The large card in the window reads "Trains Testing—Not in Service. MAX Yellow Line Opening May 1." Both ends of the Oregon Convention Center can be seen in the background; the two glass spires at its northern end date from its 1990 opening and the rounded glass roof at right is part of the 2003 expansion. (*Photograph by Steve Morgan*)

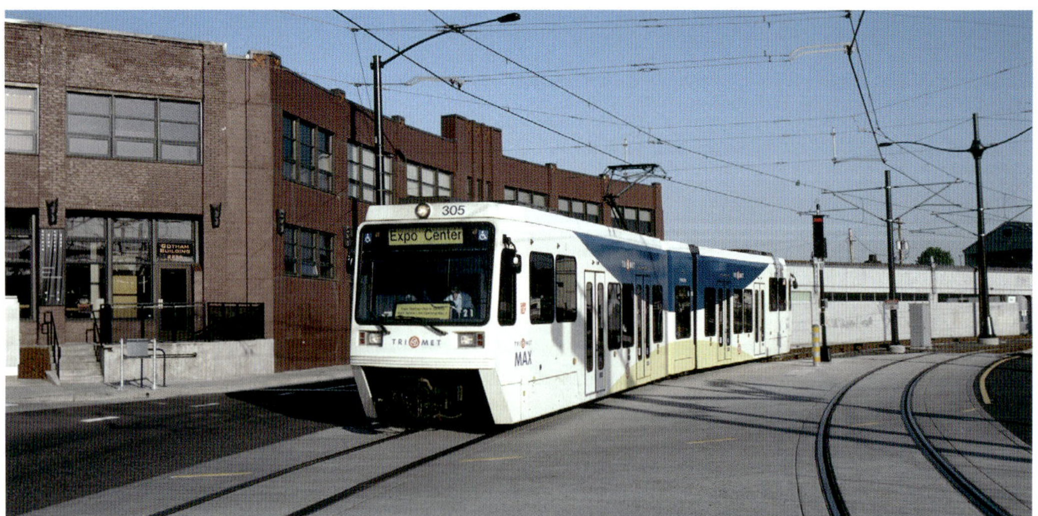

Type 3 LRV No. 305 is northbound on N Interstate Avenue at Albina Avenue running as a single car during simulated service on April 26, 2004, five days before the line's May 1 opening. During simulated service trains ran the full planned schedule but without passengers. The Gotham building in the background was also a landmark during more than thirty years of classic streetcar service along this street. Compare this picture with the one on page 76. (*Photograph by Steve Morgan*)

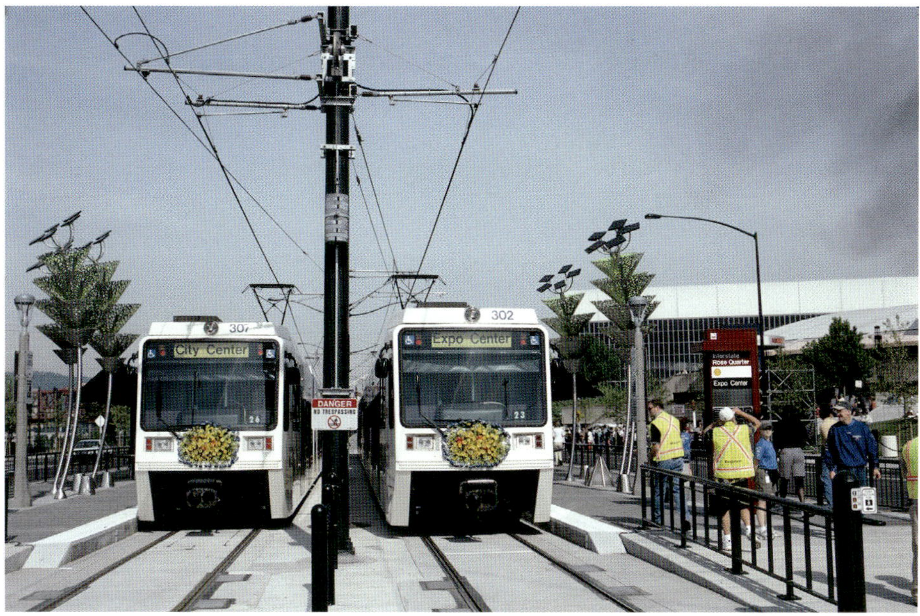

Decorated Type 3 LRVs 307 and 302 are seen at the Interstate/Rose Quarter station during the MAX Yellow Line's opening ceremony on May 1, 2004. Both are Siemens SD660s built in 2003. As can be seen on the destination signs, the cars are headed in opposite directions. The terminals at each end of the line are City Center and Expo Center. (*Photograph by Steve Morgan*)

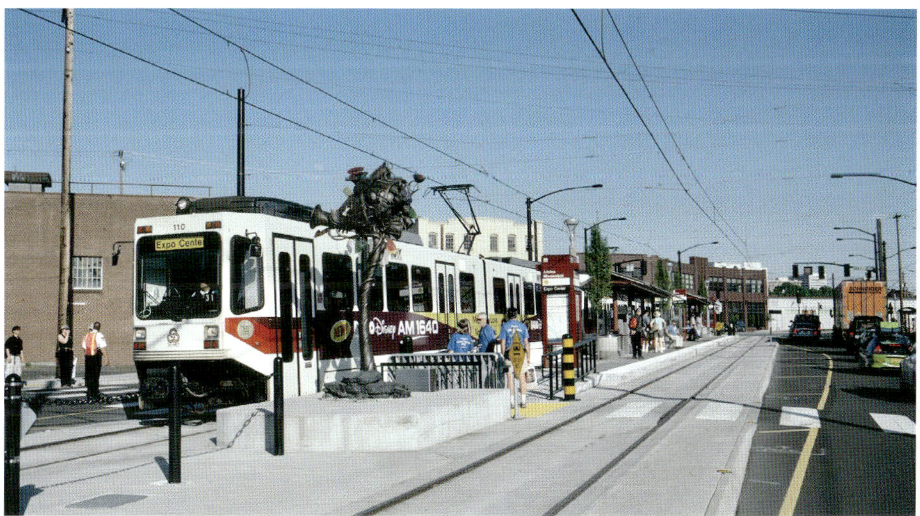

This opening-day shot of 1984-built Type 1 LRV No. 110 pulling away from the Albina/Mississippi station shows its very unusual artwork which was described by TriMet as "A bronze, tree-like vine flowering with forms representing the arts of the area," a reference to musical instruments since the area was known for several jazz clubs. The three people in blue T-shirts are TriMet workers or volunteers there to assist the public on opening day. (*Photograph by Steve Morgan*)

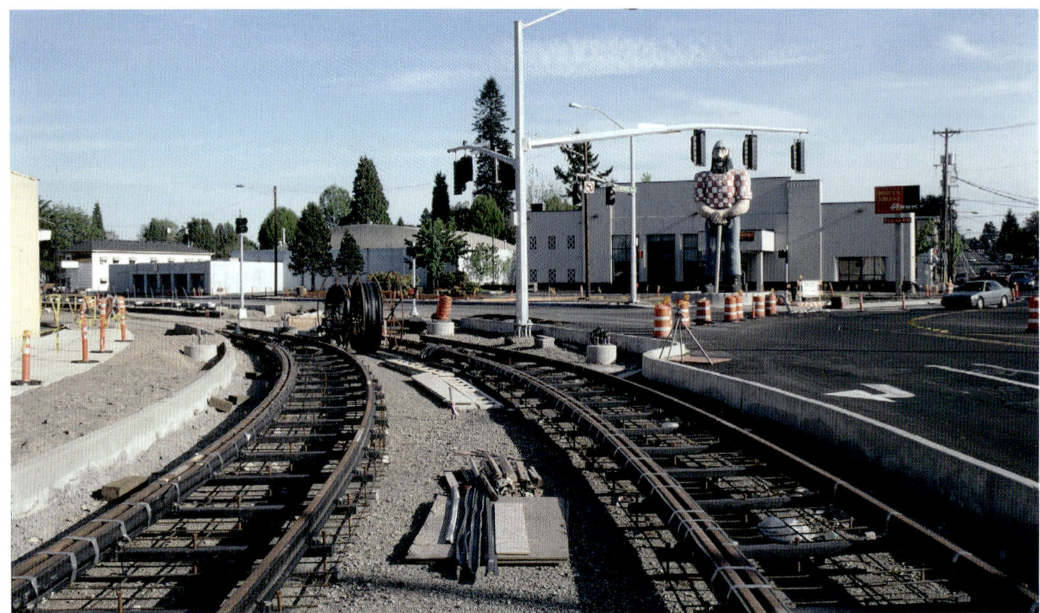

The 31-foot-tall Paul Bunyan Statue, seen at the corner of N Interstate Avenue and Denver Street during 2002 Yellow Line tracklaying in Kenton, was built in 1959 for Oregon's Centennial Exposition and International Trade Fair, which was held nearby. The metal sculpture, now listed on the National Register of Historic Places, was moved from its original location at the intersection of North Interstate Avenue and North Argyle Street. (*Photograph by Steve Morgan*)

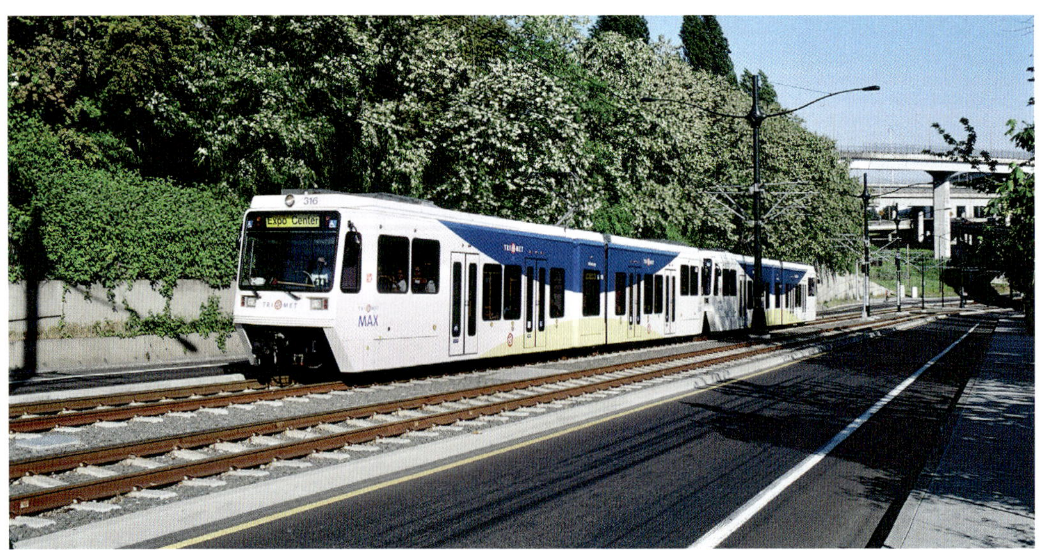

An outbound train of new (and ad-free) Type 3 Siemens SD660s led by car 316 climbs the Yellow Line's steepest grade, 6.7 percent on Interstate Avenue north of Greeley Avenue. The I-405 ramps leading to and from the east end of the Fremont Bridge are visible in the distance in this view taken on opening day, May 1, 2004. (*Photograph by Steve Morgan*)

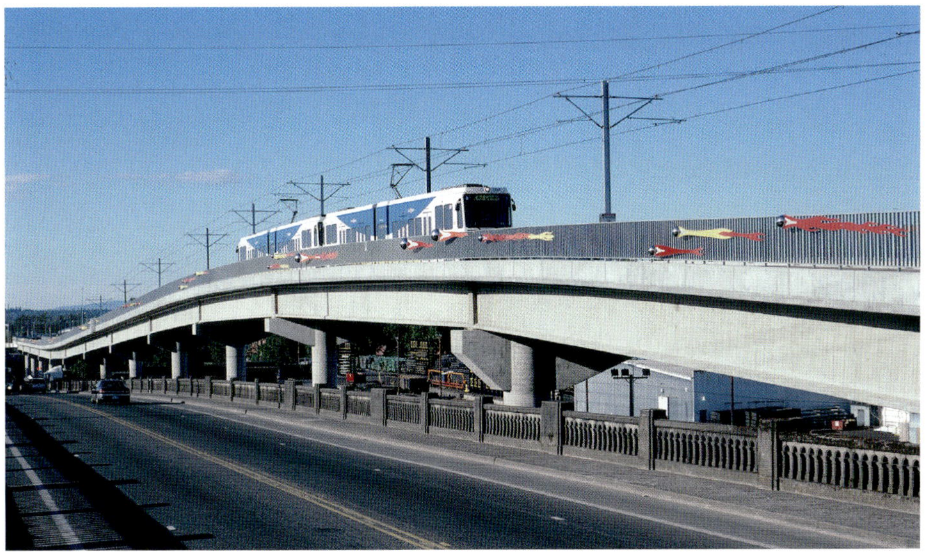

A MAX Yellow Line train is southbound on the viaduct next to N Denver Avenue near Argyle Street on May 2, 2004, the line's second day of service. The 3,850-foot-long viaduct, the longest on the entire MAX system, has been adorned with "flaming comets" artwork. The train is composed of two then-new SD660 Type 3 light rail cars built in 2003–04. (*Photograph by Steve Morgan*)

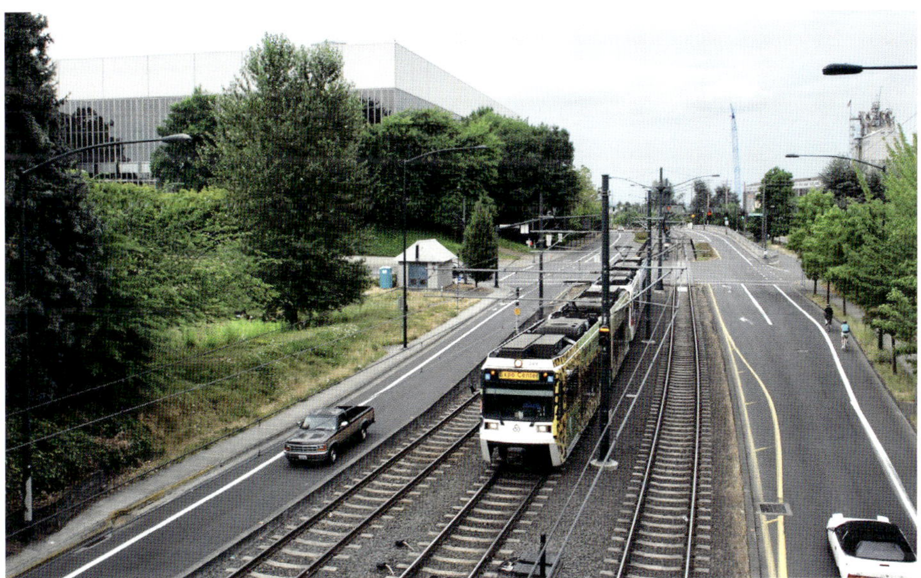

No. 249 heads a northbound train in the three-track section north of the Rose Quarter and Veterans Memorial Coliseum in a view looking south on N Interstate Avenue from the east approach to the Broadway Bridge. The easternmost track, at left, is a so-called "pocket track" where a train can be stored temporarily and put into service quickly at the end of an event at the Coliseum or the adjacent Moda Center. (*Photograph by Steve Morgan*)

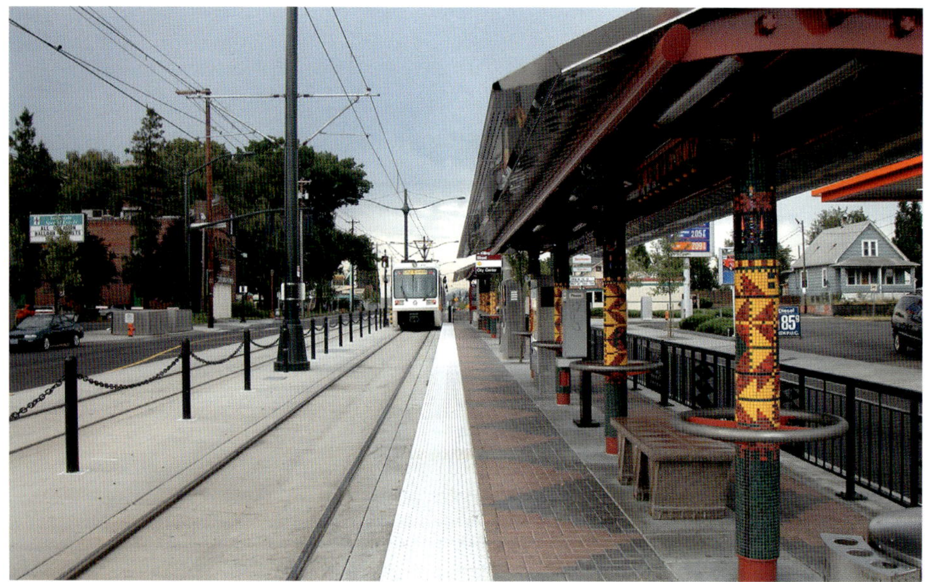

Art at Killingsworth Station celebrates the multiculturalism of the surrounding community. Its main theme, "Cultural Polyrhythms" by Adriene Cruz and Valerie Otani, features glass mosaic columns based on colorful African cloth designs, metal flags suggesting the torans of India, and guardrail panels inspired by South American textiles. Passengers can wait on concrete benches that evoke the carved wooden stools of Africa. (*Photograph by David Wilson via Wikimedia Commons*)

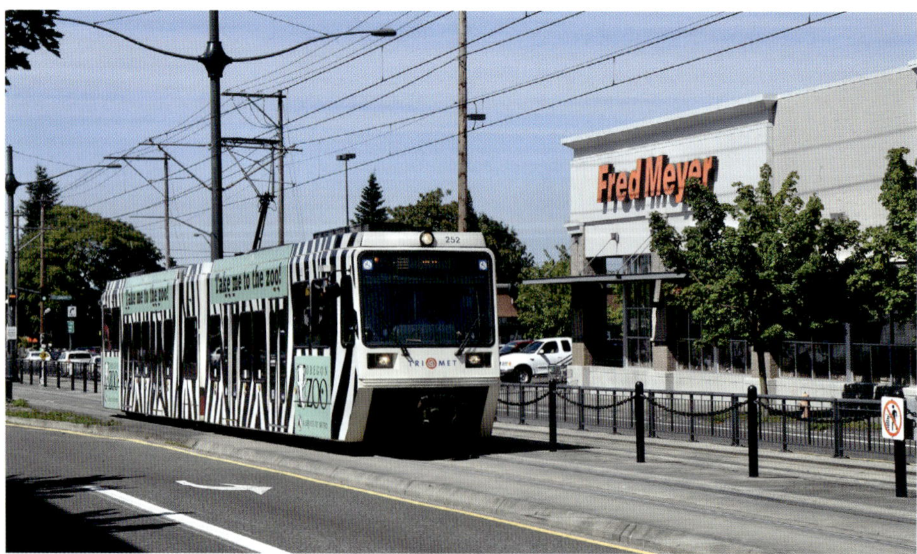

The very last Type 2 LRV, 2000-built No. 252, is southbound wearing zebra stripes for an Oregon Zoo advertisement in this June 2015 view on N Interstate Avenue south of Lombard Street in June 2015. The car's newly retrofitted destination sign is showing a yellow square and "PSU." (*Photograph by Steve Morgan*)

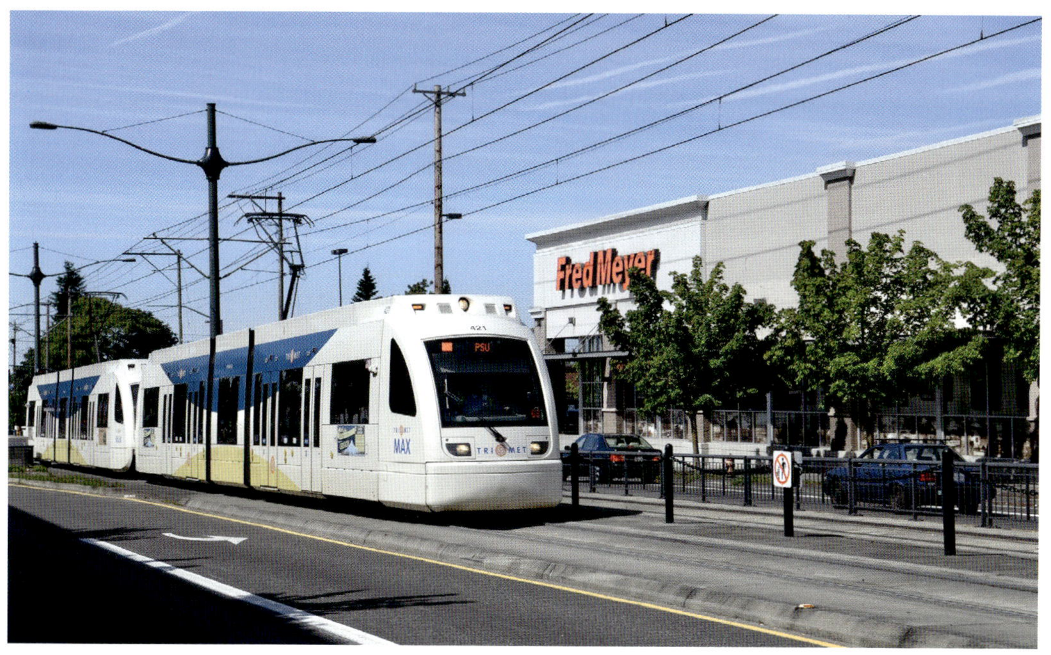

Siemens S70 cars 421 and 418 make up a train of Type 4 LRVs seen heading south in June 2015 next to Fred Meyer at Interstate and Lombard. These cars were equipped with LED destination signs that are easier to read than the new signs retrofitted to older LRVs like in the previous picture. (*Photograph by Steve Morgan*)

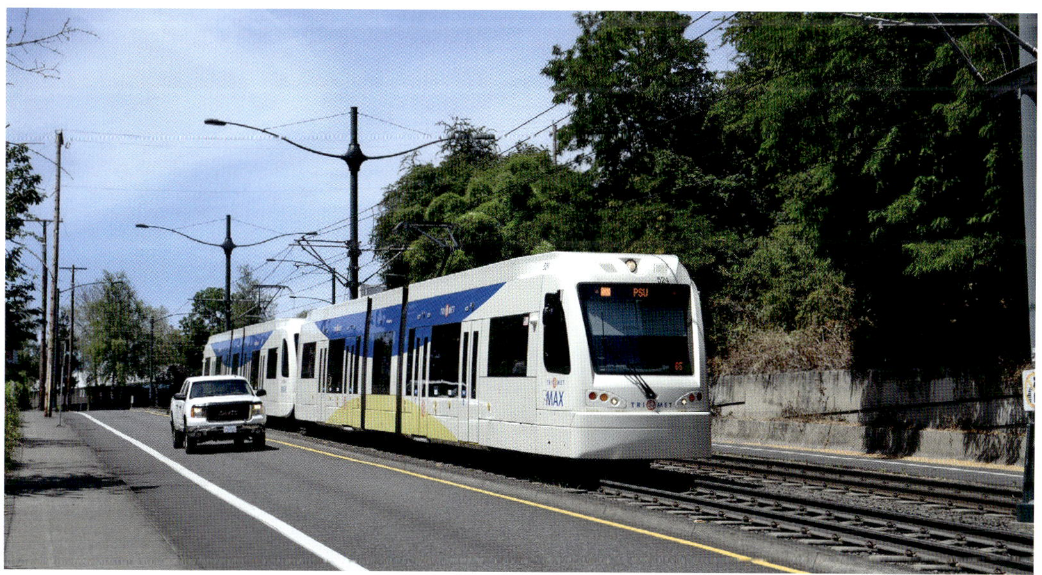

Type 5 LRVs 524 and 522 make up an inbound train on the Yellow Line's steep 6.7 percent grade on N Interstate Avenue in June 2015. In 2020, Siemens retroactively rebranded TriMet's Type 5 cars from model S70 to S700. (*Photograph by Steve Morgan*)

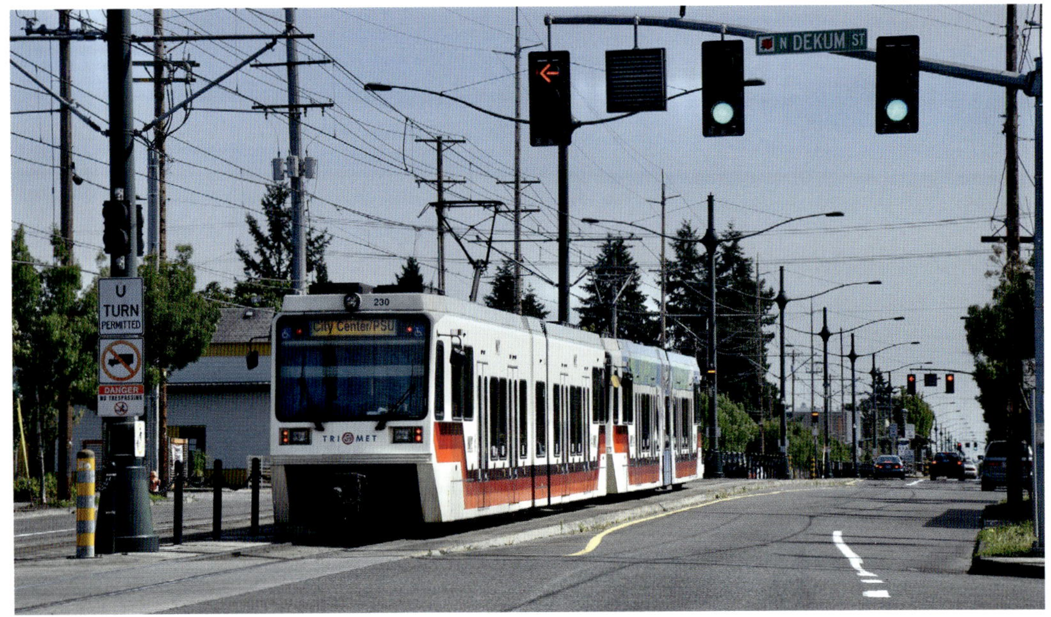

A train of Type 2 Siemens LRVs is seen heading south on N Interstate Avenue at Dekum Street on June 20, 2015. The car closest to the camera—1997-built No. 230—was part of a series that included the first low-floor LRVs in North America when placed by TriMet in 1993. In 1998, their model number was changed from SD600 to SD660 to reflect the use of motors running on AC instead of DC current. (*Photograph by Steve Morgan*)

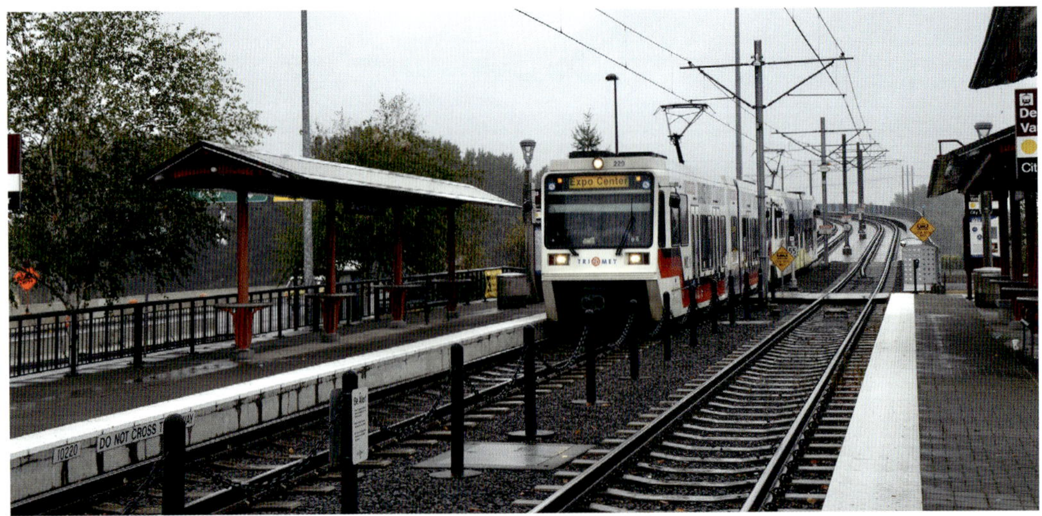

The typical Portland drizzle makes the headlights "pop" in this view of a northbound train led by car 229. The Type 2 SD660 is seen pulling into the Delta Park/Vanport station on September 6, 2015. The northern end of the long viaduct along N Denver Avenue can be seen in the background. All TriMet LRVs that originally used rollsigns were converted to LED destination signs in 2014–2016. (*Photograph by Steve Morgan*)

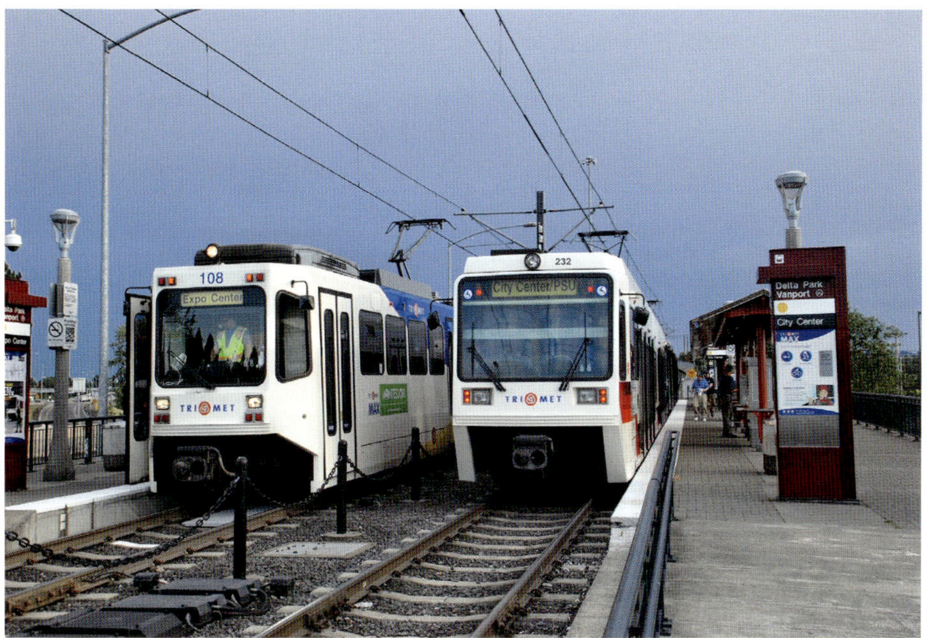

Two trains are seen passing at the Delta Park/Vanport MAX Yellow Line station. The cars at the near end in this 2013 picture are No. 108, an overhauled high-floor Type 1 LRV built by Bombardier in 1985, and No. 232, a Type 2 manufactured by Siemens in 1997. Both were still equipped with traditional rollsigns at that time. (*Photograph by Steve Morgan*)

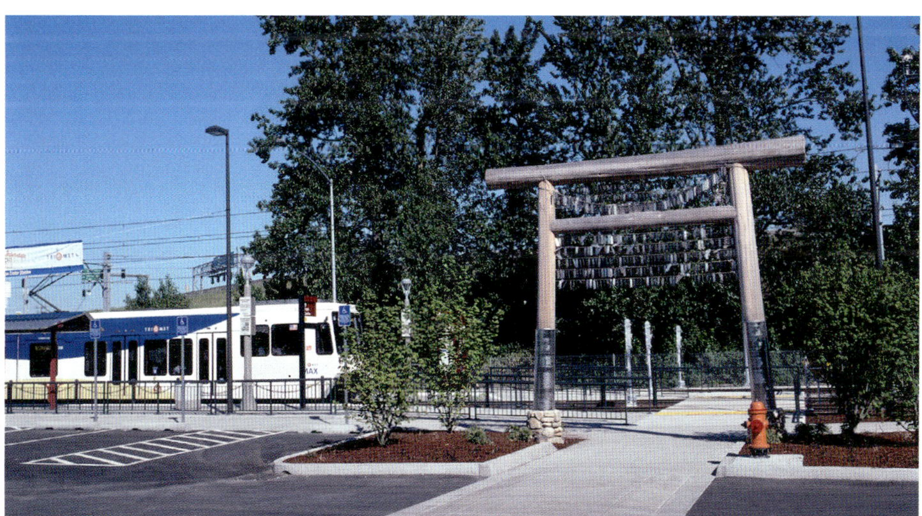

The terminal at Expo Center station, seen here on the second day of Yellow Line service, features traditional Japanese timber-and-bronze gates that serve as a memorial to those going through the World War II relocation center that was located here. Valerie Otani's artwork "Voices of Remembrance" includes metal "internee ID tags" strung between the timbers and gate legs etched with vintage newspaper articles. (*Photograph by Steve Morgan*)

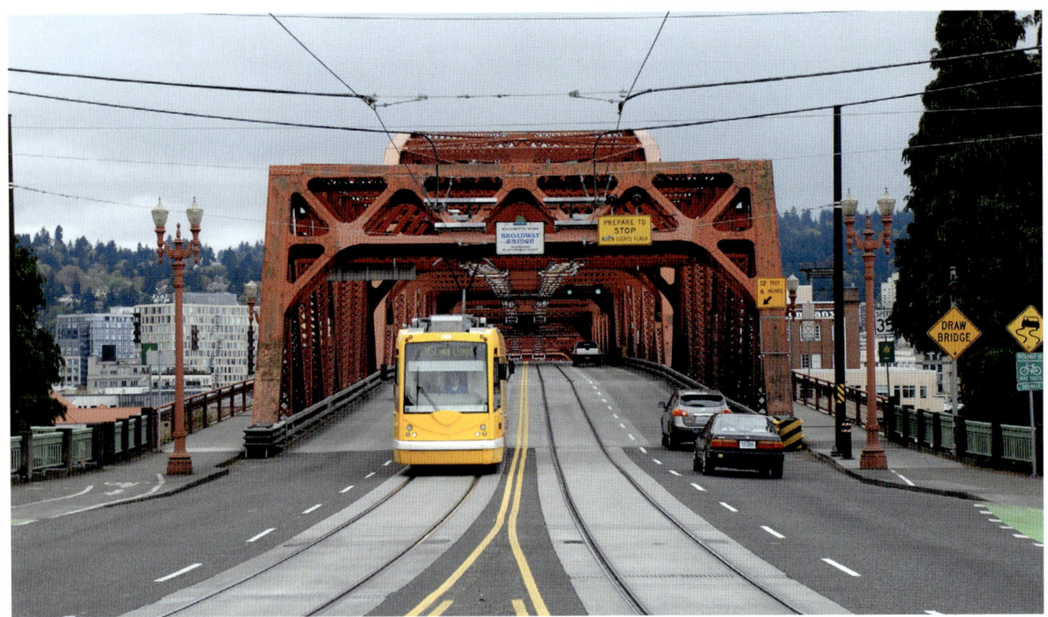

Entering North Portland on its way to the east side, Portland Streetcar car 008, built in 2007 by Inekon Trams, is coming off of the 1913-built Broadway Bridge. The 2012 opening of the CL line returned streetcar operation to this drawbridge after an absence of seventy-two years. (*Photograph by Steve Morgan*)

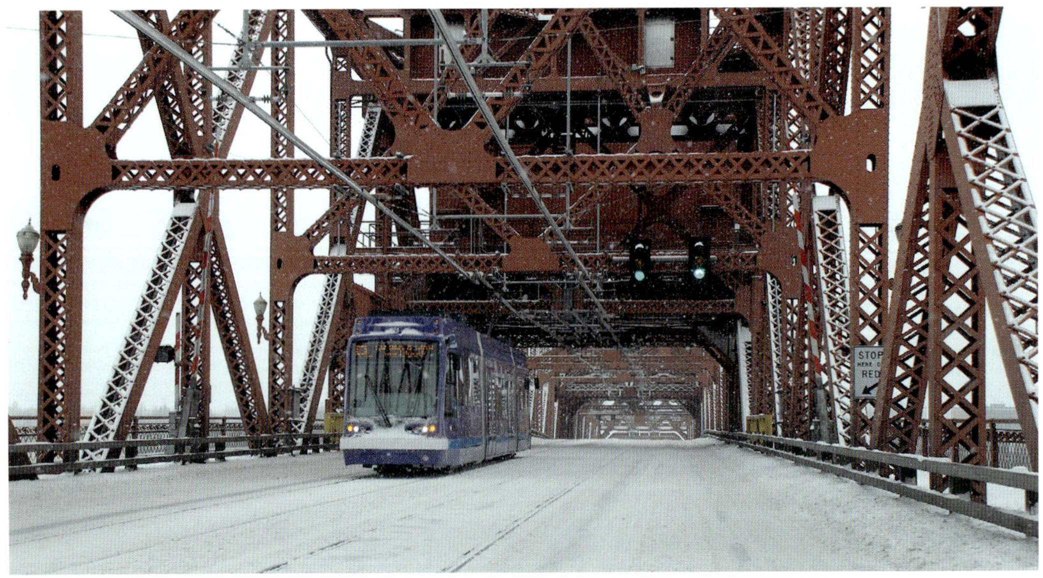

Portland Streetcar car 024, built in 2013 by United Streetcar, is crossing a deserted Broadway Bridge during a snowstorm on February 8, 2014. It was in service on the CL line, which was renamed the Loop Service in 2015. As the bridge is a drawbridge, the overhead power for the streetcars is supplied via overhead rails rather than trolley wires. (*Photograph by Steve Morgan*)

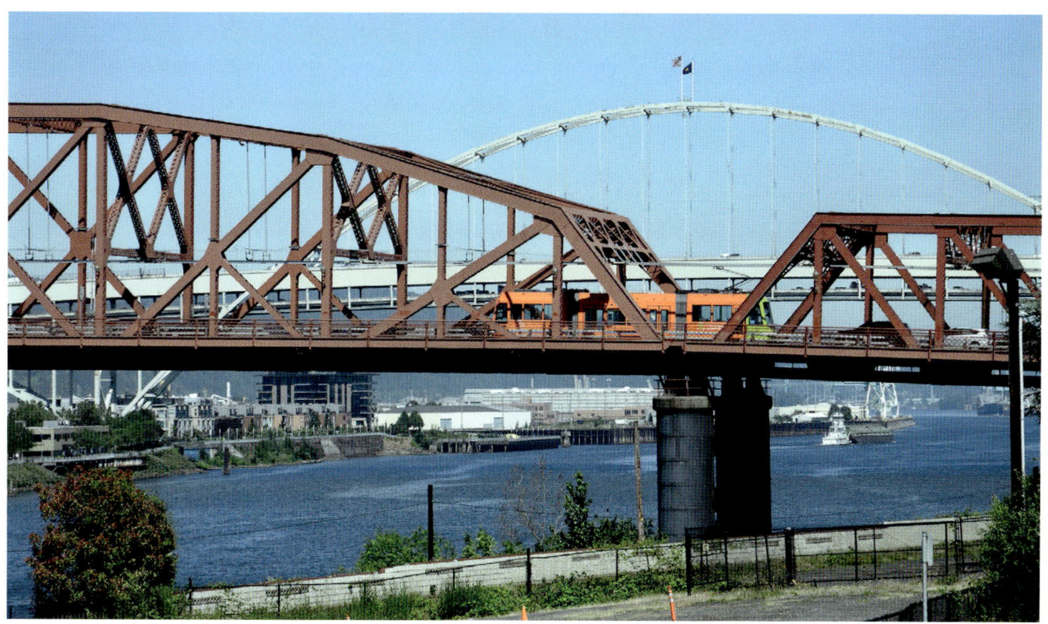

Portland Streetcar No. 022 is seen here crossing the Broadway Bridge on the CL Line in a picture taken from the Steel Bridge in June 2015. In the background is the Fremont Bridge, the longest main span of any bridge in Oregon and the second longest tied-arch bridge in the world when built. (*Photograph by Steve Morgan*)

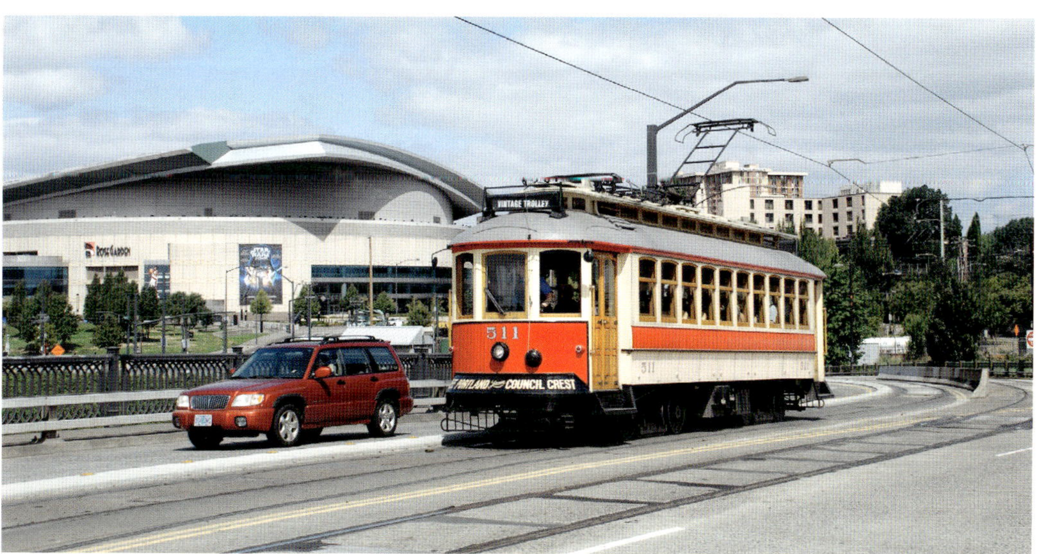

Vintage Trolley 511, a 1991 Gomaco reproduction modeled after Portland's iconic 1904 Brill Council Crest cars, is ascending the east deck of the Steel Bridge on August 23, 2009, the last day of service on this route except for deadhead trips from the carbarn at the start of each shift. The large stadium in the background is the Rose Garden, which was later renamed the Moda Center. (*Photograph by Steve Morgan*)

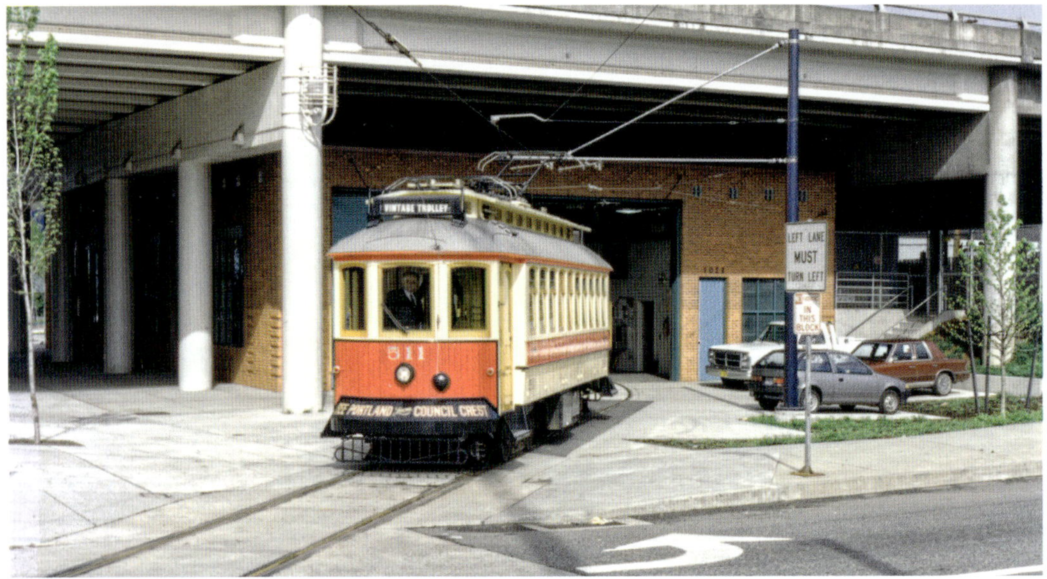

Vintage Trolley 511 is leaving the carbarn with the late Bill Wegesend at the helm in early 1992. The VT carbarn was located beneath the I-5 freeway on NE Holladay Street at 1st Avenue near the Steel Bridge in the Rose Quarter District. Since discontinuation of Vintage Trolley operation in 2014, the former carbarn has become a TriMet maintenance facility. (*Photograph by the author*)

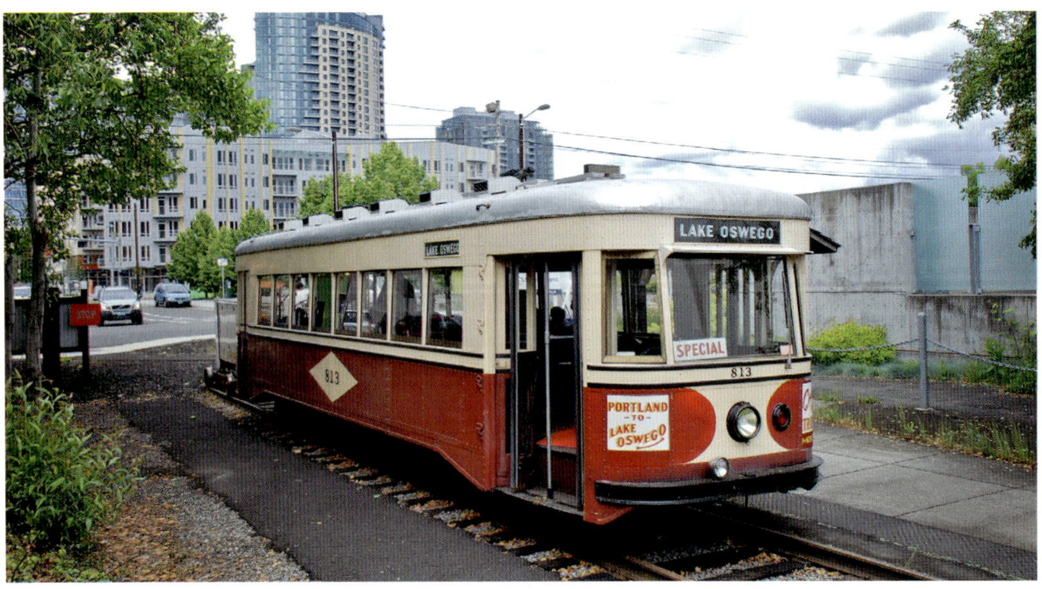

Broadway car No. 813 has been restored by the Oregon Electric Railway Historical Society and is seen at the Willamette Shore Trolley terminus on SW Bancroft Street in May 2010, during the last year it ran on the heritage line between Portland and Lake Oswego. Since there are no overhead trolley wires, operation was made possible with the tag-along power supply seen behind the car. (*Photograph by Steve Morgan*)

About the Author

Richard Thompson is a native Oregonian, whose family settled in Linn County, Oregon, in the 1880s. His interest in street and interurban railways began as a boy, when his grandmother took him for rides on Portland's last streetcar line, to Oregon City.

Thompson holds a master's degree from the University of Oregon and has worked as a historical museum director, college instructor, school librarian, archivist, educational technologist, and archaeological field worker. His favorite job was serving as crew coordinator for Vintage Trolley, Inc. during their twenty-three-year operation of Brill-replica trolleys through downtown Portland.

He is the author of eight books on electric railway history and has appeared in several documentaries, including *Streetcar City*, produced by Oregon Public Broadcasting. He has also written sixteen entries for the online *Oregon Encyclopedia*.

Thompson has been a volunteer for the Oregon Electric Railway Historical Society for nearly fifty years, operating trolleys at the Oregon Electric Railway Museum, editing and writing for their newsletter *The Transfer*, and serving on the board of directors.

Now retired, Thompson continues to indulge his passion for history and writing. He also enjoys foreign travel, ocean cruising, and reading mysteries. A resident of North Portland's Overlook Neighborhood for eighteen years, he currently resides in the Portland suburb of Cedar Mill.

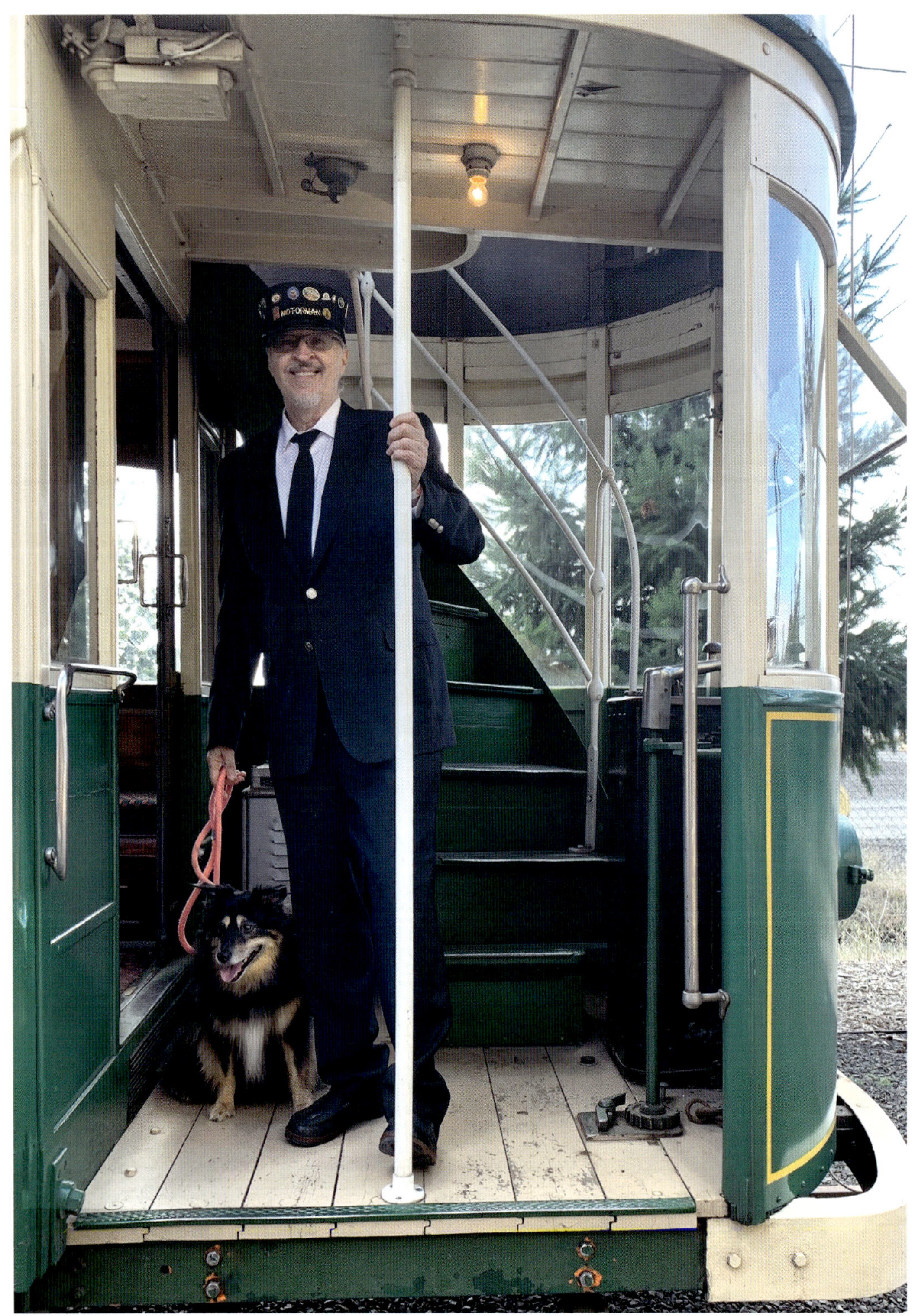
MOTORMAN